BUDDHISM ON AIR:
Televised Kaleidoscope of a Growing Religion

BUDDHISM ON AIR:
Televised Kaleidoscope of a Growing Religion

Kenneth Kenshin Tanaka

BUDDHIST EDUCATION CENTER

BUDDHISM ON AIR:
Televised Kaleidoscope of a
Growing Religion

Published by Buddhist Education Center
Anaheim, California 92804
United States of America

ISBN 978-0-9721395-9-5

Printed in the USA

To our sons and daughters
Serena, Nathan & Sandi, & Aaron

Table of Contents

Accessing the Televised Series Online

There are 3 places for accessing the videos; the first is most recommended for its easy access. (note: Prog. 49 alone is not available)

1) Website of The Society for the Promotion of Buddhism:
http://www.dharmanet.org/videobdkMSL.htm

2) Kenneth Tanaka's personal website:
http://kenneth-tanaka.life.coocan.jp/index.html

   (Click "Video Clips" and then click "Mutually Sustaining Life: A Buddhist Call to a Troubled World" (BDK Video Series), the title by which this series is also known.)

3) On YouTube: Search for "Buddhism Today: Answering to the Call of the World" for videos.

*In the unlikely event that none of the above works, please contact: chacotanaka@gmail.com or kktanaka@gamma.ocn.ne.jp

Sources for the Opening Sacred Sayings
Found at the Beginning of Each Program

Buddha-Dharma. Revised Second Edition. Numata Center for Buddhist Translation and Research, 2003. (The passages are taken from Buddhist canon.)

The Teaching of Buddha. Bukkyo Dendo Kyokai (Society for the Promotion of Buddhism), 1975. (The passages are taken from Buddhist canon.)

Numata, Toshihide. *Mutually Sustaining Life*. Bukkyo Dendo Kyokai (Society for the Promotion of Buddhism), 2000.

Notes

1) Book titles and words of emphasis are italicized in accordance with the standardized style, but in this book other words are also italicized to reflect those that appeared on the televised screen on account of their importance.

2) The expressions of some of the non-native English-speaking interviewed guests have been left uncorrected (even though they may not be grammatically or idiomatically correct) in order to capture their unique style and personality.

Preface

This book is the outcome of a televised series on Buddhism that I helped to produce. Such a series is rare, especially one that aired for an entire year. This series was shown on a Los Angeles cable network channel for 52 Sundays throughout the year 2006. Even more rare is the fact that this series was filmed in Japan to constitute, perhaps, the first-ever trans-continental Buddhist televised project of this length.

The original plan was to continue to air it in other major American metropolitan areas, such as Honolulu, the San Francisco Bay Area, Seattle-Tacoma, Chicago, and New York, but it did not materialize for a host of reasons. However, I felt compelled to put the contents of the series in writing, for I believe that the teachings and the interviews of this series had a valuable message for confronting the spiritual, religious and social issues facing all of us today. This book is, thus, the outcome of my fervent wish!

As the word "Kaleidoscope" in the subtitle indicates, this book offers—in all their respective beauty and wonder—a wide range of topics related to Buddhism, its teachings, practices, and cultural and artistic features. It even includes a program devoted just to humor! There are 52 fourteen-minutes-long programs. Half of them include interviews with Buddhist practitioners of various traditions as well as scholars.

The series aims not only to explain the basic teachings and practices of this ancient religion but also to apply them to address some of the spiritual, religious and social issues of contemporary society. As noted above, this series is not sectarian in nature, for it focuses on the teachings of early Buddhism, particularly the Four Marks of Existence, which form part of the foundation for many of the schools of Buddhism today.

I did my best to include as many of the major traditions of Buddhism as possible, but I deeply regret that I was not able to do so with the Vietnamese tradition on account of the limitations of filming the series in Japan. Also, the series has the general American audience in mind, but I believe its message appeals to audiences that transcend national, cultural and even religious boundaries. As a case in point, a Japanese translation of this book will soon be published in Japan.

The videos on which this book is based are available on the website of The Society for the Promotion of Buddhism (BDK), which sponsored and funded this series. I strongly encourage the readers of this book to access the website, for your understanding and appreciation will definitely be enhanced by the visual impact of the videos that show the guests and scenes related to the topics being discussed. (Please see separate page for website access.)

In the process of producing these programs, I played many roles including those of scriptwriter, producer, speaker and interviewer even though I had hardly any experience with any of them. Being asked to take on this project just six months prior to its first airing, I had no confidence in being able to carry it out, but I accepted this rare opportunity even while maintaining my fulltime teaching load at the university. In hindsight, it was a miracle that I managed to write the script for all 52 programs and survived the all-day shootings that took place throughout the year.

That I survived to contribute to the successful airing of this project is a testimony to the enormous support I received from the staff at The Society for the Promotion of Buddhism, my family, and all those who appeared on the series as guests. To them, I send forth my heartfelt gratitude.

I wish also to extend my profound appreciation to the Rev. Gyodo Kono Memorial Scholarship Fund for its generous financial support enabling me to bring this book to its completion. It is my sincere hope that this book contributes in some small ways toward the Kono Fund's noble mission of making Buddhism available to as many people as possible. Finally, I am deeply grateful to Marvin Harada and the other members of the publication committee of the Buddhist Education Center for accepting this book and to Arlene Kato and Janis Hirohama for their technical and editorial support.

Kenneth Kenshin Tanaka

CHAPTER ONE:
Introduction with Focus on the Growth of Buddhism in America

◆ ◆ ◆

PROGRAM 1
Introduction to the Program and an Overview of the Growth of Buddhism

There is nothing as empty as an existence in which we do not know why we were born into this world, and for what we should devote our lives.

(*Mutually Sustaining Life, p.154*)

Preface

Hello. I'm Ken Tanaka. I am honored to be able to serve as your "guide" throughout this program.

During the 52 shows of this program series, we wish to accomplish two things. First, we want to *offer basic knowledge* about Buddhism, especially the early teachings and practice as taught by the Buddha. Secondly, we want to try to address the *spiritual and religious concerns* of you and I living in the 21st century.

And it's our sincere hope that what we have to share with you, both the knowledge and the spiritual dimensions of Buddhism, will add to making your lives more meaningful, while also contributing to the peace and happiness of the world.

The Society for the Promotion of Buddhism

This program is being sponsored by the Society for the Promotion of Buddhism (or Bukkyō Dendō Kyōkai). Since 1965, this non-sectarian, non-profit organization has dedicated itself to the promotion of Buddhism throughout the world.

For example, the Society has been distributing free of charge the book, *The Teaching of Buddha*, in hotels. This book is now *translated into 41 different languages* including Swahili, Arabic, Finnish, Tagalog and English, and is in 1,100,000 rooms in 55 countries.

The Society has also established academic chairs of Buddhist Studies at 14 universities in Europe and North America that include Oxford University, the University of California at Berkeley, Harvard

University, and the University of Calgary.

Another project is to translate into English 139 main scriptures from the Chinese Buddhist Canon, which when completed will contain close to 150 volumes.

The Society is, thus, helping to actualize the meaning of the *Wheel of Dharma* that we saw portrayed at the beginning of the program. This Wheel of Dharma symbolizes the Buddha's teaching that continues to spread widely and endlessly like a rolling wheel of a cart. Today, the *Wheel of Dharma* has become the common *symbol of Buddhism.*

Self-Introduction

Allow me now to introduce myself briefly. I grew up and was educated in public schools in Northern California. My first exposure to Buddhism came at the age of 13, when I began attending the Mountain View Buddhist Temple. Soon after graduating college in 1970, I went to Thailand to live a life of a monk in a Buddhist monastery. With renewed interest in Buddhism, I returned to the U.S. to pursue graduate studies and to eventually earn a Ph.D. from the University of California at Berkeley. Since then, I have been teaching at academic institutions in the U.S. and Japan.

My primary spiritual tradition is *Jodo Shinshu*, one of the main Japanese Pure Land schools. As an ordained priest in that tradition, I also served as a temple minister for a number of years in the 1990s.

The Nature of the Program

Now, as for this program, we will periodically be inviting guests to bring expertise to a variety of areas. These shows will be introductory in nature for those who know little or nothing about Buddhism. We shall do our best to make our presentations simple and easy to understand. So as the Buddha often called out, "*Ehi passiko,*" meaning, "*come here and see*" or "gather around and check it out." We hope that you will gather around as often as you can, so that we can explore together the vital issues of life as reflected in the passage that appeared at the top of this program:

"There is nothing as empty as an existence in which we do not

know why we were born into this world, and for what we should devote our lives."

In the first segment, we will begin by discussing a very interesting phenomenon of how Buddhism is growing in America.

The Growth of Buddhism in America

Professor Diana Eck of Harvard University, who is conducting an extensive study of the various religions in the U.S., has stated, "Buddhism is now an American religion."

This leads me to begin with a question, which I bet many of you won't be able to answer correctly. Which city in the world has the largest number of Buddhist schools? You might say Bangkok, Taipei or Kyoto. The answer is, in fact, Los Angeles, where there are at least 80 different schools of Buddhism. In other words, virtually all the main schools of Buddhism in Asia are now represented in Los Angeles. This is truly amazing.

In Asia, Buddhists from different countries have rarely known each other, let alone live in the same community. But in Los Angeles, a Thai and a Korean temple are located on the same street. The same thing can be said for other major metropolitan areas such as Honolulu, the San Francisco Bay Area, Seattle-Tacoma, Chicago, and New York.

So, how many Buddhists are there? Most experts estimate this number to be around 3 million. It's been difficult to give a more exact number, as there has been no thorough study or a clear criterion for determining who qualifies as a "Buddhist." If we include the so-called "Night-stand Buddhists," those who are not members of any temples or centers but practice Buddhism in the privacy of their home doing meditation and reading Buddhist books at night (hence, the term "Night-stand Buddhists"), then the number would be much more. However, even at 3 million, this is a significant number, equivalent to little over 1 percent of the U.S. population.

Now, of those Buddhists who attend temples and centers, we can perhaps categorize them into four groups:

1. New Asian-American Buddhists (those who mostly arrived in the U.S. since the '60s: the Vietnamese, Thai, Korean,

Cambodian, Laotian, and Sri Lankan).

2. Old-line Asian-American Buddhists (those who were established before the Second World War: the Chinese and the Japanese).

3. Convert Buddhists whose main practice is meditation (predominately, Euro-Americans belonging to Zen, Vipassana and Tibetan traditions).

4. Convert Buddhists whose main practice is chanting (Sokagakkai International—U.S.A., comprised of a sizable percentage of African- and Hispanic-Americans).

Among these four groups, what draws extra attention of the media and the scholars are the convert Buddhists, especially the famous. Someone once made a comment in jest, "Hey, Richard Gere and Tina Turner don't look Buddhist!" Well, they may not fit the image, but they are Buddhists, and are very dedicated ones at that.

There are plenty more convert Buddhists, which is why some time back, *Time* magazine on its front cover had Brad Pitt, who starred in the popular movie, "Seven Years in Tibet," with a heading, "The American Fascination with Buddhism." And it dedicated a ten-page article on how and why many Americans are attracted to Buddhism.

Well, it has been said that there is a Chinese restaurant in virtually every city in America, but maybe the same is now becoming true of Buddhist temples and meditation centers.

A Humorous Encounter
of Two Buddhist Traditions

Before we conclude our show, I would like to share a humorous episode from American Buddhism, caused by different Buddhists coming together for the first time. If you don't find it funny now, hopefully you will … as you keep watching the program.

Once a Korean monk and a Tibetan Lama met for a doctrinal debate at a gathering at Harvard University as hundreds looked on. It was an impressive sight when the two eminent monks entered the stage with their flowing robes, attended by their disciples. The

Korean Zen master began by thrusting out his arm, holding an orange. He then asked "What is this?" seeking an answer, which in Zen calls for a profound spiritual understanding.

Unaccustomed to this Zen style, the Tibetan Lama seemed perplexed and turned toward his translator. As they whispered back and forth for several minutes as the hushed audience waited in great anticipation, the Tibetan translator finally addressed the crowd: "The Master says, 'What is the matter with him? Don't they have oranges where he comes from?'"

The debate went no further.[1]

Thank you for joining us. Please visit our website for more information. In our next show, we'll be discussing meditation with a guest. We hope to see you next week.

---

[1] Mark Epstein, *thoughts without a thinker* (Basic Books, 1995), pp. 13-14

PROGRAM 2
Reasons for the Growth of Buddhism: Meditation

Oh Ananda, the Buddha remains unaffected by the eight things of this world: profit, harm, defamation, honor, praise, slander, suffer ing, and pleasure.

(Dhammapada Atthakathā)

Three Reasons for the Growth

In our last show, we talked about the growth of Buddhism in the U.S. Today, we want to ask "why?"

I believe there are three main reasons. The first is the healthy attitude of Buddhism when dealing with the *negatives of life*, such as old age, death and "losing." People clamor for youth, life, and winning, but there is reluctance, even taboo, in dealing with old age, death and losing. Buddhism, on the other hand, sees them as a *natural part of life* that needs to be affirmed and accepted. When there is youth, there is old age; when there is birth there is death; and when one team wins the other team loses. It's so simple, yet so difficult to see them in that way. But by seeing them as a natural part of life, we're able to deal more effectively with them and even turn what we inadvertently perceive as "negatives" into a springboard for living a fuller life.

Secondly, Buddhism gives much value to the *personal understanding* of the individual. This is because the teaching cannot come alive and make real sense without it speaking directly to our unique experience. We must test how it works in our everyday life. The Buddha once cautioned his disciples: "Do not accept a statement on the grounds that it is found in our books… or because the teacher said so."

The third major reason lies in people's attraction to *meditation*. Many find Buddhist meditation easy to do, therapeutic and empowering. Sitting meditation, in particular, is the main practice in Zen, Theravada and Tibetan schools, which have attracted the largest number of converts to Buddhism.

Today, I am pleased to have a guest to help us better understand

Vipassana or Insight meditation, which comes to us from the *Theravada tradition* of Southeast Asia.

Guest Interview

KT: Our guest is Jonathan Watts who is practicing in the Theravada tradition, which is mostly found in Sri Lanka, Burma, Thailand, Cambodia and Laos. Hi, Jon, welcome.

Jonathan Watts: Nice to be here.

KT: Let me ask you. How long have you been practicing Vipassana, and how did you get started?

Jonathan Watts: I've been practicing since about 1990, when I had a chance to live in Thailand. While I was there, I went to southern Thailand and was able to practice in the Thai forest tradition with a teacher named Buddhadāsa, whose student now, Santikāro, teaches in Chicago.

KT: Can I ask you about Vipassana? What do Vipassana and also Samatha, what do they mean. And what is their relationship?

Jonathan Watts: In Theravada meditation, we talk of two different styles, Samatha and Vipassana. Samatha means "calming," and Vipassana means "clear intuitive insight." And so, usually, we do the Samatha practice first, calming of the breath, the mind and body. And under those conditions, we can engage in insight. So that would be insight into one's mind and insight into one's breath and body.

And then technically we also talk about insight into three factors, which is the ever-changing nature of all phenomena, which we call "impermanence." And then that insight leads us to the insight that attaching to any of these impermanent phenomena lead to suffering. That's the second insight.

And then the third insight follows that, which is that all ever-changing phenomena—if we understand self like that—that is not self. That actually liberates us to act in the world as freely, as free beings.

KT: Well, I wonder if you could show us how meditation is done.

Jonathan Watts: Sure. Okay. Now, when we get started, we want to find something comfortable to sit on, something like this (cushion). So, there are a couple of different ways of sitting. We can use the full lotus, but that is usually too difficult for most people. So, we can use the half lotus, which is one leg [folded] over the top [of the other leg]. And again you can use this way, too [the other leg over the top of the other leg]. Also there is the Japanese style which is called *"seiza"*, which is putting your legs [tucked under your buttocks and pointing] behind like this and having the pillow support you like that [under your buttocks].

Okay, now that we have gotten comfortable in our sitting position, we want to get our hands together. And we just want to have them in a comfortable place. Here on the thighs [hands on one's thighs] is a good way, except in hot weather our hands tend to sweat [when placed] on our thighs. So another way we can do it is this way with our hands just here [left hand on top of the right and both hands placed on the lap]. Basically we just want to have them in a comfortable place.

And the next thing is your eyes. Preferred way is to usually to keep your eyes three quarters shut like this, with the line of your sight off the tip of your nose. Now we can begin the practice.

Another name for this Vipassana meditation is *ānāpānasati*, which means mindfulness, *sati*. Inbreath, *āna* and outbreath, *apāna*. And when we do this, we just bring our mindfulness or concentration, just called *sati*, onto our breathing. Watching it go in and out. And we study the inbreath, and we study the outbreath. We study the deep breath and the shallow breath. Together, not forcing it, just following the breath in and out. And when you breathe, we are not breathing deeply from here [chest], like after you've been running [breathing from the chest] like "ha …," but it's a deeper breath from down here [lower belly], kind of like you're drawing the breath down into your belly. But again, there is no need to force it, because naturally your breath will calm down, the longer you sit.

So there is another method that we call "guarding." And when we become accustomed to the breath, we notice that there might be a certain place where it's sensitive. Where we notice it. Maybe here, on the top of the lip or up here on the tip of the nose, or back of the nasal cavity or perhaps down on the throat. There is a certain one spot that is very easy to notice, and so we bring our mindfulness, our *sati*, to that point. And we just guard it like a gate keeper. We notice when breath passes it on the inbreath and when it passes it on the outbreath.

And this guarding practice can also be very helpful for studying other points of what we call "contact." So there is not just contact of the breath on the nose but also the contact of, perhaps, a pain on our knee or an itch back behind our ear. And these are the places where we can also put our mindfulness.

We can also put our mindfulness if there is what we think of a distracting noise. So that pain becomes the point of mindfulness, and the noise outside becomes the point of mindfulness. So what we actually thought was an obstacle becomes actually something that helps us in our practice.

Now the final point here with guarding is—in general all of this Vipassana meditation—is that the mind often wanders. Mind often goes off on to thoughts and feelings. Maybe even a song comes into our head. And the point is not to get too upset with oneself. Just come back. Keep coming back. Keep coming back to mindfulness. And that is the practice, when we come back.

KT: Well, Jon. Thank you very much. That was very helpful. What do you gain when you meditate?

Jonathan Watts: Well, you gain a number of things. The basic from the *samatha* meditation, we gain a lot of stress reduction. And I think that's why a lot of people meditate nowadays. Specifically, that can help with things like insomnia and sleep, especially if we meditate just before we go to sleep. On a deeper level, when we do insight meditation and also we learn to bring, come back to ourselves to the guarding through the development of mindfulness, we learn how to stop. And that happens spontaneously during the day when we build up our meditation practice. So that stopping can help us stop, when we get involved in various difficult situations when our greed is getting out of control, or our anger is getting out of control. Or we are just sort of lost in our life, suddenly we find ourselves coming back to ourselves. Stopping and cut back, and stop from falling into our greed and anger.

KT: Well, thank you, Jon.

Jonathan Watts: My pleasure, Ken.

Closing Remarks

It can be said that in this regard, one of the outcomes of meditation is the peace and calm in the face of the ups and downs and the good and the bad, as seen in today's opening passage:

> *Oh Ananda, the Buddha remains unaffected by the eight things of this world: profit, harm, defamation, honor, praise, slander, suffering, and pleasure.*

Thank you for joining us. In our next show, we will look at the uniquely American innovations, with a focus on one of the largest and oldest schools, Jodo Shinshu.

PROGRAM 3

The Developments in American Buddhism: Jodo Shinshu as an Example

I live here and now, not by myself, but along with many other "lives." When "life," which causes and sustains my existence, achieves happiness, I, too, will become happy.

(*Mutually Sustaining, Life, p. 14*)

Jodo Shinshu School

In our last show, we discussed Vipassana meditation that comes to us from Southeast Asia. Today, I would like to focus on the teachings of *Jodo Shinshu,* a tradition that comes to us from Japan and one that is part of the Mahayana branch of Buddhism.

Jodo Shinshu (also known as Shin or Shinshu or Pure Land) also happens to be the tradition in which I was ordained, hence this robe I am wearing today. This is the robe that Jodo Shinshu priests in the United States wear for ordinary ceremonial purposes. As you can see, I am wearing a necktie, a shirt and a pair of pants, which represent a combination of the traditional and the modern, or the East and the West.

This is different from how most Jodo Shinshu priests dress in Japan, and is another example of how Buddhism has continued to change from the practices in Asia in adapting to the American circumstance.

It is this topic, the distinctive American form, that I wish to talk about today.

In order to understand this topic, I would like to initially provide a birds-eye view of the development of Buddhism from the time of the Buddha.

Roots of Buddhism:

A Very Brief Overview of the Development of Buddhism in Asia

The beginning of Buddhism, of course, starts with the Buddha who lived approximately 2,500 years ago, and about whom we will talk about in greater detail later on. Around 260 years later, by the third century before the Common Era, Buddhism, under the support of *King Ashoka*, spread throughout India, and even beyond its borders.

It is said that King Ashoka's son, Mahinda, went to Sri Lanka to introduce Buddhism. This was the beginning of the southern branch known as *Theravada* or the *"School of Elders,"* and today is found mostly in Sri Lanka, Burma, Thailand, Cambodia and Laos. The monks are well known by their saffron or orange-colored robes.

The northern branch is called *Mahayana, the "Larger Vehicle."* It mostly spread by way of the so-called "Silk Road" through ancient Central Asian kingdoms. And by the first century of the Common Era, Buddhism had begun to trickle into China. By the end of the fourth century, Buddhism became a state religion of the Northern Wei kingdom. Ever since, Buddhism has remained an important pillar in the religious life of China, alongside Confucianism and Taoism.

The Chinese then transmitted Buddhism to Vietnam in the second century and to Korea in the fourth century. Then, in the sixth century, Buddhism made its way to Japan from Korea.

As for Tibet, Buddhism was introduced directly from India a little later, around the seventh century.

American Buddhism: Four Phases

Let me now paint a quick picture of Buddhist development in the U.S., which can be divided into four phases.

The first phase, of the intellectuals, began in 1844 when Henry David Thoreau translated a chapter from the *Lotus Sutra*, one of the most important scriptures, from French into English.[1] He was followed later by people such as Henry Olcott and Paul Carus, both of whom became Buddhists and devoted their lives to propagating Buddhism.[2]

The second phase, which overlaps with the first to a great ex-

---

[1] The long-held view that Thoreau was the translator was recently academically demonstrated to be historically incorrect. I regret that this revision did not reach me in time for this program. The actual translator was Ms. Elizabeth Peabody.

[2] One cannot say that Carus was exclusively a Buddhist, but he was certainly an enthusiastic promoter of Buddhism with enormous results.

tent, refers to Buddhism brought over by Chinese and Japanese immigrants in the second half of the 1900s, who established numerous temples, mostly on the West Coast, serving as important centers of their community life.

The third phase refers to the convert Buddhists that began with *"Beat Buddhism"* in the 1950s, as represented by such individuals as Allen Ginsberg and Gary Snyder. They paved a way for more full-fledged groups of the '60s and '70s such as the Tibetan institutions founded by Thartang Tulku and Chogyam Trungpa Rinpoche, the San Francisco Zen Center founded by Shunryū Suzuki Roshi, and the Insight Meditation Society founded by Americans Jack Kornfield, Joseph Goldstein, Sharon Salzberg and Jacqueline Schwartz. We should also include in this phase, the emergence of Sōkagakkai, which succeeded in creating the most ethnically and racially diverse organization.

The fourth phase does not lag too far behind the third phase, for it refers to the Buddhists who arrived in this country from the second half of the 1960s from such places as Taiwan, Vietnam and the other Southeast Asian countries.

"Golden Chain": An American Creation

The transmission from Asia across the Pacific to the U.S. called for major changes and innovations. The case in point is found in the Jodo Shinshu school. More specifically, on the mainland and in Hawai'i, the nationally organized *Buddhist Churches of America* and the *Higashi Honganji*, as well as the statewide *Honpa Hongwanji Mission of Hawai'i*, are the longest, continuously run institutions.

Within the Jodo Shinshu temples such as these, we find a uniquely American expression of its teachings called the *"Golden Chain,"* which, very interestingly, is not known at all in Japan.

This "Golden Chain" is very often recited together at services. It is probably the most popular and most well-known among the statements of Jodo Shinshu belief. This is especially true among the younger generation.

So that you can perhaps understand and feel its meaning, permit me to recite this slowly, as follows:

"I am a link in Amida's Golden Chain of love that stretches around the world. I will keep my link bright and strong. I will be kind and gentle to every living thing and protect all who are weaker than myself.

I will think pure and beautiful thoughts, say pure and beautiful words, and do pure and beautiful deeds.

May every link in Amida's golden chain of love become bright and strong, and may we all attain perfect peace."

I would like to briefly explain each line of this Golden Chain.

"I am a link in Amida's Golden Chain of love that stretches around the world. I will keep my link bright and strong."

This line tells us that each of us is part of a set of interconnected relationships that encompasses the whole world and beyond. And the very nature of this interconnectedness is boundless compassion, which is referred to as "Amida" or "Amida Buddha."

I would like to point out that the truth of "compassion" is expressed here as "love," which is a more familiar term to Americans. Also, here we cannot help but notice a strong sense of social or spiritual responsibility as he or she vows to do one's part to sustain this golden chain of interconnection by keeping one's link bright and strong.

"I will be kind and gentle to every living thing and protect all who are weaker than myself."

Here a person pledges to treat not only humans but all living beings with respect, including animals, birds, insects, and fish. There is no mention of the "rights" of humans to rule over other creatures, but rather humans are to co-exist with them. And in so doing, one vows to go to the aid of those in need, whether humans or other creatures.[3]

"I will think pure and beautiful thoughts, say pure and beautiful words, and do pure and beautiful deeds."

In Buddhism, the worth of a person is determined not by birth or one's class but one's deeds. So our spiritual happiness also depends on how one acts and sees the world, and is not determined by pre-

---

3 This respect for other creatures actually extends even to inanimate objects, such as mountains, rivers, grass and trees. This is principally true for Buddhists of the East Asian traditions, who believe that Buddha nature resides in all living beings and entities.

destination or by chance or by divine beings. We have the ability to determine our happiness, through what we think, how we speak and how we act.

> *"May every link in Amida's golden chain of love become bright*
> *and strong, and may we all attain perfect peace."*

It concludes with one's concern for the welfare of all others, wishing for all beings to reach the ultimate Buddhist goal of becoming Buddhas or attaining nirvana or enlightenment. This line is rooted in the realization that one cannot be truly happy if others are not also spiritually happy.

This is precisely what was being expressed in today's opening passage:

> *I live here and now, not by myself, but along with many other*
> *"lives." When "life," which causes and sustains my existence,*
> *achieves happiness, I, too, will become happy.*

These are my thoughts and feelings on the "Golden Chain," which for me personally has been an inspirational guiding force. Again, our Jodo Shinshu counterparts in Japan have never heard of it. Naturally, the reason for this was that the "Golden Chain" was composed on American soil, probably in Hawai'i prior to World War II at a time when openness and optimism flourished.

And so, once again, here too, is a prime example of a uniquely American form!

Closing Remarks

In our next show, a guest will talk about "engaged Buddhism," a movement that seeks to bring the teachings to address social problems and concerns. It promises to be a thought-provoking show, so please be sure to join us once again.

PROGRAM 4
Characteristics of American Buddhism: With a Focus on Engaged Buddhism

Because it recognizes the mutual relationship of every being, it accounts for the gratitude that arises from the realization of this interdependency. It produces the volunteer spirit to repay these invisible obligations.

(*Mutually Sustaining Life, p. 90*)

Other Characteristics of American Buddhism

This show is the last in the series of four shows on how and why Buddhism has been growing in America. Today, we would like to explore one of the interesting characteristics of American Buddhism, what is being called "engaged Buddhism."

Engaged Buddhism refers to the effort to apply the teachings to address social issues and problems in order to build a more equitable and peaceful world. This emphasis on the outer and the social differs from the traditional Buddhism that has emphasized the inner and the mental.

Before we begin with our main topic, let me briefly mention some of the other distinctive characteristics of American Buddhism.

First, there are definitely more women in leadership roles, as they make up half of the teachers in some of the convert groups. As discussed earlier, women helped to found the Insight Meditation Society, and women now hold top leadership positions at San Francisco Zen Center and elsewhere.

Secondly, monks and nuns are the norm in the Buddhist world in Asia, but American Buddhists have largely rejected celibacy in favor of married priests or priests in long term relationships.

Thirdly, psychology and psychotherapy have proven to be one of the "channels" through which Buddhism is being understood and adopted by many Americans. The reasons are due to the obvious similarities in their focus on the mind and inner workings.

Finally, the American love of humor has also impacted the

Buddhist world. For instance, I heard a Buddhist joke even on a mainstream radio station: "Why couldn't the Buddha vacuum clean under a sofa?" Well, the answer is ... are you ready? ... "because he had no attachments!"

Well, I think it's pretty good! If you don't get it, please keep watching this program as I will explain in due course.

Today, I am pleased to have with us a guest to help throw greater light on the topic of engaged Buddhism.

Guest Interview

KT: Our guest is Professor David Loy, who has written extensively and lectured world-wide on Buddhist philosophy, especially as they apply to social issues of the day. David, thank you for joining us.

Prof. Loy: Thank you, Ken. It's my pleasure to be here.

KT: Let me begin by asking a question about how you got started with Buddhism and when.

Prof. Loy: I was a part of large wave of young Americans, who became Buddhists in the late 60s and early 70s. I think it was a natural development out of the cultural transformation that occurred then. Not only politically but also spiritually, I think many of us became open to new possibilities. And for me personally, as a philosophy major in college it wasn't such a big jump from existential philosophy to something like Buddhism, which, as you know, is a very existential religion. It has a lot to say about death, meaning of life, and anxiety and such things.

KT: I know you've written a number of books. I wonder if you can say a few words about some of the books that you've written, specifically on engaged Buddhism.

Prof. Loy: Thanks for the plug!

KT: You're welcome.

Prof. Loy: There are two main books. One of them is historical, and it tries to use Buddhist principles to look at how it was that the history of the West developed in the way it did. The title of that one is *A Buddhist History of the West*. It doesn't talk about Buddhism in the West but uses Buddhist ideas. And the other one is more recent.

That one is called *The Great Awakening: A Buddhist Social Theory*. And that again tries to elaborate Buddhist principles into the social understanding. As you know, Buddhism doesn't really have a social theory that we can extrapolate from the basic Buddhist teachings to look at social issues and social problems. That's what that book tries to do.

KT: I see. Well, on that point that Buddhism is lacking social philosophy, that there are some people who claim that Buddhism should not be so concerned with the social. Rather it should focus more on the inner and the mental. How do you respond to that?

Prof. Loy: I think that is a very good question because, of course, many people do think that way. But the really important response is "Can we really separate them? Can we really separate the personal from the social?" In fact you can argue that it's really inconsistent with basic Buddhist teachings to try to do that. As you know, Buddhism is all about awakening, awakening toward our true nature. And awakening involves overcoming this sense of duality between inside and outside, this sense of separation that I am in here, and the world is out there. Buddhism emphasizes interdependence of everything, that there is no self apart from the world. So, the danger then is if we are thinking that we are just looking after our own liberation, our own awakening, then we are really reinforcing in our practice what we are trying to overcome.

KT: Let me ask you. Are there organizations that are specifically dedicated to socially engaged Buddhism?

Prof. Loy: Yes, there are quite a few now. The two that I am most familiar with are first the International Network of Engaged Buddhists, which is based in Bangkok, Thailand. It's primarily an Asian organization, so it has branches in South Asia, Southeast Asia, Japan, Korea, and Taiwan. But the main group for Americans is the Buddhist Peace Fellowship, which is based in Berkeley, California. It started about 25 years ago. And it's an umbrella group encompassing all different types of Buddhism. In fact, you don't even have to be Buddhist to be involved as long as you are committed to the same basic principles of peace and justice that they are concerned about.

KT: Can I ask you more specifically, what are some of the issues? You know, the environment, etc.

Prof. Loy: Sure, as you can imagine, peace and justice issues are a very important part of their work, especially in the last few years dealing with things like Afghanistan and Iraq and terrorism. They've also been very involved with matters working with prison groups. There are a lot of people, lots of Buddhists, for example, now in prison. We have a huge prison system in the United States. They do a lot with homelessness and other issues of poverty. And they also try to address other peace and justice issues like gender and racism. So, it's really dealing with a large number of issues. In addition to all that, they are trying to develop social analysis from a Buddhist perspective that would help us understand these problems.

KT: Fascinating … one of the recent concerns is, of course, Iraq war. And I know you've written extensively and have spoken widely in different parts of the world. Could we hear a little bit about your thoughts on Iraq?

Prof. Loy: Well, as you could imagine, Buddhism and the Buddha had a great deal to say about issues of peace, non-violence and hatred. One of the most interesting and important things he said was that, "hatred is never ended by hatred." Hatred, the original term is *"vera,"* is always ended by non-hatred, often translated as "love" or "compassion." Now the interesting question for us today is: if that's true personally and the Buddha said twenty-five hundred years ago that this was an ancient law, if it's true personally, is it also true collectively? Can't we see it operating in Iraq right now? It's a sad thought, but the truth is that the United States is probably more disliked in many quarters, more hated as a result of our very military response to terrorism than we were three years ago (in 2001) before September 11th. It seems to be exemplifying what the Buddha was getting at, that when your response to terrorism is killing terrorists, you can't be surprised that others are springing up out of the network in response to that.

KT: David, is there a final point that you'd like to make?

Prof. Loy: Buddhism is all about suffering and how to end our suffering. Traditionally, this was understood in a very personal way. How do I address my own greed, my own ill will, and my own delusion? Again, these three are roots of evil. But the situation that we find now is quite different, I think. We have to find ways to address the institutional forms of these three poisons. We are now in situations where we have institutionalized greed, institutionalized ill will and institutionalized delusion. And that's really the *"koan."* That is really the challenge for contemporary Buddhism. Can we understand how to address them as well as our personal problems?

KT: Well, thank you, David, for sharing your thoughts and insights with us.

Prof. Loy: Thank you, Ken.

Closing Remarks

Obviously, in Buddhism there is no one position that all Buddhists must adhere to on social matters. Each person must arrive at his or her own opinion. What is fascinating, however, is that on the American soil, we are witnessing a blossoming of the social dimension of Buddhism in what is called "engaged Buddhism." However, this spirit is not an American invention, for it goes to the very heart of Buddhist spirituality, which was expressed in today's opening passage:

> *Because it recognizes the mutual relationship of every being, it accounts for the gratitude that arises from the realization of this interdependency. It produces the volunteer spirit to repay these invisible obligations.*

In our next series of shows, we will move away from the topic of American Buddhism and take a look back to the beginning of Buddhism in ancient India, as we explore the life and the teachings of the Buddha.

CHAPTER TWO:
Shakyamuni Buddha: Life and Images

PROGRAM 5
Buddha's Birth, Renunciation and Ascetic Practice

The luxuries of the palace, this healthy body, this rejoicing youth! What do they mean to me?" he thought. "Someday we may all be sick, we shall become aged; from death there is no escape. Pride of youth, pride of health, pride of existence—all thoughtful people should cast such pride aside.

(*The Teaching of Buddha, p. 8*)

Background of the Buddha

Previously, we looked at the state of Buddhism in America. Well, over the course of the next four programs, we'll be going back to the very origins of Buddhism, focusing on the life of the Buddha, the founder of Buddhism. *The Buddha was a human being, not a god.* He lived in the northeastern area of the Indian subcontinent some 2,500 years ago.

The records tell us that the Buddha was born a prince of a kingdom located on the present-day borders of India and Nepal. His given name was *"Siddhartha"* (Siddhārtha), meaning *"he whose purpose is accomplished,"* and his family name was *"Gautama."*

In Sanskrit, the language of ancient India, the term "Buddha" meant *"one who has awakened."* So, "Buddha" is actually a title used to refer to anyone who attains ultimate awakening, which is the goal of all Buddhists, past and present. In another words, in Buddhism, there are as many Buddhas as there are awakened people. Yet normally, when we say "the Buddha," we are referring to the Indian prince who became the founder of Buddhism. To avoid any confusion, he is often referred to as "Shakyamuni Buddha" (Śākyamuni); "Shakya" in *"Shakyamuni"* refers to the name of his clan and "muni" means the "sage," thus, *"The sage of the Shakya Clan."*

Birth and Youth

According to Buddhist legend, one night the prince's mother, *Queen Maya (Māyā)*, had a strange dream, in which she dreamed that a white elephant entered her womb through the right side of her chest, after which she conceived. Nine months later when Queen Maya was returning to her parents' home to have the baby, she took a rest in the Lumbini (Lumbinī) Garden, finding herself captivated by the beautiful flowers of the *Ashoka* (Aśoka) *trees*. As she reached up for a branch, it is said that the tree bent itself down to meet her hand, and she gave birth standing up.

And as soon as the prince was born, he is said have taken seven steps and proclaimed, "In the heavens above and heavens below, I alone am the honored one!" But the joy of birth was short-lived, as Queen Maya suddenly died. The prince was, then, brought up by his stepmother, *Mahaprajapati* (Mahāprajāpatī).

By many accounts, the young prince was a sensitive child. Once, he sat under a tree, watching a farmer plowing the ground. Soon the birds began to sweep down to prey on the earthworms. This shocked the young prince, and he was saddened by the fact that creatures have to prey on others.

Given the sensitive nature of the young prince, his father, King *Shuddhodana* (Śuddhodana), was probably not surprised when a hermit prophesized that his son would be either a great king or an eminent spiritual leader. The king was fearful that his son might abandon the kingdom in favor of seeking the spiritual path, so he did everything in his power to shield him from experiencing pain and suffering. In this way, the prince was surrounded only by young, healthy and beautiful people, and sheltered by a life of pleasure within the pristine confines of the palace.

Renunciation: The Four Sojourns

However, this all came to an end when he wandered outside the palace gates four separate times.

On his first journey, accompanied by his driver, Prince Siddhartha rode out from the *east gate* in a chariot. He then came upon an *old person*, bent over and barely able to walk even with a cane. Having never seen anyone like him before, the prince was puzzled and asked the driver who the old person could be? Well, the Prince was told that everyone would be like him, if one lived long enough. Shocked, the prince asked, "I, too?" and the reply was, "Yes, you too, sir."

On another day, the prince left from the *south gate*. Shortly, the prince came upon a very *sick person* lying on the side of the road in great pain and agony. Shocked again, the prince asked, "I, too?" and the reply was, "Yes, you too, sir."

The prince left yet a third time from the *west gate*. He came upon a *deceased person* being carried by his family to the funeral pyre. Shocked once again, the prince asked, "I, too?" and the reply was again, "Yes, you too, sir."

On another day, the prince left from the *north gate*, where he came upon a *wandering monk*. This time, the monk's serene and composed features captivated the prince's attention to such an extent that he felt compelled to be like him and seek the spiritual life.

The Start of Buddha's Search

Soon thereafter, he made the difficult decision to leave behind his family, along with the life of luxury and pleasure, in search of an answer to the question of suffering and how to overcome it. His motivation to do so is expressed in today's saying:

> *"The luxuries of the palace, this healthy body, this rejoicing youth! What do they mean to me?" he thought. "Some day we may all be sick, we shall become aged; from death there is no escape. Pride of youth, pride of health, pride of existence—all thoughtful people should cast such pride aside."*

Then the prince headed off for the forest. He was 29 years of age.

Guest Interview

KT: In today's modern world, many of you may wonder why and how one follows a spiritual calling. To take us on her personal journey, our guest today is Reverend Jiho Sargent, who is a Zen priest. Reverend Sargent, thank you for coming today to be a part of our program.

Rev. Sargent: Thank you for inviting me.

KT: You're welcome. I have a number of questions to ask you. The first one is, how long have you been a priest?

Rev. Sargent: Well, I was a priest trainee for ten years and fulfilled the qualifications of being a priest with a temple. And I've been fully ordained for 15 years.

KT: What made you go so far as to become a priest? You didn't have to be a priest.

Rev. Sargent: Well, no. Just by circumstances, I found myself one time as the leader of a *zazen* (sitting meditation) group for Westerners, and it finally occurred to me that I had absolutely no idea what I was doing. I was the leader simply because the meetings were in my house. It wasn't really much help in dealing with people. So, I wanted to become an apprentice priest and have the training that nuns undergo to help me.

KT: Let me ask you about your robe. You know, Buddhist priests and monks and nuns dress differently.

Rev. Sargent: Our robes, interestingly, I think, are a commentary on the history of Buddhism in its passage from India to Japan and then to the West because the outermost robe that we wear is an Indian Buddhist robe. This is a miniature version of it, but the full size one ties over the shoulder. Yours is even more of a miniature version than mine.

KT: Although this one and that one, in essence, if I open mine up, it's very similar inside. It looks a little different.

Rev. Sargent: Different, yes.

KT: So, Indian outside …

Rev. Sargent: Indian outside, then Chinese on the second layer, and then under that, you can't really see it, Japanese kimono style garment. And those of us who come from the West, I think, mostly wear a layer of Western underclothes under that. But, of course, once we get under the skin, we are all the same.

KT: Oh, very good! Tell me, Buddhist monks and priests often shave their heads, monks especially or definitely. Why do they shave their heads?

Rev. Sargent: Well, it's basically a symbol of cutting off attachments to worldly things, and it's also a way of identifying a Buddhist priest. In earlier times until the 1870s, the Japanese government required that almost all Buddhist priests have their heads shaved. And Jodo Shinshu was an exception, even at that time. But most of the other denominations required it so that you could identify them.

KT: I see. Interesting…let me ask you about the Buddha. What do you find attractive about the Buddha?

Rev. Sargent: Well, what I find most attractive and what attracted me in the first place is that the Buddha didn't ask us to believe in him or anyone else or in his teachings for that matter. He simply asked us to act in a way that is friendly to other beings, whether human or not. And that leads to a peaceful universe. That, I think, is a good thing to have.

KT: So, it's not so much what you believe but how you act in the world.

Rev. Sargent: Yes.

KT: Reverend Sargent will be joining us next week as we explore the second half of the Buddha's life journey. I look forward to seeing you again.

Rev. Sargent: Thank you.

PROGRAM 6
Buddha's Awakening, Teaching and Passing On

When the morning star appeared in the eastern sky, the struggle was over and the Bodhisattva's mind was as clear and bright as the breaking day. He had, at last, found the path to Enlightenment.
(The Teaching of Buddha, p. 14)

Buddha's Ascetic Practices

When Prince Siddhartha left the palace in search of truth, he went to study with various teachers. From this point on, he was no longer a prince, but rather became a *Bodhisattva*, or in other words, a *seeker of enlightenment*. Despite these well-known teachers, he found none of their ways to be completely satisfactory; instead, the Bodhisattva joined other seekers to engage in severe ascetic practices. These austere practices were so demanding that his body became extremely emaciated, to the point where his arms and legs became so thin that they were like the jointed stems of a bamboo.

Unfortunately, yet again, he was making no progress whatsoever, giving him no choice but to abandon this path. Hence, both the lives of the pleasures of the palace and the six years of ascetic life could not bring peace.

Buddha's Offerings from Sujata

The Bodhisattva then regained his physical strength by receiving an offering of milk and rice by a young woman named *Sujata* (Sujātā) from a nearby village. Thereafter, the Bodhisattva sat under a Pipal (Pippala) tree, which came to be called *"the tree of awakening"* or Bodhi tree, and resolved not to leave the spot until he had realized the state of awakening. In the shade of the tree, he then settled into a state of deep meditative calm and peace.

Buddha's Battle against Mara

There are many accounts of what actually took place, but one that I find easy to understand and appreciate is explained in a story of the Bodhisattva's encounter with a figure called *Mara* (Māra). *Mara* means *"the bringer of death,"* and one that symbolizes our mental and emotional attachment. In this tale, Mara appears before the Bodhisattva with various temptations to get the Bodhisattva to give in to his *greed, hatred and ignorance.*

For example, Mara sends an army of demons to attack him with many kinds of weapons. However, the Bodhisattva perceives the demons and their weapons as representing the attachment of hatred and anger.

Consequently, he did not react to them and so the rain of weapons hurled at him by the demons turned into a rain of beautiful flowers. In this way, the Bodhisattva saw that people suffer because they let these attachments run wild and overwhelm them.

Mara then approached the Bodhisattva directly to challenge him and asked, by what right he sat under the tree of awakening? The Bodhisattva replied that by the right of having practiced the spiritual path for a long time. Mara countered him by saying that he, too, had done the same. Besides which, he had all his armies to vouch for this fact; but who, he asked, could vouch for him?

Buddha's Awakening

The Bodhisattva, then, lifted his right hand and touched the ground, calling on the very earth as witness in what has come to be known as the *"earth-touching gesture."* This signalled Mara's defeat and the Bodhisattva's awakening as the Buddha.

This is obviously not the whole story of the Buddha's awakening, but rather gives us a glimpse into the nature of that awakening, as described in today's opening passage:

"When the morning star appeared in the eastern sky, the struggle was over and the Bodhisattva's mind was as clear and bright as the breaking day. He had, at last, found the path to Enlightenment."

He had become the "Awakened One," the Buddha!

Buddha's First Teachings: Turning of the Wheel of Dharma

Once he decided to share what he had discovered, the Buddha met up with five fellow ascetics, with whom he had trained together previously. At first, they shunned him, but Buddha's demeanor and his words won them over as they heard the Buddha deliver his first sermon. Convinced by the truth of his awakening, they became the Buddha's first disciples.

From there, the Buddha journeyed around the country sharing his teachings. His charisma and compassion led many to seek him as their teacher, and his number of disciples swelled. According to some accounts, his *wife, Yashodhara* (Yaśodharā), *son, Rahula* (Rāhula), *stepmother, Mahaprajapati* (Mahāprajāpatī), and his father also became members of the *Sangha* (saṁgha), the *order of monks and nuns.*

The Buddha's Passing

For the next 45 years the Buddha wandered throughout the region to share, to teach and to nurture. When he was 80 years old, he became deathly ill after eating some food offered by a layman. Lying between two large Sala (Śāla) trees, he continued to teach until his last moments of life. As his disciples, lay supporters and even the animals wept amid the sadness of the imminent death of their teacher, the Buddha spoke these famous words:

"Make yourself the light. Rely upon yourself. Do not depend upon anyone else. Make my teachings your light."

Guest Interview

KT: We are honored to have Rev. Jiho Sargent back with us again. Reverend Sargent, thanks for coming back. Good to have you back.

Rev. Sargent: My pleasure.

KT: You know, Buddhists have been accused of over-emphasizing unsatisfactoriness and suffering. But I tell such critics that that's just the beginning; that's where you start from. What is important is where you end up, which is enlightenment and awakening. And so, you yourself having become a priest in search of that awakening,

32

what differences have been made in your life, having been a priest?

Rev. Sargent: Well, mostly I don't know the differences until afterwards, and life just seems to proceed more smoothly than it used to. Perhaps that's from cutting attachments to concepts as well as cutting attachments to things like hair.

KT: Like hair? So, it's not just attachments to hair but cutting attachments to concepts. Is there any example you have, when you say cutting attachments to concepts?

Rev. Sargent: Well, one is my attachment to certain words. And it's much more relaxing for everyone else and for me when I let that attachment go some.

KT: So, breaking attachments to concepts is what Buddha taught, and that's what he did as he taught for forty-five years of his life. And, in so doing, there were women involved in that process. For example, his family members participated. Can you say something about the role of women in early Buddhism?

Rev. Sargent: Well, the important thing, I think, is that there was a role for women in early Buddhism. And it was a role in both the "home-leavers" and "house-holders" sections of the Buddhist sangha. We think now that Buddhism is something that doesn't exist for women, but that's not true. There have been women in Buddhism, we say, ever since the time of Shakyamuni Buddha himself.

KT: And women have become enlightened; they have reached the highest stages, haven't they?

Rev. Sargent: Yes. There are records from India of both women and men who recorded their awakenings.

KT: Speaking of women, there is another important woman in his life, who is Sujata, the young lady who provided milk-rice when he left the mountain.

Rev. Sargent: And then, that gave him the strength to be able to awaken.

KT: A related topic is how Buddha taught and how he got involved with people. Can you say a little bit more about that?

Rev. Sargent: Yes, we often seem to think of Buddhism as a rather passive thing, but Shakyamuni Buddha traveled extensively throughout the rest of his life and interacted with all kinds of people and taught them by both words and examples of his own way of life. So, this interaction with other people was a primary part of his teaching.

KT: So, often in the West, in the olden days, Buddhism was accused of being indifferent and withdrawn, but that's not really what it was in the beginning, or even now.

Rev. Sargent: That's true. Buddhism was very much involved with all kinds of beings from its start.

KT: Unfortunately, our time is up. It's been very informative and quite enjoyable the last two times. And I would like to thank you for joining us.

Rev. Sargent: Thank you.

Closing Remarks

The Buddha's life confirms that life at its core is fundamentally good. When we awaken to the true nature of life, we experience greater joy, gratitude and a sense of oneness with others. We realize that we are a part of the world and not separate from it.

As I leave you with thoughts of oneness, allow me to close with a little humor. Well, a Buddhist monk wanted a hot dog; so he walked over to a hot dog vender on a busy street corner. The vender asked, "What would you like sir?" The monk answered, "Make me ONE with EVERYTHING!" Well, hopefully you liked that one.

In the next two shows, we'll be looking at images of the Buddha with a guest. Please be sure to join us.

PROGRAM 7
Images of Shakyamuni Buddha

Do not seek to know Buddha by his form or attributes, for neither the form nor the attributes are the real Buddha. The true Buddha is Enlightenment itself. The true way to know Buddha is to realize Enlightenment.

(The Teaching of Buddha, p. 48)

Images of Shakyamuni Buddha

During the previous two shows, we looked at the life of the Buddha and related spiritual themes.

In the next two shows, we will continue to look at these themes through the images of Buddha and Bodhisattvas. These images, whether of statues or pictures, are probably the single most visible artifacts of Buddhism.

Most everyone even outside of Asia is familiar with the images of the Buddha. While such images are so common today and play such important roles in the religious lives of Buddhists, it's very interesting that the practice of representing the Buddha in *human form* did not begin for several hundred years after the Buddha had passed on.

A number of reasons for this have been offered. One view is that the Buddha was too sacred and beyond conceptual thinking to be limited to human form. This idea is actually similar to the views held in other religions, such as Judaism and Islam.

But, this did not mean that in the centuries immediately after the Buddha that there were no representations or *symbols for the Buddha* at all. For example, we find the use of *parasols* and the *empty throne*, which symbolized the Buddha's royal background. Another popular symbol was the *footprint* of the Buddha. And of course, the *Wheel of Dharma* that we see at the beginning of each of our shows, symbolizing the Dharma, or the teachings, which continue to spread widely and endlessly like a rolling wheel of a cart.

Guest Interview

KT: To tell us more about Buddha images, we have with us today a guest. Her name is Monika Dix. And Monika is presently affiliated with the Department of Asian Studies at the University of British Columbia. So, Monika, thank you for being with us.

Monika Dix: Thank you very much for inviting me on your program.

KT: The first, I'd like to ask you, to begin with, what did you find appealing about the Buddha images that you've been working with for so long?

Monika Dix: The most appealing aspect is the variety of Buddhist images we have. Like we see in the background, Buddha is represented in various kinds of images. All of them represent various aspects of his life and his teachings. This is done especially through paintings, sculptures, engravings, and in a lot of other forms of artifacts in order that we can come to better understand the complex and abstract Buddhist doctrine in more comprehensive ways.

KT: Yes, Buddhist teachings tend to be very difficult. So it is through the images, statues and paintings that we are able to convey the thoughts of Buddhism.

The first image that we'd like to talk about is what is known as the "Baby Buddha," one hand up, one hand down. Can you tell us more about this?

Monika Dix: Yes, this is a small bronze sculpture of the Baby Buddha. He has one hand pointing up and one hand pointing down, and he is uttering the sentence, "In the heavens above and the heavens below, I alone am the most honored one. This is the final birth. There is no further rebirth." There are various interpretations of the sentence, but I take it to mean that every person is unique and every person has the full possibility to attain enlightenment.

This particular representation of the Buddha is important to Buddhists in East Asian traditions because every year and on occasions of celebration of Buddha's birth day, which is April 8th, the devotees pour sweet green tea over the sculpture. This is symbolic for the sweet rain that fell upon the Buddha's birth in Lumbini (Lumbinī) Garden.

KT: Thank you. When I see this image with his hand up, it reminds me of a humorous story. Once a man I knew at a Buddhist temple that I used to serve came up to me and asked, "Is the Buddha a football fan?" I said, "Why do you ask that?" He said, "Well, because he has his hand up like this, he looks like those guys at the San Francisco Forty-niners' football games with those fingers and saying, 'We are number one! We are number one!' Well …"

So, Monika, the second image that I'd like for you to talk about is the one that is called *"Emaciated Buddha."* Could you tell us more?

Monika Dix: Yes, this is an image of emaciated Buddha, also called "[the] Buddha descending from the mountain." This image relates the story that following the Buddha's encounter of an old person, a sick person, and a dead person, he departed from his family, and he took up the residence in a mountain to practice ascetic meditation. In this image, you can see the bones are protruding underneath his body. His body is very emaciated, skinny, undernourished, and he is wearing or having a beard, which is a sign of wildness or like a wild recluse. Images like this are particularly popular in Japanese Zen Buddhist art.

KT: I see. Beard, that's interesting, especially since he left being a prince and having spent six years of austere practices.

The next Buddha is one that is probably the most well-known, particularly in Southeast Asia. And that's the one that depicts the moment of enlightenment. And we have an image here of the white Buddha. This is a Thai image, and it's called the "Buddha with the *earth-touching gesture."* Could you tell us more about that?

Monika Dix: Yes, the story about this particular Buddhist image relates to the victory over the demon god Mara (Māra). And the Buddha made a hand gesture or *mudra* (mudrā) of calling the earth to witness, meaning one hand is pointing down to the ground and the other hand is on his lap. "Calling the earth to witness" refers to the fact he accomplished good deeds in his past lives, and that he accumulated merits in his current life in order to occupy the lotus throne at Buddha Gaya. (Buddha Gayā/Bodh Gayā)

KT: So, what I like about this particular image is the gesture of touching the earth, and the earth and all of nature giving witness to his experience. So there is that strong connection between Buddha's enlightenment or awakening with the natural world, which I personally enjoy.

The next one I'd like to ask you about is the "Sermon Buddha" where he is giving his first sermon, and it's often called the *"Turning the Wheel of Dharma Buddha."*

Monika Dix: Yes, according to the story, the Buddha taught his first sermon at the Deer Park in Sarnath (Sārnāth) near Banaras (Banāras). And he taught his five primary disciples. And this image shows the Buddha teaching and discussing the Buddhist law in front of his five disciples. And it's called the "Turning the Dharma Wheel" because the Dharma Wheel is symbolic of the Buddha's teachings.

KT: The Dharma that's always turning like a wheel of a cart.

Monika Dix: That's right. This image of *Entering Nirvana (Nirvāṇa)* shows us the Buddha lying on his death bed and surrounded by his mourners. Particularly in Japanese paintings sculptures of mourners include not only his disciples but all kinds of lay people and animals. And sometimes his mother, Queen Maya (Māyā), is painted coming from the right corner and watching over the Buddha's death.

KT: So, the last Buddha I'd like to ask you about is the so-called "Laughing Buddha." And we have an image here. And so, can you tell us about this.

Monika Dix: Yes, Chinese *Laughing Buddha* which has a happy disposition, a fat belly and, in this image, he is wearing a bag. But sometimes he is depicted surrounded by many children. He is considered a form of Maitreya. However, this attribution is rather problematic because originally this particular deity was a Chinese fertility figure. It did not belong to the traditional Buddhist canon. And his Chinese name is Budai Heshang, meaning the "hemp-bag monk." And in China, he is seen at street corners and temples, and people rub his belly in order to aspire for good luck and prosperity.

KT: Like this (while rubbing the belly of the image)? Will it bring me luck, do you think?

Monika Dix: I think so.

KT: I hope so. Here we have an example of a native Chinese god, who has been incorporated into Buddhism, and which makes him very different from some of the other images that we saw, for example the Emaciated Buddha. There's quite a contrast between the two.

So, as you can see, these images are not idols to be worshiped as they themselves don't hold any special power. Instead, through the images, we are inspired to be like him. Even if we cannot be exactly like him, what is important is that we aspire in our own way to realize awakening. Hence we have today's passage,

Do not seek to know Buddha by his form or attributes, for neither the form nor the attributes are the real Buddha. The true Buddha is enlightenment itself. The true way to know the Buddha is to realize enlightenment.

Monika will be joining us once again next week as we continue to take a look at the images of Buddhism.

KT: Monika, thank you for being with us. See you next week.

Monika Dix: I'm looking forward to joining you again.

PROGRAM 8
Images of Buddhas and Bodhisattvas

The Spirit of Buddha is that of great loving kindness and com-
passion. The great loving kindness is the spirit to save all people
by any and all means. The great compassion is the spirit that
prompts it to be ill with the illness of people and to suffer with
their suffering.

(The Teaching of Buddha, p. 28)

In this week's program, we will continue to explore the images
of Buddhism. If you know anything about Buddhist images at all,
you will know that these images are not simply confined to that of
Shakyamuni Buddha. Today, we will look at images of Bodhisattvas
and Buddhas other than Shakyamuni.

Let's begin with the *Bodhisattvas*. "*Bodhi*" means "*awakening*" and
"*sattva*" means "*beings.*" They are, thus, "beings of awakening." This
carries at least two meanings, the first of which means "those who are
in search of awakening," as we saw in the case of Prince Siddhartha
when he left home to become an ascetic.

In its second meaning, Bodhisattva refers to those who have
reached high spiritual levels but are not yet fully Buddhas. Actually,
many Bodhisattvas put off becoming Buddhas in order to voluntarily
stay closer to the people they wish to help. In fact, their very existence is dedicated to assisting others, which is reflected in the first of
the Four Universal Vows of the Bodhisattvas, "No matter how large
the number of beings, I vow to deliver them all."

For many devotees, the Bodhisattvas are more accessible than the
Buddhas, who are sometimes regarded as being too transcendent to
help with their more mundane requests, like curing their sickness
and protecting them from danger. Such "savior" Bodhisattvas have
been the object of popular devotion.

Next, how are we to understand the Buddhas other than
Shakyamuni (Śākyamuni)? Well, soon after the passing of Shakyamuni, Buddhists began to believe that there were many Buddhas,

the so-called *Past Buddhas*, who lived on earth prior to Shakyamuni Buddha. Hence, Shakyamuni, the founder of Buddhism, was one in a long line of Buddhas who preceded him.

This then led to the belief that there would appear a *Future Buddha* called *Maitreya* to revitalize the spiritual state of the world. The exact time of the arrival of the Maitreya ranges from 5,000 years to even one billion years into the future. Until the appointed time, Maitreya now waits in Tushita (Tuṣita) Heaven as a Bodhisattva until he is able to descend to earth as a Buddha.

At the same time, there soon emerged a belief in *Contemporary Buddhas*. They, unlike the past and future Buddhas, lived in the present and in realms beyond this world. The most popular among these Contemporary Buddhas is *Amitabha* (Amitābha), who is the object of devotion of Pure Land Buddhism, one of the largest schools of Buddhism.

Guest Interview

KT: We are pleased to have Monika Dix back with us again to help us sort out what can be a very confusing topic. Well the first, let's begin with the first question about the Earth-encompassing Bodhisattva.

Earth-encompassing Bodhisattva

Kshitigarbha (Kṣitigarbha) (Sanskrit), Dizang (Chinese), Jizo (Japanese)

Monika Dix: Bodhisattva Jizo, whose name is Earth-encompassing Bodhisattva, is central for Pure Land Buddhism. He is considered the master of the world of rebirth, and he consoles the souls which fall into hell. But the Jizo also plays the role in terms of dead children. He is the saint of dead children. And various temples in Japan, you can see stone sculptures of the Bodhisattva Jizo. He is wearing a bib, usually a red bib, and toys are laid on his feet by the parents who pray for their dead children.

KT: I see. Jizo, especially in Japan, we see a lot of him on the road side, and you mentioned the Jizos at the temples. Why are there so many Jizos in various temples?

Monika Dix: Because usually stone images like in this picture, the families can actually commission these images. And in addition to being a popular Buddhist deity, he is also related to Japanese folk belief. Because Jizo is a Bodhisattva who looks like a monk, so it appeals to people because of his human character.

KT: So, he has a shaven head.

Monika Dix: Yes, that's right. And he holds a staff and a jewel usually.

Bodhisattva of Future Buddha

Maitreya (Sanskrit), Mile (Chinese), Miroku (Japanese)

KT: The second Bodhisattva I'd like to ask you about is the so-called "Future Buddha" or "Bodhisattva of Future Buddha," also known as Maitreya in Sanskrit or Miroku in Japanese, Mile in Chinese. So, could you tell us more about that?

Monika Dix: Yes, Maitreya is the Future Buddha, who resides in the heaven, Tushita Heaven, which is his paradise. And he will come down to this world after a certain period of time, and he will be the new Buddha. And actually in this image, Maitreya is depicted as a young handsome Bodhisattva because he is not the Buddha yet, but once he descends to earth, he will be the future Buddha.

KT: We do not know exactly when he is coming but there are different versions or ideas as to when he'll be coming. Isn't that right?

Monika Dix: That's right. It's at the center of the idea of *mappo* (the last period of Dharma), and there are different dates as to when *mappo* started. But it's generally considered that we are still in the age of *mappo*. And once *mappo* is over, the Buddha of the future will come.

Bodhisattva of Compassion

Avalokiteshvara (Avalokiteśvara) (Sanskrit), Guanyin (Chinese), Kannon (Japanese)

KT: I see. Well, *mappo* is an idea that has evolved over a long time and maybe it is too complicated to talk about it now, but…The next Bodhisattva is the one that is very well known, probably the most well-known Bodhisattva. And he or she is the Bodhisattva of compassion or Avalokiteshvara (Avalokiteśvara) in Sanskrit, Guanyin in Chinese, and Kannon in Japanese.

Monika Dix: Yes, I should say that he is the most worshipped Bodhisattva. And Kannon can have thirty-three different forms. But the most common form is one that is standing like in this image, holding a vase, a rosary and usually a lotus flower. And the characteristic of Kannon is in his crown; he has an image of Amida because he is related to Amida Buddha. Especially in China, where Kannon is the most popular and where he is the most worshipped, sometimes she is portrayed as a mother figure holding a little child. So, in China, actually, sometimes she is seen to take on female characteristics.

KT: That's the interesting part, where it shifts gender sometime around a thousand years ago. Isn't that right? And it became more of a female figure as you mentioned.

You know, speaking of Kannon, in Sanskrit it's called Avalokiteshvara, literally meaning "someone who looks over the world," and there is a humorous story. There were these three religious people. One is a Christian, one is a Muslim and one is a Buddhist. They went to heaven, and in order to get into their respective heavens they had to pass a test. The first question for the Christian was, "Spell God." "Oh, it's G-o-d." He easily passed and got in. And next, for the Muslim, the question was "Spell Allah," and he answered, "A-l-l-a-h." He, too, easily passed and got in. And then finally the Buddhist, the question was, "Spell Avalokiteshvara Bodhisattva." Well, it was [the most] tough one [to answer.] Hopefully, he got in.

Buddha of Immeasurable Light and Life

Amitabha (Amitābha) or Amitayus (Amitāyus) (Sanskrit), Amituofo (Chinese), Amida (Japanese)

Okay, the next question has to do with [the topic where we are] actually moving from Bodhisattva to Buddhas. The first Buddha is the Buddha of immeasurable life and light, Amitayus (Amitāyus) or

Amitabha (Amitābha) in Sanskrit, Amituofo in Chinese and Amida in Japanese.

Monika Dix: Yes, Amida is the central deity of Pure Land Buddhism, and he occupies the Western Paradise known as the Pure Land of Extreme Peace and Joy. And he is the Buddha of the death after life and beyond. His worship which belongs to the school of Pure Land Buddhism is very popular in Japan and it was especially strong in the Kamakura Period. And people worshipped him because they wanted to be born in his Pure Land. Pure Land is a glorious place with palaces, [jeweled trees and it's a place for Amida Buddha to lead the devotees to enlightenment]. So it is a very promising outlook for the devotees.

Great Illumination Buddha

Vairochana (Mahāvairocana) (Sanskrit), Dari (Chinese), Dainichi (Japanese)

KT: I see. And of course, as you mentioned, the Pure Land Buddhism in East Asia is one of the major branches of Buddhism with many followers. Now there is the Great Illumination Buddha called "Vairochana" (Mahāvairocana) in Sanskrit and "Dainichi Nyorai" in Japanese. Can you tell us about him?

Monika Dix: Yes, he is the principal deity in both Womb World Mandala and Diamond World Mandala of Esoteric Buddhism. And he is called the Buddha of great light and truth, and he resembles the absolute. In this image he makes a hand gesture or mudra (mudrā) of teaching, which resembles that of the Buddha's teachings at Deer Park at Saranath (Sārnāth) (the place of his first teaching). So, basically, he is the absolute representation (of enlightenment).

KT: So, he is both a teacher and the one that represents the absolute

Monika Dix: Yes, the truth and enlightenment.

KT: Interesting. Well, Monika, thank you very much for joining us for these two shows.

Monika Dix: Thank you. It was my pleasure.

Closing Remarks

Because the state of awakening lies at the center of Buddhist teachings, Buddhists speak often of wisdom. But that is half of the story, for awakening also entails compassion. Wisdom and compassion are like two wings of a bird. And the images we saw today have given compassion a voice and expression that touched the hearts of millions of ordinary people throughout the centuries.

> *The Spirit of Buddha is that of great loving kindness and compassion. The great loving kindness is the spirit to save all people by any and all means. The great compassion is the spirit that prompts it to be ill with the illness of people and to suffer with their suffering.*

Please watch us again, as we proceed next week to explore the basic teachings of the Four Noble Truths.

CHAPTER THREE:
Teachings of the Four Noble Truths

◆ ◆ ◆

PROGRAM 9
Four Noble Truths - Relationship Among the Four Truths

All those who are seeking awakening must understand the Four Noble Truths. Without understanding these, they will wander about interminably in the bewildering maze of life's illusions. Those who understand these Four Noble Truths are called "the people who have acquired the eyes of awakening."

(The Teaching of Buddha, p. 76)

Hello, we're glad you could join us again. And for those of you watching us for the first time, welcome!

In our last series of shows, we looked at the life of the Buddha and the Buddhist images and statues. Here in today's show and in the following shows, we'll turn our attention to the *teachings* of the Buddha or what the Buddha *taught*, the real "meat" of Buddhism!... Well, maybe "meat" wasn't a good expression, for Buddhists are perceived as being vegetarians. Actually though, Buddhists are not all vegetarians. Even the Buddha wasn't. Well, we'll take this up in one of our later shows!

Four Noble Truths

Among his teachings, the most basic is the *Four Noble Truths*. They were the main topic of the Buddha's *first sermon*, which he delivered to the five mendicant monks with whom he had once trained together during the six years of his ascetic life. And we are told that after hearing the Buddha's sermon, all five of them attained full awakening on the spot. So, the Four Noble Truths were the topic of his first sermon *and* were also the very teachings that led to the first awakening of his first disciples.

Moreover, I feel that for people in the West being introduced to Buddhism, the Four Noble Truths offers a bird's eye view and a comprehensive framework for better understanding the Buddha's teachings. In other words, it's a great place to start!

Let's, then, look at what the Four Noble Truths are. They are traditionally stated as:

The first truth of suffering
The second truth of the cause of suffering
The third truth of cessation
The fourth truth of the path

I would like to restate these truths in more colloquial terms that are easier to understand:

First truth = We all experience suffering.
Second truth = Suffering is caused by greed, hatred and ignorance.
Third truth = There is a state of awakening where suffering ceases.
Fourth truth = There is a path for realizing awakening.

First Truth = We All Experience Suffering

The Buddha specified 8 kinds of suffering. They are **1)** *birth,* **2)** *aging,* **3)** *illness,* **4)** *death,* **5)** *having to face what one does not like,* **6)** *having to separate from what one likes,* **7)** *not getting what one wants,* and **8)** *attachment to the five physical-psychological components that make up my experience.* If these are not clear to you, please don't worry, for I will explain each of these in later shows. But three of these are quite clear, for if you were with us, it was seeing an old person, a sick person and a deceased person that shocked and then motivated Prince Siddhartha to go forth to seek the spiritual path.

Here, perhaps, a clarification is in order. Suffering here refers to a person's *response* to a condition, and not on the *conditions* themselves that lead to suffering. For example, getting old is simply a condition. The Buddha is not bothered by it at all, but many ordinary people fret and worry about it. So they suffer from their aging. Suffering is, thus, their *response* to a condition.

So suffering for the Buddha had to do more with the *inner dimensions of our experience,* particularly in relation to "*existential* difficulties or conditions" such as illness, aging and death, rather than suffering caused by social condition or natural disasters. Though having said that, if the Buddha were alive, he would like everyone else be horrified and saddened by the tsunami disaster. His enormous capacity for compassion for others would be directed in words and deeds to all the victims. He would not be *indifferent* to their pain and suffering, just as when he spoke out against the tyranny of the caste system of his day.

Second Truth = Suffering is Caused by Greed, Hatred and Ignorance

So, how is this first truth related to the second?

The second truth is that suffering is *caused by greed, hatred and ignorance*. Greed, hatred and ignorance, sometimes referred to as the *"Three Poisons,"* are the *cause* or *reasons* for our suffering. For example, the prince, before he became the Buddha, experienced extreme pain, shock and suffering upon witnessing a deceased person. And his response was rooted in his desire (or greed) to want to live, or in his own words, due to his "thirst for existence." And this was compounded by his ignorance about the truth of impermanence, that is, that everything including our body is subject to change.

Now, we can certainly empathize with him, for this *desire to live is universal* and is a powerful drive in virtually all of us. But however common and universal the thirst for life is, it is still greed, nevertheless. This truth discovered by the Buddha will probably be hard to swallow. It certainly was for me, when I was rudely awakened in my early teens that we all have to die eventually. I recall vividly feeling that it was unfair, and it wasn't how it was supposed to be. And the Buddhist teaching wasn't much of a consolation *initially* when it taught that *my discomfort with death was due to my greed and attachment to life*. However, the teaching has since helped me to see that the root of my suffering regarding death lies within me.

Third Truth = There is a State of Awakening Where Suffering Ceases

Now, let's move to the third truth of cessation, there is a state of awakening in which suffering ceases. This is the state realized by the Buddha under the Bodhi tree, and is also known as *"nirvana."* I am sure that nirvana is a term that many of you have heard, for it's become part of the English language to express a sense of "extreme happiness, bliss, freedom and/or liberation." You can now find it in your dictionary as an *English* word. There was even an internationally famous rock band named "Nirvana."

Fourth = There is a Path for Realizing Awakening

This awakening or nirvana is attained by consummating the fourth truth, which is, there is a way for realizing awakening. The way is called the *Eightfold Noble Path*. What are the eight? They are *Right View, Right Thought, Right Speech, Right Conduct, Right Livelihood, Right Effort, Right Mindfulness and Right Concentration*. We shall return in later shows to explore each of these in greater depth. But for now, they give us a sense of what is required in order to attain awakening.

So, between the fourth and the third truths, there also exists a *cause and effect* relationship. By practicing the Eightfold Noble Path, the fourth truth, one can achieve nirvana or awakening, the third truth, when suffering ends.

So, the Four Noble Truths are comprised of *two sets of cause and effect relationship*. The second truth is the cause of the first truth, and the fourth truth is the cause of the third truth. And, mostly importantly, when the third truth (awakening) is attained, the first truth (suffering) ceases or is lessened.

When we evaluate the Four Noble Truths, they are *empirically and logically based*. They do not require us to believe in something that we cannot experience in our lives. They note the fact that we experience suffering, and then proceed to identify their causes. And then they propose a path for us to think, speak, and act in the right way. When we practice them, we are then able to lower the level of our suffering as well as that of others.

Now, let's see if we can bring the Four Noble Truths, especially the first two, to a level where even children can understand. For that, stories are very effective. While there are traditional Buddhist stories, today I wish to draw from a Western source.

Aesop's Fable of *The Greedy Dog*

It's that famous Aesop's fable of *The Greedy Dog*. I am sure that you know the story but let me tell it here. Once upon a time a hungry old dog saw a puppy carrying a juicy bone in its mouth. Wanting this bone, the greedy dog barked and growled until the poor puppy dropped the bone and ran away. The old dog carried the juicy bone in its mouth to find a quiet place to eat. On his way, he walked over a bridge, and as he looked over the side he saw *another dog* with a bone in its mouth. Not realizing that *that* other dog he saw was *actually* himself reflected in the water, he wanted that bone and barked at the other dog. As he did, "splash" went his own bone as it fell into the river, leaving the dog with no bone and hungry once again!

Well, the causal relationship is obvious. *Greed got the best of him.* Not only did he take someone else's bone, which had caused suffering for that puppy, but he also ended up losing the bone and went hungry.

Applying the Truths to Our Circumstance

Well, some of you may be saying to yourselves, "what a stupid, greedy dog!"

But are we so different? Don't we sometimes find ourselves in the same situation? Aren't we swept away by our greed for more and more things? As a result, we become overburdened with huge debts that put undue pressure on the family and forcing us to overwork. So, there isn't enough time to spend with our families and friends. Not having enough time for each other, many couples grow distant and end up in divorce. Or the stressful life can take a toll on the mind and body, leading to psychological and physical illness.

We could blame our greed on the consumer economic system in which we live. Certainly, we have the most affluent society in the history of humankind, where many middle class people are able to live in four-bedroom homes with three-car garages. And many of these houses are located miles away from places of work, school, and shopping, requiring multiple cars and a lot of gas. *Our living style rests on a very high level of consumption*, which if we are not mindful can bury us under the weight of the burdens of our greed.

But *to walk the Buddhist path means to be self-directed, not to blame others, and not to feel victimized.* We can choose to help change the system to encourage a life style of less consumption. We can do that in the spirit of engaged Buddhism, in which we are inspired to take the Dharma from the personal to the societal level.

And, of course, *we can and we should on a personal level work to control our greed.* We could let our greed get out of control, like the greedy dog, and suffer. Or we can apply the Four Noble Truths to our lives, to see the various temptations in our lives, and take appropriate ways as found in the Eightfold Noble Path. This is why the Buddha stressed the Four Noble Truths as today's scriptural passage indicates:

> *All those who are seeking awakening must understand the Four Noble Truths. Without understanding these, they will wander about interminably in the bewildering maze of life's illusions. Those who understand these Four Noble Truths are called "the people who have acquired the eyes of awakening."*

Whether you suffer or not is up to each of us. This idea is expressed in the statement, "suffering is optional," which I now see has become quite popular. Actually, I first came across this over 10 years ago among the graffiti scribbling in, of all places, a public restroom in a park. It read, *"Difficulties are inevitable, but suffering is optional."*

We look forward to having you watch us next week, when we invite a guest to discuss some of the subtleties of the Four Noble Truths. See you then.

PROGRAM 10
Four Noble Truths: Interview

Buddha leads people, merely by indicating to them the Four Noble Truths. Those who understand them properly will attain awakening. They will be able to guide and support others in this bewildering world, and they will be worthy of trust.

(*The Teaching of Buddha*, p. 78)

We're once again pleased to have you join us. We hope that your weekend has been relaxing and enjoyable, and that you are looking forward to a new week.

Being Grateful *Just to Be Alive*

I know that sometimes Mondays are a *real drag*. No wonder it's called a "Blue Monday."

When I was young, I used to say to myself, "Yeah, that's *really* true." But since I began seriously walking the Buddhist path, I have rarely felt that. That's because I feel most of the time that *I am grateful just to be alive*, with a ceiling over my head, enough food to eat, people whom I care about, and a general sense of spiritual well-being.

The other day, I saw a TV program about an African country wracked by civil war, where one-fifth of the children die before the age of 5 due to malnutrition and illness. A Christian nun running an orphanage was asked why the children seemed so happy despite their lot, and she replied without any hesitation, "*The children know that killing and deaths are real and are everywhere. So they **truly** feel lucky, **just to be alive**.*"

In my view, this phrase, "Just to be alive," is related to our on-going discussion of the Four Noble Truths, for such a view of life is so different from that of the greedy dog in the Aesop's fable brought up during our last show. Wanting more and more does not assure happiness but, in fact, will probably invite unhappiness.

Now, by making this point, I am in no way condoning the civil war or the plight of those children in Africa. Those societal conditions need to be improved and changed, and they can't come soon enough.

Karma

Now, there is another important point related to suffering that needs to be addressed. And that has to do with Karma, a Sanskrit term that has now become part of everyday English language, but one that is generally understood incorrectly, having departed from the original meaning. How is it then used incorrectly? Well, there are, unfortunately, many people who understand Karma as "fate" resulting from some kind of punishment or retribution, expressed commonly as "Well, that's his karma." In such usage, the suffering is their fate or even their fault! In their eyes, the suffering of these children in the African country or those people who died in that devastating tsunami were the result of some negative deeds they had done previously, either in this life or in some prior lives. This is outright wrong and must be corrected!

The correct Buddhist meaning of Karma is "action." This action takes three forms: **1)** intentional thoughts, **2)** speech, and **3)** bodily action. In other words, karma refers to what a person thinks, says, and does, primarily in the religious context. Karma is actually very optimistic in that it encourages us to realize possibilities that affect the course of our spiritual lives. This clearly differs from the notion of fate, predestination or retribution.

Also, karma should be applied primarily to oneself (in the first person). It should not be a means to judge others (in the third person), especially to explain why some people find themselves in unfortunate or disadvantaged conditions. For example, the outcastes, untouchables, and slaves were often told to accept their social status because their situation was their own doing, the result of negative karma created in their past lives.

Unfortunately, such understanding of Karma existed in the past and exists even today. I believe it's a reflection of our human tendency to blame others for misfortunes as well as the practice, especially in the past, of the ruling class to maintain order and justify the inequities of their society.

At any rate, karma represents a complex issue that calls for more detailed explanation, which we hope to provide in one of our future shows. I just felt the need to dispel any gross misunderstanding of this now well-known *English* word, particularly in relation to people in suffering.

Rev. Kodo Matsunami, Jodo Priest

Today, we are pleased to have as our guest, Rev. Kodo Matsunami. He is a priest of the Jodoshu School and a university professor teaching religious studies.

Jodo School or the Pure Land School was founded by *Honen in late 12th century Japan*. Honen was the charismatic and learned monk who made Pure Land Buddhism an independent movement, gathering many capable disciples who went on to form schools of their own. One of them was *Shinran, the founder of my school, Jodo Shinshu*. So what's the difference between Rev. Matsunami's Jodoshu and my Jodo Shinshu? Well, his means the "Pure Land School" and mine means the "*True* Pure Land School."… Actually, Shinran never intended to found a new school, for when he was advocating his views he had no other intention but to correctly convey the "true Pure Land" teachings of his beloved teacher, Honen … So, I should be more respectful to Rev. Matsunami.

Rev. Matsunami has also written numerous books, both academic and popular. One is on the *Dhammapada*, one of the Buddhist classics that contain the sayings of the Buddha. I am also impressed by books such as *Light in Dark Times: 108 Wise Buddhist Thoughts* and *Buddhist Sages Speak: On Dealing with Today*. In this second book, there are short chapters, such as "For People Greedy for Money," and "For People Who Cannot Feel Grateful for Being Alive."

Interview

KT: Let's begin with this intriguing chapter, "For People Greedy for Money." What is your advice for such people in the context of the Four Noble Truths?

Rev. Matsunami: I happen to know an old man who passed away recently. He had practically nothing when he started his business. He went around town to collect second-hand articles. He was obsessed by money, and *he would often say, "Without money, we can do nothing. Money is everything."* He neglected his family life. With the accumulated money, he purchased land and became a millionaire by taking advantage of the boom in land prices. Yet he continued to live in a small house.

Then this old man died suddenly due to a heart attack. Immediately after his death, his sons, who had not seen him for some time, rushed to their father's house to attend the wake service. It was thought that they had come to pay their last respects. On the contrary, they quarrelled over the inheritance, even going so far as to argue in front of their father's remains. When I saw this, I asked myself, "What on earth had the old man worked so hard for?"

We cannot, of course, live without money and things and gadgets around us. But *we should remember that these are only tools for living.* I understand our desires for more and more things, but time has come for each one of us to reconsider what true happiness is all about. I believe the most important things are such things as love, trust, kindness, good health, freedom and peace of mind, none of which we can buy with money.

KT: There is a well-known scriptural passage, "Don't be greedy and realize that you already have enough." Maybe that dog in Aesop's fable should've known this.

Rev. Matsunami: Yes, *once we cross the line of moderation, nothing good can happen.* When we do whatever we want, forgetting that we live in relation to others, then we cross the line into excesses without even noticing it. Then we have to pay the price. If we drink too much alcohol or eat too much, then we will be tormented by drunkenness and stomach-ache. If we blame others without considering their feelings, then people will feel anger toward us.

I am not saying that it is best to tolerate adversity, only that you should ask yourself. "Am I doing too much? Am I going too far?" If the answer is, "I might be," then consider it a red light. And for the sake of yourself and for others, exercise enough self-control not to cross over into excess. Thus, you should ask yourself, "Too much? One sided? Immoderate?" If the answer is "yes" to any of these three, don't wait for someone to criticize you. Create some space to carefully reflect on your actions.

KT: Some people say that the Buddha was overly concerned with suffering. But I say that he was honest and clear about his mission, for he pronounced in effect, "I speak about suffering, its cause and ways to overcome it, and nothing more." Then he uses the metaphor of the *"Man with a Poison Arrow."* Can you comment on this?

Rev. Matsunami: The story of the "Man with a Poison Arrow" goes like this. Suppose a man was pierced by a poisoned arrow, and his relatives and friends got together to call a doctor to have the arrow pulled out and the wound treated.

The wounded man objects saying, "Wait a moment. Before you pull it out, I want to know who shot this arrow. What was the bow made of? Was it a big bow or small bow? Was it made of wood or bamboo? Before you pull out the arrow, I want to know all about these things." Then, what will happen? The poison will have time to circulate all through the system and the man may die. *The first duty is to remove the arrow, and prevent its poison from spreading.*

The Buddha's teaching contains what is important to know and practice and not what is unimportant. That is, it teaches us that we, too, have been pierced by an arrow. So we must take it out. We must learn the teaching and practice it. It's a practical way of life, rather than a theoretical understanding of life.

KT: What do you say to people who say that suffering is not only done unto oneself but also caused by other people and social systems (crime, war, etc.) and natural disasters (typhoon, earthquake, tsunami, etc.) that are done to us? Maybe an answer is to be found in the now famous phrase that I found in a public restroom, "Difficulties are inevitable, but suffering is optional."

Rev. Matsunami: The phrase "Difficulties are inevitable, but suffering is optional" is saying that it is up to us as to how we deal with the situation that confronts us here and now. *What is important is our action in response to the difficulties.* When we are wounded and are in pain, we have to, first of all, get immediate medical treatment for the wound.

Our everyday life is just like driving our car. While driving, we have to always watch out at every corner, and steer the car by adjusting the accelerator and the brake pedals. If there is a stumbling block ahead of us, we have to either stop, remove the block, or go around it in order to avoid an accident.

Therefore, first of all, we have to have an intuitive and well-controlled mind, and take appropriate action. The Buddha instructed us that absent-minded, delayed action would lead to grave results.

KT: Some people claim that Four Noble Truths are not creeds to believe in but a road map to proceed in life, especially for dealing with difficulties. How do you respond to that?

Rev. Matsunami: When confronting suffering, we have to, first of all, find the cause of suffering and sum up all possible ways and means for solutions. Likewise, when we are confronted with political or social problems or issues, we should never give up our effort.

We have a tendency to want to change the world at great cost and effort, before changing ourselves. *Shantideva (Shāntideva)*, a Buddha's disciple, once said,

> "Smoothing out the earth with leather sheets cannot be done
> for lack of enough hide. Just put a bit of leather on your feet;
> it's just like you have covered the entire world."

Likewise, there are two ways to transform ourselves as stated in this stanza, "We can change the world, or we can change perspective." There are so many pettiness and corruption of social and political injustice, and we are sickened and disgusted, but we should never be discouraged or give up our hope. If the people who are involved in the affairs have their intentions clean and pure, we should honor them and help them in doing their work. The Buddha once told a parable:

> "Here is a dirty cloth. A dyer desires to dye it. The dyer dyes
> it indigo, crimson, red or perhaps yellow. And he throws it
> into his dyeing trough. It is apparent that this cloth shall not
> come out dyed in fresh colors. Why is that? It is because the
> cloth was not clean. Likewise, if your hearts are not clean
> and pure, you cannot expect good results."

It means that whatever we say can say or do, our motive or intention is more important than anything else. *If the motive is impure, then the result will be like dyeing the dirty cloth.*

As we thank you for being with us this week, I'd like to close by again reciting today a passage that reiterates the high evaluation that the Buddha had for people who came understand the Four Noble Truths:

> *Buddha leads people, merely by indicating to them the Four Noble Truths. Those who understand them properly will attain awakening. They will be able to guide and support others in this bewildering world, and they will be worthy of trust.*

PROGRAM 11
Four Noble Truths: Twelve Links
of the Chain of Dependent Arising

Following the path of the Four Noble Truths is like entering a dark room with a light in the hand. The darkness will all be cleared away and the room will be filled with light.

(The Teaching of Buddha, p. 78)

Hello there. For those of you who were with us last week, did your past week go a little better, based on a greater sense of gratitude for "just being alive"? We would be very pleased, knowing that was the case.

Well, this week, we will continue our discussion on the Four Noble Truths.

A Lesson to Be Learned
From the Four Noble Truths

I want to focus on a very important lesson we can learn from the Four Noble Truths and that is this: by learning to let go of our greed, hatred and ignorance, we can lessen our suffering for myself and for others. This is an *optimistic message* even though we, as lay persons living in the modern world, would not be able to completely let go or eliminate greed, hatred and ignorance like the Buddha. Nevertheless, by putting the Four Noble Truths into practice, there will be a significant difference in our lives. The difference will become apparent for those who put them into action in their daily lives.

In this connection, we should not misunderstand the aim of the Four Noble Truths. Just because the first truth has to do with suffering, it does not mean that it's the most important or that the Four Noble Truths *conclude* that life is full of suffering. If it were, it would truly be pessimistic and would not have inspired millions over the centuries, and many to achieve true happiness as symbolized by the serene and peaceful smile on the faces of the Buddhist images that we saw in our earlier shows.

Twelve Links of the Chain
of Dependent Arising

In this show, we shall begin by introducing an important teaching, which explains the process by which **1)** suffering arose and **2)** suffering can be eliminated. The Buddha expounded this in an important teaching called the *Twelve Links of the Chain of Dependent Arising* (pratītya-samutpāda). It offers a detailed description of the process, which is very much psychological in nature. The process is comprised of twelve links. They are technical in nature and cannot be readily understood in the short time that we have, but allow me to mention them now so that you can get at least the general idea. They are: **1)** *ignorance*, **2)** *intentional action*, **3)** *consciousness*, **4)** *mind and body*, **5)** *the six senses*, **6)** *sense-contact*, **7)** *feeling*, **8)** *craving*, **9)** *attachment*, **10)** *becoming*, **11)** *birth*, and **12)** *aging, dying, lamentation, grief, pain, sorrow, despair, etc.*

These twelve links can be seen as an elaboration of the relationship between the 2nd and the 1st Noble Truths. If you recall, greed, hatred and ignorance were the cause that led to suffering. Here ignorance is listed first, while greed and hatred are included as dimensions of intentional action, the second link. These then generate the rest of the links, ending in suffering, which constitutes the 12th link. So, the Twelve Links of the Chain of Dependent Arising explains how suffering arises.

Now, this teaching also serves as an elaboration of the relationship between the 4th and the 3rd Noble Truths. If you recall, the 4th Truth was the path or set of practices for eliminating greed, hatred and ignorance, which when completed leads to the 3rd Truth, which is none other than awakening or nirvana (nirvāna). So, much like dominos, by eliminating ignorance, suffering is eventually eliminated.

What is important to remember here is that each link cannot arise independently but is dependent on another. They are, therefore, related to each other on the principle of causality. They are conditioned, relative and interdependent. So, suffering too is not absolute but relative, and therefore can be lessened, if not eliminated, by our practice and effort.

Tom's Struggle with His Wife's Death

Once I was invited to talk about Buddhism at a local TV cable network. After the show, Tom, the host of the program, told me about the loss a few years earlier of his wife of 30 years. Tom appeared to be in his mid-60s and was not a Buddhist. Since I had talked about the truth of impermanence (that all things are subject to change) in the program, he must have felt even more compelled to confide in me of the impact of his wife's death. *Her death had devastated Tom* to a point he could not work for more than a year and suffered mentally and emotionally ever since.

Her death was totally unexpected. But when I asked Tom, surely, he must have thought about death, his answer was that he, of course, knew that we all eventually had to die but never thought about it occurring so soon to him or to his loved ones. *Death was in the distant future and hardly ever entered his mind.* His words were, "We were having too much fun and enjoying life." As I heard Tom talk about his life style and outlook, I had flashes from the Buddha's life when he led a life of luxury and enjoyment of the palace before the prince left for his spiritual search.

Then, Tom told me that he wished he had known about the teachings of impermanence. I wished he had too. Even though he would not be able to get his wife back, we agreed as we talked that *had he been more aware, he would not have suffered so unduly.* Of course, it's extremely sad, and it's natural to be sad, and it's OK to be sad. But he could have avoided the extreme debilitating suffering.

I don't intend to be insensitive or overly clinical, but I believe we can look at his situation through the teaching of the Twelve Links of Dependent Arising. [**1)** *ignorance,* **2)** *intentional action,* **3)** *consciousness,* **4)** *mind and body,* **5)** *the six senses,* **6)** *sense-contact,* **7)** *feeling,* **8)** *craving,* **9)** *attachment,* **10)** *becoming,* **11)** *birth,* and **12)** *aging, dying, lamentation, grief, pain, sorrow, despair, etc.*] He had experienced the 12th link, where he felt extreme grief and despair. And the source of his extreme suffering ultimately lay with ignorance, the 1st link. Due to his ignorance concerning the truth of impermanence, his wife's death triggered a chain of psychological reactions (links 2 to 6). He then experienced a deep and abiding unpleasant feeling (link 7), followed by a craving or desire to have his wife as before (link 8). He further became attached (link 9) to his wish of having his wife alive and regaining a life with her. This attachment, of course, clashed with the reality that his wife was no longer around, causing him to experience extreme suffering filled with grief, lamentation and despair (links 10-12).

However, had he known about the truth of impermanence and had trained his mind accordingly, *greater wisdom would have replaced ignorance,* and the rest of the psychological and emotional chain reaction would not have occurred with such intensity. He would ultimately not have experienced such extreme degree of grief, sorrow and despair to a point where he couldn't work or lead a normal life for such a long time.

As ordinary people who lead a lay life, we will surely feel the sadness and grief at the loss of our loved ones. But as ignorance is replaced by wisdom and understanding, we can avoid what Tom had gone through which was rooted in ignorance about the real nature of life.

Wisdom helps us to *"see things as they really are"* and not *"how we wish to see them."* Wisdom helps us to cope better in times of personal loss, but, as we will discuss more later, also inspires us to live our present lives more fully with a greater sense of joy, gratitude, and compassion.

A Mother and Daughter Conflict

Let's look at another example, this one of a conflict between a parent and a teenage child. I am sure many of you can identify with that.

This is a situation where a mother gets into another heated argument with her teenage daughter over violin practice. Mother is unhappy that the daughter has not practiced as much as she had promised, while the daughter disagrees. It's upsetting for both of them. The mother, who is a violinist herself, has always expected her children to play the violin well, thinking of their welfare and benefits in life. The daughter had complied with the mother's wishes up till now, but she has hit the rebellious years, and she now resists.

In Tom's case, he wished he had dealt with the death of his wife differently. And the same would be suggested for the mother. In her case, she would no longer make her daughter continue the violin lesson to avoid the conflict and suffering. This would be the traditional approach.

But I believe in Buddhism, one has a choice, particularly for lay people who don't live in the pristine environment of monasteries. The choice is 1) to have the daughter quit violin altogether or 2) to press on with the practice. Suffering would be eliminated with the first choice as the source of conflict would be eliminated, but the daughter would lose out on acquiring an important skill that could benefit her life.

In the case of this mother, she chose the latter, out of her conviction that violin would be good for the daughter. She felt that the benefits for the daughter outweighed any arguments and conflicts that were bound to continue. The mother decided that *"suffering" with a purpose and awareness* was better than giving up on something important just to avoid the suffering.

Here, the mother also realized something very important. And that is this: her insistence on her daughter learning violin, *no matter how well intentioned, is still greed*, and it's *her, the mother's,* greed. So, when conflicts do arise, she would not be bewildered and lament, "Why is it happening to me!" She would proceed with humility and clarity rather than self-righteousness and delusion.

The mother provides for the rest of us an important lesson. *We should not delude ourselves in thinking that when we do things for others that we are doing it for them, for ultimately we are doing it for ourselves.* This view will avoid unnecessary suffering when people do not acknowledge our "sacrifice," and will also enhance the effectiveness of our efforts.

Well, in choosing to press on with the violin, the mother also made some practical adjustments and compromises. They together set up a more flexible practice schedule. Then the mother communicated to her daughter all the reasons for wanting her to continue. These efforts helped her daughter to become a *willing* partner.

Lesson in Other Aspects of Life

The same approach can be taken when we try to accomplish anything we think is important at home, at work, at school, or in the community. That could range from bringing about improved ways of communicating at work or at school, or instituting ways to help the environment by how our garbage is collected. In regards to these challenges, the way the mother applied the teachings of the 12 Links in the Chain of Dependent Arising and the Four Noble Truths can serve as an inspiration, a beacon for us, as today's sacred words convey:

> Following the path of the Four Noble Truths is like entering a dark room with a light in the hand
> The darkness will all be cleared away and the room will be filled with light.

Please watch us again next week, when we explore the fascinating topic of inter-religious dialogue in the growing diverse and global world that we live in.

PROGRAM 12
Inter-religious Dialogue

The world is like a lotus pond filled with many varieties of the plant; there are blossoms of many different tints. Some are white, some pink, some blue, some yellow; some grow under water, some spread their leaves on the water, and some raise their leaves above the water.

(The Teaching of Buddha, p. 128)

How are you today? We're glad that you could join us.

Today, we would like to take a break from our on-going discussion of the Buddha's teachings, focused recently on the Four Noble Truths, to discuss the topic of *inter-religious dialogue,* particularly between Buddhists and Christians.

Greater Religious Diversity

Before we begin the discussion with our guest, I would like to say a few words about this topic. *There has been no greater time than today for inter-religious dialogue,* for virtually all the religions of the world are now present in the United States. As mentioned previously, Buddhism alone has at least 80 different schools represented in Los Angeles. In many communities we find numerous religions that do not fall within Jewish-Christian traditions.

Note, by the way, that I did not say, "Judeo-Christian," a term that Christians coined but one that some Jews do not subscribe to; they prefer "Jewish and Christian traditions" [*not "Judeo-Christian tradition" but "Jewish and Christian traditions."*] The same goes for "Old Testament," for which "Hebrew Bible" is preferred [*not "Old Testament" but "Hebrew Bible"*]. These discoveries were the fruit of my involvement in inter-religious dialogue.

On account of the growing diversity, numerous communities have inter-religious associations. When I served as a temple priest, I became a member of the Interfaith Council comprised of clergies of that area. We met for lunch meetings and organized joint services and activities, which broadened my knowledge about other religions and strengthened my contacts in the larger community.

If religious pluralism marks the communities, then the same can be said for families. With greater degree of inter-marriages, our families are no longer of the same faith. It is no longer uncommon for families to have among their members Christians, Jews, Muslims, and Buddhists. This situation surely calls for a need for people to be more aware of each other's religious beliefs and practices.

Inter-religious Groups

Greater understanding is also needed on a national and global level. There are a number of interfaith organizations at these levels. My efforts have focused on the Buddhist-Christian interaction, particularly in an academic setting. My focus on Christianity stems, obviously, from the fact that Christianity is the dominant religion in this country.

There exists an active academic group called the *Society of Buddhist-Christian Studies* comprised of about 400 members, which meets annually and publishes a journal. And there is also the *International Buddhist Christian Theological Encounter,* which has met annually for 2-3 days for the past 20 years. The themes at these gatherings of approximately 10 Buddhists and 10 Christians have centered on doctrinal topics such as the nature of the ultimate and religious practices, but since my participation began 7 years ago the themes have shifted to social issues such as the environment, violence, and consumerism.

Inter-religious Gatherings

At inter-religious gatherings, I am reminded of the *World Parliament of Religions* which took place in Chicago in 1993, one hundred years after the epoch-making gathering in 1893 also held in Chicago. It was at that first gathering over a hundred years ago, where impressive speeches by Buddhist representatives such as *Anāgārika Dharmapāla from Ceylon* and *Shaku Soyen from Japan* helped to "put Buddhism on the map" in the eyes of many Americans.

More recently, I was fortunate enough to participate in *The Day of Prayer* a few years ago, convened by *Pope John Paul II* partly in response to the tragic events of September 11th. It was held in the Italian city of Assisi, the home of *St. Francis*, known the world over as a man of peace. I was able to meet representatives of many religions, including the Pope, which made me realize, not just with my head, that we really do live in a world with people of many different religions.

When I met the Pope, though very briefly, I shook his hand and told him, "Having come to Assisi, I feel compelled to work harder for peace." The Pope then nodded with a firm grip and a great bodily gesture of confirmation. If I had more time, I wanted to share with him the famous Buddhist statement about a solution for peace from the well-known scripture, *Dhammapada*, "*Hatred is not overcome by hatred. Hatred is overcome only by abandoning hatred.*"

Our Guest Rev. Kodo Matsunami

And there is no better person to explore today's topic than Rev. Matsunami, a Jodo priest, who has graciously agreed to join us again. Rev. Matsunami is active in inter-religious conferences, and whenever I talk to him it seems that he is either going or has just returned from Rome or New York, often to participate in inter-religious functions. And I understand that he will soon be leaving for South America.

KT: What have been your thoughts and impressions of having attended these inter-religious meetings?

Rev. Matsunami: I have not attended as many inter-faith gatherings as I would like, but I believe that the sharing and understanding that take place at these gatherings are very important to break through the barriers that religions are assumed to have. *We can no longer afford to be ignorant about others.*

I also feel the present world-wide crises, happening everywhere, particularly in the Middle East, are not directly caused by religious differences, but rather by national, ethnic, social or economic differences. *The real roots of the conflicts are based on these non-religious differences, where these various groups happen to be of different religions.* I must admit, however, that some religious leaders reinforce the differences without helping to bring about reconciliation and peace among these groups. That's why people of various faiths must work together to understand each other.

KT: Which gathering stands out the most?

Rev. Matsunami: A few years ago, I was privileged to attend the *Religious Summit meeting at the Vatican*. I met many leaders of different faiths, namely, Roman Catholic, Protestant, Jewish, Islam, Hindu and Sikh. I was fortunate to exchange our ideas with them on the pertinent problems and issues for world peace. They were all good people with profound thoughts. We discussed many issues intensely in order to reach common understanding, though our ideas or standpoints differed slightly on some issues.

KT: What can Buddhists learn from other religions?

Rev. Matsunami: As a Buddhist, I learn a lot from other religions, and I fully respect them from the bottom of my heart. I believe that the differences of religious creeds or teachings are not all that important. What matters most is following the path of being who and what we are. *What matters is being compassionate and not clinging to the idea that we alone know the truth and are superior to others.*

KT: What do you think Buddhism can offer to the world?

Rev. Matsunami: According to Buddhism, our world is nothing but the manifestation of the *Oneness of Life, where all beings—animate or inanimate—exist interdependently.* We are just like the small icebergs sticking up from the surface of the ocean, but we are actually part of the big iceberg under the surface of the ocean. Recent discovery of DNA, which is laden in every sentient being, has proven this point.

However, people impose distinctions and separate what is mine from what is not mine. This discrimination arises from an attachment in man called blind craving that differentiates Oneness from the plurality of many-ness. Consequently, conflicts, misunderstanding, or frictions arise within people themselves. From blind craving comes the conscious self, affirming the fundamental selfishness.

Since people go against Oneness by responding to the blind craving within themselves, *they create the illusory world of many-ness, which is not the real world but a world created in their own imagination.*

Therefore, Buddhism refutes such egocentric habit of separation and confrontation. Instead, it teaches that our true nature is empty, dynamic, infinite, unifying, pervading and inherent. I believe that by pointing out the basic flaws in the way we view each other and the world, Buddhism can contribute in addressing the world crisis facing our societies and the world.

Well, we sincerely hope that our shows are having some positive impact in your lives. If the answer is yes, do tell your friends about this show.

And we hope you will be with us again next week, when we delve further into the basic teachings of the Buddha.

CHAPTER FOUR
Teachings of the First Mark of Existence

✦ ✦ ✦

PROGRAM 13
First Mark of Existence: The Nature of Suffering

Ordinary people in the world sooner or later run into difficulties, and consequently most people suffer. However, those who have heard the Buddha's teaching do not suffer because they understand that these difficulties are unavoidable.

(The Teaching of Buddha, p. 94)

Hello. It's good to have you watching us.

Four Marks of Existence in
Relation to Four Noble Truths

Starting today, we will explore the teaching of the *Four Marks of Existence*. These Four Marks make up an important segment of the *Four Noble Truths*, the overall framework for understanding the core Buddhist teachings, which we discussed in our last series of shows.

How then do the Four Marks of Existence relate to the Four Noble Truths? Well, the Four Marks of Existence constitute a dimension of the Fourth Noble Truth or the Eightfold Noble Path.

Four Noble Truths

1st truth of suffering
2nd truth of the cause
3rd truth of cessation
4th truth of the path (Eightfold Noble Path —— Four Marks of
Existence

Now, among the eight categories of the Eightfold Noble Path, the Four Marks fall under *Right View*.

Eightfold Noble Path

Right View → *Four Marks of Existence*
Right Thought

Right Speech
Right Conduct
Right Livelihood
Right Effort
Right Mindfulness
Right Concentration

The aim of Buddhist teaching is to help seekers awaken to truth, and to do so, one needs to view our experiences in the right or correct way, thus, Right View. And the Four Marks of Existence show us the details of how to do so.

The Four Marks of Existence

What are the Four Marks of Existence? I will for each of the four give the traditional statement, followed by an everyday expression for easier understanding.

The First is **1)** *All Conditioned Phenomena are Suffering.*
Rephrased, *"Life is a bumpy road"*

The Second is **2)** *All Conditioned Phenomena lack substantial entity.*
Rephrased, *"Life is interdependent"*

The Third is **3)** *All Conditioned Phenomena are impermanent.*
Rephrased, *"Life is impermanent"*

The Fourth is **4)** *Nirvana (Nirvāna) is peaceful and tranquil.*
Rephrased, *"Life can be great"*

Teachings of the First Mark of Existence

We will concentrate today on the first mark.

Let me begin by asking you, "How do you feel about life? Is your life one of happiness? Or is your life one of suffering? Or do you feel life is a combination of the two?" I bet most of you would say that life has its share of *both* happiness and suffering. That is why I've often expressed this as *"Life is a bumpy road."* It really is, isn't it? At times, everything goes your way and you feel life is hunky-dory! Then at other times, things just don't go your way. We have our highs and our lows. Life is, indeed, a bumpy road!

However, our human nature makes us accentuate the highs or the smooth part of the road while ignoring the lows or the bumps on the road. And our cultural and economic environment reinforces this tendency.

The Buddhist message is, then, to balance this tendency to address the bumps, for only by so doing, can we attain real spiritual peace and freedom. That is why Buddhism places the issue of suffering on the "front burner."

Now, speaking of "suffering," some feel that the word "suffering" is an improper translation of the original, which is *"duhkha"* (duḥkha) in Sanskrit. But *duhkha* has too many multiple shades of meaning to be translated into just *one* English word. Some people prefer, for example, *"pain," "unhappiness,"* or *"unsatisfactoriness."* In any case, no one word or phrase can do justice to the word *duhkha,* but I shall use "suffering," as I believe it's still the best translation.

Let's now proceed to explain the first Mark of Existence by referring to a best-selling book, *Freddie the Leaf.*

I'm sure many of you have read or heard about a picture book *The Fall of Freddie the Leaf: A Story of Life for All Ages* by Leo Buscaglia? It's about a leaf named Freddie, who experiences the ups and downs of life. In the spring he is "born" on a branch of a tree in a park, and as summer comes he finds himself working together with his fellow leaves to create shade for the people who come to enjoy the park. Freddie is really happy with his life, surrounded by good friends and engaged in the meaningful work of bringing joy to others. Then, suddenly, fall brings the cold and the frost and Freddie learns that he must soon leave the tree against his will. Freddie fights and resists at first, but gradually comes to accept his predicament, for he learns that *though all things must change and die, they are part of a greater Life* (with a capital L), *which lasts forever.* So, having found inner peace, Freddie departs from the tree *gracefully* ... to join the ongoing process of Life.

I believe that the enormous popularity of this book was due to the very simple and approachable way of addressing the fears and anxiety surrounding death, aging and change. In some ways, this book broke a taboo by talking openly about a subject people and society felt uncomfortable addressing; similar, in my view, to what Buddhism has been doing for the past 2500 years.

Basic Set of Conditions that Lead to Suffering

Speaking of uncomfortable topics, the Buddha spelled out what he meant by the First Mark of Existence, that is, "All conditioned phenomena are suffering" or "life is a bumpy road." They include, 1) *birth,* 2) *aging,* 3) *illness,* 4) *death,* 5) *being united with what one does not like,* 6) *separation from what one likes, and* 7) *not getting what one wants.* I will return to the first example, "birth," later. And we have previously looked at aging, illness and death. On death, Freddie expressed his fears to his friend Daniel, "I'm afraid to die. I don't know what's down there." I am sure many of us can identify with Freddie on this point.

As for suffering stemming from "being united with what one does not like" refers, for example, to *associating with difficult people.* Don't we all have the experience of having to work with a demanding boss or hard-to-get-along-with co-worker? For Freddie, he was united with a situation, where all the leaves had to go.

On the other hand, "separation from what one likes," refers, for example, to *having to move away from a great neighborhood or school* due to a parent's new job. For Freddie, he was perfectly happy being in the tree with all his leaf friends, working together to bring joy and comfort to the old and the young who came to enjoy the park. But with the arrival of fall, Freddie would be torn away from his friends, his work, and his home.

Now, suffering stemming from "not getting what one wants" is a more generic category that refers to a case of your efforts not bearing fruit. For instance, can you recall liking someone very much? So, *you did everything possible to get that person to like you,* but he or she just did not look your way. As for Freddie, he wanted to remain on the tree so much and fought as hard as he could, but in the end, he could not realize what he wanted.

Now, let's return to the "birth" to ask why the Buddha included this as an example of suffering, when birth of a baby is a reason for celebration. This is a tough question to answer in such a limited time, with potential for misunderstanding.

In short, according to the general traditional Indian religious view, unless spiritual awakening is attained, one is born again and again in a *cycle of birth and death* (saṃsāra), commonly known as *transmigration or reincarnation*. The Buddhists, too, subscribed to this general view. So, to be born into human life, *even though it is considered rare and precious*, meant that one is still wandering in the cycle of transmigration, which is a proof that one has *failed* to achieve awakening, the supreme goal of the Buddhists. For that reason, birth was included as an example of suffering.

To use an analogy, to ride on a *ferris wheel* is fun, but it would be horrifying if you continue to go in circles for one day, for one month, for one year, and endlessly! So, to be born into this never-ending cycle is suffering.

Well, at any case, you will have to develop an appreciation for the Indian religious worldview that I have just described in order to understand why *birth* is included among the examples of suffering.

Facing Up to Our Suffering and Aspire for Awakening

All this talk of suffering is not the end of the story, for acknowledging that "life is a bumpy road" as the First Mark of Existence teaches is the first step toward a solution, as we saw in the Buddha as well as in *Freddie the Leaf*. When we do, we awaken to the fact that the difficulties that can lead to suffering are unavoidable and we cannot run from them, as aptly expressed in today's scriptural passage:

> *Ordinary people in the world sooner or later run into difficulties, and consequently most people suffer. However, those who have heard the Buddha's teaching do not suffer because they understand that these difficulties are unavoidable.*

Of course, one's suffering doesn't disappear just by hearing the teachings, but it does propel us on the path where the level of our suffering decreases.

Please join us next week, when a Theravada monk will show us how to meditate to deal with our difficulties and suffering. See you then. Good bye for now.

PROGRAM 14
Teachings of the First Mark of Existence: Interview

People can get rid of mistaken views and resulting worldly pas-
sions by careful and patient observation of the mind.

(The Teaching of Buddha, p. 228)

Needless to say, a program like ours holds little value without viewers to watch it. So, we are especially grateful that you have joined us today to give value to what we do.

Our Guest Venerable Alubomulle Sumanasara

We are very fortunate today to have as our guest, *Bhikkhu* Sumanasara, whose name means "pleasant mind." Venerable Sumanasara belongs to the Theravada school, which is found mainly in Sri Lanka and Southeast Asia. Venerable Sumanasara was born in Sri Lanka and was ordained as a novice monk at the age of fourteen. And, he has been a bhikkhu for 46 years.

Interview

KT: Well, Venerable Sumanasara, thank you very much for being with us.

Ven. Sumanasara: It is a very good pleasure that we can have a talk like this.

KT: The pleasure is ours. Bhikkhu Sumanasara, "Bhikkhu," means, well, it refers to monks, but literally doesn't it mean "beggar"? Isn't it a little pejorative?

Ven. Sumanasara: Literally it means "beggar," and it may be a pejorative term. But the Buddha meant people who don't possess anything and *don't get attached to anything*. That means "absolutely free people." So with that in mind he purposely used this word for us, his disciples or bhikkus.

KT: So, if you don't have possessions, you are free, free to go anywhere. You don't have to worry about possession and guarding it. I think I understand that.

Now, you became a novice monk at age fourteen. That's very young to be a monk. Can you tell us a little bit about your motivation for becoming a monk or novice monk?

Sumanasara: In my country to become a monk is not a big problem because it was a natural process. From our earliest period, about 3 years, 4 years, our parents taught us about the basic principles of Buddhism. For example, when we play with animals and catch ants and like that, she got very angry. She said, "Every life is equal" and "Don't harm anybody!" It is the same as you. When I quarrelled with my brother, [she said] "Don't do stupid things. Let it go." So, like that. When I questioned about our life, they said, "Life is meaningless. Just people study and do their job and grow old and die." Then, once again when I asked, "What is the meaning of life," she said, "There is no meaning, but *you have to make life meaningful.*"

KT: So, one of your motivations is seeking a meaning in life for you.

Ven. Sumanasara: Yes, maybe.

KT: So, in Sri Lanka, at a young age, parents teach you to respect all life, including cats and dogs.

Ven. Sumanasara: Yes, entire life, even ants.

KT: Even ants?

Ven. Sumanasara: Yes. I couldn't be even allowed to press [step on] ants.

KT: So, Venerable, our program right now has to do with duhkha (duḥkha / dukkha) or suffering. And so, what kind of duhkha or suffering do most of your followers or students feel?

Ven. Sumanasara: When I talk with people, I found that many people complain about some type of fear. So, they say they feel fear in the ordinary sense. When I ask them further, they say fear of job, their family, about their health, and people fear their death ... so many things. And even younger people also, for they feel very strongly unsatisfied. They are not satisfied with everything that's going on. So, it becomes a very mental torture for them. So that's why they come to me and ask for help. And they can find out what it [the answer] is.

KT: They don't know the reason [for their suffering].

Ven. Sumanasara: Yes. They don't know the reason, the real reason. Because they are very intelligent, so they know that they cannot avoid death; they cannot avoid the problems of their job; they cannot avoid the problems of the family. But they are not really facing up to them.

KT: So, what is your solution? What do you teach them?

Ven. Sumanasara: So, the solution is that...we have a lot of imaginations and daydreaming and a lot of functions in the mind. Everything is unnecessary.

KT: A kind of obsessive thinking?

Ven. Sumanasara: Obsessive thinking and endless thinking, aimless thinking...purposeless. Just mind is turning, turning and turning endlessly. So, our mind is full of these *unnecessary loops* of thought patterns or thought cycles.

KT: [They are] kind of stuck, attached.

Ven. Sumanasara: So they can't stop that pattern. So they don't have time to face the life. All the energy is going down. So, it's a sheer waste of time. So our solution is very simple. We *cut all these loops of the mind*.

KT: Cut the loops of the mind. Okay. How do you do that?

Ven. Sumanasara: So that is what *Vipassana [meditation]* is for. So, the meditation that I introduce is called Vipassana, which means observation. So, we observe our mind and cut all the loops. So the point is like this. We face at the right moment and stop other thinking. So, should I explain it also?

KT: Yes.

Ven. Sumanasara: Simple practice is, for example, here we can imagine that there is a glass of water. I want to drink it. So, I slowly move my hand without thinking. To stop thinking, I have to mentally note every minor action of hand. So, I say [in my mind], "stretching, stretching, stretching, touching, touching, touching, feeling of touch, raising, raising, raising, raising, raising ...." So you feel the touch on your lips, and you take one gulp and drink, [noting to yourself] "Drinking, drinking, drinking, returning, returning, returning."

KT: So, this sounds like *mindfulness*. Is this mindfulness? Sati? We really concentrate on what's now in front of you?

Ven. Sumanasara: In front of you, at this right moment. So, that is very simple.

KT: So, you don't think of other obsessive thoughts.

Ven. Sumanasara: We purposely cut off other unnecessary thoughts.

KT: And you have to train your mind for that, and that's Vipassana.

Ven. Sumanasara: When you train this, we can think properly. So, you have a lot of energy preserved for life.

KT: You mentioned Vipassana. And there are different forms of Vipassana. One of them is walking Vipassana or meditation, which anyone can do. Can you please show us how to do that?

Ven. Sumanasara: Yes, it's my pleasure. I will explain.

So, I am going to introduce you to one aspect of Vipassana meditation. We call it [Vipassana] walking meditation. One is expected to do at least one hour a day. Within two weeks, I think you can enjoy happiness of your mind and calmness of your mind. So, when you practice this meditation, first you have to straighten our back. The way to straighten your back is that you have to move your body one millimeter and not fast, very slowly. And you have to tell yourself, "Stretching, stretching, stretching, stretching, stretching, stretching, stretching…" Something like that. So, you talk these words in your mind without moving your lips. After you have straightened your back, it is better to keep the hands held like this or in the back. And afterward, without moving the body, we move only the legs, only the foot.

And we say, "Right, raising, moving, pressing, left, raising, moving, pressing, right, raising, moving, pressing, left, raising, moving, pressing, right, raising, moving, pressing, left, raising, moving, pressing, right, raising, moving, pressing. Stop. Turning, turning, right, turning left, turning, right, turning left. Stop. Walking. Right, raising, moving, pressing, left, raising, moving, pressing, right, raising, moving, pressing, left, raising, moving, pressing, right, raising, moving, pressing, left, raising, moving, pressing. Stopping. Turning, left turning, right turning, left turning, right turning,"

We have to practice at least about one hour; or at least 30 minutes may be also all right. For example, if you walk one hour, you may feel walking slowly a little bit boring, then you can do little bit faster like this, repeating the words in your mind, you can walk like this.

For example, if you feel like walking very fast, you can say [to yourself], "Right moving, left moving, right moving, left moving, right moving. Stopping. Left, right, left, right. Left moving, right moving, left moving right moving, left moving." You can practice this very simple method. It is a very simple practice, but the effect is very great. Thank you very much.

KT: Wow, that was very nice. Thank you so much for showing us the walking Vipassana.

As the Venerable said, meditation helps us to realize the sense of *calm and clarity*. As you saw, these practices can be carried out by anybody and at any time. We hope that you can apply even a tiny bit of what the Venerable demonstrated today.

In our next show, we will continue our discussion on the First Mark of Existence and how to turn suffering into a resource for living a fuller and deeper life.

PROGRAM 15

First Mark of Existence: Turning Suffering into a Resource for Living

In Buddhism, suffering refers to a condition where one is restrained and without freedom. Accordingly, regardless of how difficult one's condition might be, it is not suffering if one's life is not restricted and freedom exists in daily life.

(Mutually Sustaining, Life p. 76)

It's great to have you join us as we take a final look at the topic of the First Mark of Existence, "All conditioned phenomena are suffering," or as many of you have heard me say by now, "Life is a bumpy road."

In previous shows we looked at the various kinds of suffering and stressed the need for us to face up to them. Last week as well, we learned some meditative techniques for dealing with our suffering.

Turning Suffering into a Resource for Living

Today I would like to continue with this positive approach to the issue of suffering. In doing so, I wish to restate a point: the Buddha did not promise that by following his Dharma, the teachings, people would be able to *prevent* aging, illness, death, being separated from loved ones or having to meet up with people we dislike.

These *conditions* that lead to suffering are *simply a part of life*. In life, they just happen. We can't avoid experiencing them. However, what we can control is how we *respond* to them. We can respond either by suffering or by not suffering. This is another way of expressing, once again, one of our favorite phrases, "Difficulties are inevitable, but suffering is optional."

For this reason, the *Buddha did not perform miracles*, such as bringing the dead back to life or curing illness. Some people may say, therefore, that the Buddha was weak, lacking spiritual powers. Well for me, it is precisely for this reason that I find him realistic and believable.

Metaphor of One Water and Four Views

Given this position that the Dharma, the teachings, helps to us to determine how we *respond* to difficulties, we all have the potential to turn our experiences of suffering into a resource for living more deeply and for experiencing life closer to how "life truly is."

The potential to do so is supported in a Buddhist metaphor known as *One Water and Four Views*. Well, let's say there is water, like this. This water would appear differently to those at four different levels of spiritual development. A *hungry ghost*, who is the least developed among them, would see the water as *pus and phlegm*, certainly, not something to be desired. A *fish* would see the water as an *abode*, a place to live. For a *human being*, the water is *a drink*, something to be had to satisfy our bodily needs.

And for a *heavenly being*, viewing from the highest spiritual level, the water appears as a pond filled with *shimmering jewels*! The heavenly beings are not yet fully awakened like Bodhisattvas or Buddhas but are highest spiritually among the four, higher than the human beings. For them, therefore, the water appears like a bed of jewels, which is a far cry from the pus and phlegm of the hungry ghosts!

In real life, aren't there such differences among the people we know? Some, like the hungry ghosts, are always taking a negative point of view and forever complaining about anything and everything. On the other hand, there are others, like the heavenly beings, who face difficulties in life with the right view and are able to *turn them into a resource for living life more deeply and fully*. So, let us make it our challenge to approach life's difficulties with the perspectives of the heavenly beings.

I wish to share with you the cases of two inspiring individuals, whose lives brim with the "water of a pond of shimmering jewels."

Tuesdays with Morrie

The first example of someone who dealt with suffering to live deeply and with insight is Morrie Schwartz, an inspirational person and the subject of the best-selling book published some years ago entitled, *Tuesdays with Morrie: an old man, a young man, and life's greatest lesson.* The book is mostly a conversation between a college professor and his former student named Mitch Albom, who is also the author of the book. Morrie Schwartz is the college professor, who learns that he has ALS or Lou Gehrig's disease, leaving him less than one year to live.

Mitch had become a successful and busy newspaper sports columnist. He had not kept in touch with his professor as he once promised at his graduation some 15 years ago. Then, one day by chance, Mitch saw Morrie on a nationally televised program. Morrie had drawn attention for his acts and words of courage and inspiration in the face of fatal illness. For Mitch, here was the one professor in college who had touched and inspired him. In learning of the professor's situation, Mitch felt compelled to go see him.

Thereafter, the two of them decided to meet on a regular basis from then on. In the course of their weekly Tuesday meetings, Morrie shares his thoughts on many topics including family, friends, and death. In the course of these discussions with Mitch, Morrie, who is not a Buddhist by the way, introduces some Buddhist ideas.

One that is pertinent for our discussion has to do with his understanding of not becoming attached to things because all things are impermanent. Morrie then goes on to explain that non-attachment does not mean to become *indifferent* or to *avoid* things out of fear or pain. Instead, Morrie encourages one to *immerse oneself in the fear, to experience the fear to its fullest.* By doing so, we are better able to accept our illness or death, which then we would be much better able to see in a larger perspective and let go of the fear and pain. Consequently, Morrie suggests, with the mental space provided by our act of stepping away, we would be in a better position to deal with our illness or death more effectively with openness, patience and even humor.

Morrie stresses that this approach applies to other difficulties in life, such as feelings of loneliness or our inability to express our true feelings to our loved ones. He encourages us to *"Turn on the faucet. Wash yourself with the emotion."*

Well, his expression may be somewhat unorthodox from the standpoint of traditional Buddhism. However, Morrie, in my view, epitomizes the spirit of the First Mark of Existence of turning difficulties into a resource for living deeper and fuller lives. And Morrie conveys this so well when he says to Mitch, "But it's like I keep telling you. *When you learn how to die, you learn how to live.*"

Christine's Overcoming of Suffering

Christine is another person who faced up to her encounter with suffering. She was a member of the Southern Alameda County Buddhist Church in Union City, California, where I spent a wonderful and memorable three years as the resident priest of that temple. When I met her, she struck me as an extremely lively and cheerful person. She had been confined to a wheel chair for at least ten years as a result of a car accident in her late teens. Christine herself told me how the Buddhist teachings had helped her through the difficulties, and she truly had gone through unbelievable tough times.

One day I was told that Christine was suffering from a severe case of bedsores, and that she would have to be confined to her bed for an entire year! I just couldn't imagine how she would feel being confined to her bed for 365 days!

I immediately paid her a visit, armed with all the appropriate things to say to comfort her. As I entered her room, her cheerful demeanor surprised me. Then we chatted for about half an hour about this and that, including her condition and how she would spend that year in bed. Then, as I said goodbye and was about to leave, Christine cheerfully said to me, "Sensei, don't worry about me. I'll be just fine. *I have eyes*, so I can read books, watch TV and gaze out onto the field and trees outside the window. *I also have ears*, so I can listen to my favorite music and programs on the radio. And *I have a brain*, so I can think and imagine about a lot of things. So, don't worry about me." I found that our roles had been reversed, for I left Christine more inspired and energized than before I went. She taught me something very important.

Christine, if you happen to be watching, please know that you were a Buddha to me, and your words continue to inspire me!

Mental and Spiritual Freedom

So, we have Morrie and Christine, two inspiring individuals, who despite their condition were mentally and spiritually free and unrestrained. Both of these [cases] serve as shining examples that show us that difficulties do not automatically have to become suffering, as stated in today's scriptural passage:

In Buddhism, suffering refers to a condition where one is restrained and without freedom. Accordingly, regardless of how difficult one's condition might be, it is not suffering if one's life is not restricted and freedom exists in daily life.

Let us then exercise our mental and spiritual freedom to consider the message of the First Mark of Existence, and acknowledge that "Life is, indeed, a Bumpy Road." Next, we must face up to and transform the bumps on the road as a resource for living our lives more fully and deeply, with greater wisdom and compassion for ourselves and for others.

In our next show, Venerable Sumanasara, a Buddhist monk, will rejoin us to share ritual chanting from the Theravada tradition. You'll find it melodic, soothing and inspiring. Do join us. I'm sure you'll be glad you did.

PROGRAM 16
Three Treasures: Interview

When they take refuge in the Buddha, they should seek his wisdom.
When they take refuge in the Dharma, they should seek its truth,
which is like a great ocean of wisdom.
When they take refuge in the Sangha, they should seek its peaceful
fellowship unobstructed by selfish interests.

(The Teaching of Buddha, p. 410)

Today I would like to talk about a slightly different topic than the first of the Four Marks of Existence, which have been the focus in the past three shows.

More specifically, let's turn our attention to the *Three Treasures, Tri-ratna in Sanskrit*. They are also translated as "Three Jewels," but I shall be referring to them as the Three Treasures. The Three Treasures refer to *Buddha, Dharma and Sangha* (Saṃgha).

The Buddha refers to "one who has Awakened," and for many the Buddha refers to Shakyamuni Buddha. However, for others, the Buddha also refers to other Buddhas and awakened people.

Dharma points to the teachings, which serve as the map or path for becoming Buddhas. The word, Dharma, has already come up before as in the "Wheel of Dharma," which you see at the beginning of each of our shows. Dharma has a number of meanings other than "teachings," for example, "truth," "reality," and "rules." Actually, you may already be familiar with this word, for many of you have probably watched the popular TV sitcom, "Dharma and Greg."

And Sangha refers to the group of monks and nuns, who serve as models for us to emulate as well as the transmitters of the Dharma. In some groups, particularly in the West, Sangha has come to have a wider meaning to mean "a community of all Buddhists," including the lay people, not just the ordained monks and nuns.

The Three Treasures are extremely important in Buddhism because the act of *"Taking Refuge in the Three Treasures"* is the expression of one's trust and commitment to Buddhism. In many denominations and schools of Buddhism, the taking of refuge in the Three Trea-sures constitutes an initiation as a Buddhist. And once a Buddhist, the taking of refuge is recited often at religious services by monks, nuns, and the lay people alike.

The taking of refuge is important for another reason. It is *common* to all schools of Buddhism today. In fact, this is the one ritual that Buddhists of all denominations can do together at inter-denomina-tional gatherings. Of course, the various schools take refuge in their respective language, and the wordings are phrased slightly differ-ently. However, the core expression of this act goes as follows:

"I take refuge in the Buddha. I take refuge in the Dharma. I take refuge in the Sangha."

Interview with Venerable Sumanasara

Today, we are pleased to have back with us, Venerable Sumanasara, who was born in Sri Lanka and has been a Buddhist monk or bhik-khu for 46 years. As we explore the Three Treasures, the Venerable will be chanting in an ancient language called Pali (Pāli), which ac-cording to his Theravada (Theravāda) tradition, was the language used by the Buddha.

KT: So, Venerable Sumanasara, thank you for being with us again.

Ven. Sumanasara: Thank you, and it's a pleasure to be here.

KT: We're doing [a show on the] Three Treasures today. Do you have comments on taking refuge in the Three Treasures?

Ven. Sumanasara: When you say "taking refuge," it's a little bit awkward. But actually for the Buddhists, it means three guidelines, our manual of living. Whenever we have a problem of how to live and how to address our problems, we take an example from these three refuges.

KT: When do you recite the Three Treasures in your tradition?

Ven. Sumanasara: This is a big problem because we don't have any particular time. Whenever we have a chance, we recite these three verses, because we need guidance all the time. So, [we recite it] in the morning, in the evening, and again when we have some ceremonies. We do it whenever we do something by first chanting it.

KT: So [you chant] not just at rituals or ceremonies, but all the time, anytime.

Ven. Sumanasara: Yes, anytime, even at schools. Before school starts, students chant these things. When we have a social ceremony or whatever it may be, [it is chanted].

KT: So, even at schools, it is chanted. Venerable, could you chant it for us now?

Ven. Sumanasara: Okay, it would be my pleasure.

Pali Chanting of the Three Treasures

Ven. Sumanasara:

Buddhaṁ saraṇaṁ gacchāmi, Dhammaṁ saraṇaṁ gacchāmi, Saṁghaṁ saraṇaṁ gacchāmi

"I take refuge in the Buddha. I take refuge in the Dharma. I take refuge in the Sangha."

Dutiyampi Buddhaṁ saraṇaṁ gacchāmi, Dhammaṁ saraṇaṁ gacchāmi, Saṁghaṁ saraṇaṁ gacchāmi

"For the second time, I take refuge in the Buddha. I take refuge in the Dharma. I take refuge in the Sangha."

Tatiyampi Buddhaṁ saraṇaṁ gacchāmi, Dhammaṁ saraṇaṁ gacchāmi, Saṁghaṁ saraṇaṁ gacchāmi

"For the third time, I take refuge in the Buddha. I take refuge in the Dharma. I take refuge in the Sangha."

Sino-Japanese Chanting of the Three Treasures

Now, I wish to share with you what we chant in my Jodo Shinshu tradition during a formal ceremony. I believe similar chanting is also found in other traditions that originated in East Asia.

Shi shin kei rei Na mo shou chiu fu
With sincere heart-mind of reverence and obeisance
I take refuge in the eternal abiding Buddha

Shi shin kei rei Na mo shou chiu ho
With sincere heart-mind of reverence and obeisance
I take refuge in the eternal abiding Dharma

Shi shin kei rei Na mo shou chiu so
With sincere heart-mind of reverence and obeisance
I take refuge in the eternal abiding Sangha

Blessings: In Pali

Whatever beings there may be,
weak or strong, without exception,
long, large,
middling, short,
subtle, blatant,
seen & unseen,
near & far,
born & seeking birth:
May all beings be happy at heart.　　　(*Sutta Nipāta, 146, 147*)

Let no one deceive another
or despise anyone anywhere,
or through anger or resistance
wish for another to suffer.　　　　　(*Sutta Nipāta, 148*)

May all worries be wiped out. May all sickness be cured.
May you never encounter with any dangers. May you enjoy
happiness, long life.　　　　　　　(*General Blessing*)

KT: It's been a great pleasure and honor to have a bhikkhu from the Theravada tradition to join us and to share your thoughts and chanting with us. Thank you so much.

Ven. Sumanasara: Thank you. It was a pleasure to be with you.

We are pleased to be able to share with you the chanting of our respective traditions. It's our hope that you got a glimpse of the ritual dimension of Buddhism, which plays a vital role in the lives of many Buddhists throughout the world.

In our next show, our discussion will move to the Second Mark of Existence on the interdependence of all things, one of the hallmarks of Buddhist teachings. Thanks for joining us and hope to see you next time.

CHAPTER FIVE:
Teachings of the Second Mark of Existence

◆ ◆ ◆

PROGRAM 17
Second Mark of Existence: The Universe and I

*As a net is made up by a series of knots, so everything in this world
is connected by a series of knots. If anyone thinks that the mesh of
a net is an independent, isolated thing, he is mistaken.*

(*The Teaching of Buddha, p. 82*)

Second Mark of Existence

Today, we are ready to talk about the second of the Four Marks of
Existence, which is, *All Conditioned Phenomena lack substantial entity.*
Or rephrased, *Life is interdependent.*

I should qualify here that these expressions differ slightly from
a more common English translation of this mark, which is usually
rendered *"non-self"* or *"non-ego."* However, "non-self" and "non-ego"
can not only be misleading but be difficult to explain fully in the
limited time that we have. For this reason, I have opted for what I
consider easier terms to understand, which is once again, "All Conditioned Phenomena lack substantial entity" or "Life is interdependent."

"All Conditioned Phenomena" refers to all the objects of our experiences through our senses and thoughts. "Substantial entity" refers to anything that comes into being all by itself or exists on its own,
without being dependent on anything else. However, the Buddha
awakened to the truth that there is no such entity, for every thing
comes into being dependent on something else. For example, all living beings are born from a set of parents or at least from some preced-
ing forms. And their very existence depends on others.

Indra's Net of Jewels

This is illustrated in a well-known Buddhist metaphor of the Indra's Net of Jewels. The metaphor speaks of a net that extends endlessly throughout the whole universe in all directions. At each "eye"

of the net is a jewel. And all the jewels on the net produce together a galactic bed of glistening and shimmering jewels. Each jewel illuminates its unique light. However, no one jewel can shine on its own, for it can shine only by receiving the illumination of the other jewels. And every other jewel is the same, for it has no ability to shine on its own. Hence, the jewels are *mutually sustaining*, reminding us of the overall title of this television program!

Our Breath, the Sun and the Universe

Now, let me cite an example that is intimately close to us. Please hold your breath. Hold it for a few seconds. Then hold it a little longer. ... Now, please take a breath. Had we gone much longer holding our breath, we would all have started experiencing physical discomfort. It goes to show how little we can go without depending on air. We know this in our head, but are not fully aware with our whole being.

Let me ask you, "How many times did you breathe in the last 24 hours?" Let's count each time you inhale and exhale as one time. If we time ourselves, most people inhale and exhale about 30 times a minute, which means 1800 times an hour, totalling 43,200 times a day. That's quite a few times, don't you think? So, in a sense, we are "dependent" on air 43,200 times a day.

Now, conversely, the air itself is dependent on others, including us. As many of you know, oxygen in the air that we breathe is produced through a process called photosynthesis that takes place in vegetation. And that vegetation requires water, sunshine and carbon dioxide, and carbon dioxide comes partly from what we humans exhale. Hence the very production of oxygen is dependent partly on us. There is again a mutually sustaining relationship.

Within this awareness of the mutually sustaining nature of our existence, I am constantly reminded of our connection to and relation to the sun. Without it, we would obviously not be able to exist. Besides the many indispensable benefits it provides, the sun also is present in every breath we take, for the sunlight is required in the production of oxygen. While we breathe with our lungs, the source of that breathing lies some 93 million miles away. And if we see that the sun is part of the greater solar system, which in turn is part of the Milky Way Galaxy, which further is part of this immense universe, from this perspective, we can say that the entire universe participates in each breath that we take!

Emptiness

As the "story" of our breath shows, all things are *interdependent, interconnected and inter-related*. All things originate as a result of a number of factors coming together. Nothing can emerge on its own and be sustained by itself. This truth is also expressed in the Mahayana branch of Buddhism as "All conditioned phenomena are empty of their own nature" or *"emptiness"* (śūnyatā). This has been translated also as *"nothingness."* Hence, Buddhist teachers are often associated, particularly in the West, with the teaching of "emptiness" or "nothingness."

This reminds me of a humorous greeting card that I recently saw about the *Dalai Lama*. It's his birthday. He is surrounded by a group of his top disciples who look pleased with the present they had just handed him. The Dalai Lama appears elated as he looks down into the bag holding his present. However, apparently there is no present in the bag, but the Dalai Lama exclaims, "Wow, this is just what I wanted ... nothing!"

Well ... this greeting card does not correctly convey the significance of the second mark of existence, for "emptiness" does not mean an absence of things but an absence of anything that exists completely independent of anything else.

And this truth is not pessimistic, world-negating or nihilistic. It, in fact, recognizes how we humans are intimately connected to our natural and social world.

Wes Nisker's book, *Buddha Nature*

This outlook is presented in one of the most provocative books of Buddhism in recent years, Wes Nisker's *Buddha Nature*. This work by a teacher in the Theravada-based Insight Meditation tradition makes effective use of the findings in the physical and biological sciences to reinforce the Buddhist claim of interconnectedness, particularly of our body with the *physical world and other living beings*. He shows how we are related to our physical world through the traditional Buddhist categories of the *four fundamental elements*: earth, heat, water and air.

The *earth element* is characterized by solidity, hardness, and mass. One of the earth elements is gravity, something that is ubiquitous but taken for granted and rarely noticed. It is this gravity that is holding us down to this earth when sitting, lying or walking.

The *heat element* is best expressed in the process we call photosynthesis and burning. In photosynthesis, the plants produce foods and oxygen by the combination of sunlight, carbon dioxide, and water. The other process that he calls "burning" explains how plants and animals transform the sunlight into heat energy needed for fueling their lives.

The *water element* is readily apparent as 75% of our body's mass is made up of water. Life began in the sea, and its chemical make-up is similar to the blood and sweat flowing through our veins and flesh.

The *air element* is characterized most prominently in our breathing. With each breath, we inhale the essential oxygen molecules into our body and then exhale carbon dioxide molecules.

Our Connection to Other Living Beings

Biological studies have shown with much greater clarity that in the process of human evolution, we came to embody the characteristics of the previous forms of life from the reptiles to other mammals to previous human-like beings. So, every human body replicates the entire evolutionary process during our embryonic maturation in the womb. The history of evolution is expressed in this very body.

A similar pattern is seen in the makeup of our brain. Our brain is composed of three main parts: *reptilian, mammalian, and primate*. While in our mother's womb, these three parts develop sequentially; the first to develop is the reptilian, followed by the mammalian, and the last to develop is the primate brain.

The reptilian part is basically the same as that found in the reptiles. It is this section that regulates functions such as breath, body temperature, pain perception, hunger, sexuality, and a basic nervous system program of stimulus-response. It largely determines our feelings of pleasant or unpleasant.

The mammalian brain is, as the term suggests, shared by other mammals. It permits experiences of what we now call emotion; for example, loyalty and affection, not detected in reptiles.

The development of the third brain "expanded the power to learn and remember and a sense of agency and individuality." Then, it was the human beings that leaped forward, away from all ancestors with the development of "complex language, long-term planning ability, abstract thought, and a very strong sense of individuality and control over the world."

Wave and the Ocean

When we see ourselves in this light, we cannot help but to feel a sense of deep kinship and oneness with the world and all living beings. This very body is a byproduct of the entire world. Each of our bodies is like a wave in an immense ocean. Each wave came out of the ocean and continues to be sustained by the ocean. And when the conditions lead to the breakdown of this body in what we call "death," the body is no longer an autonomous being. But that does not mean that the body disappears, but, like the wave, it merely changes form to rejoin the rest of the ocean, of which we had always been an integral part. Conversely, a person is bound to experience fear and isolation if he sees himself only as the wave and not as part of the immense ocean. This is the message being conveyed to us in today's scriptural passage:

> As a net is made up by a series of knots, so everything in this world
> is connected by a series of knots. If anyone thinks that the mesh of
> a net is an independent, isolated thing, he is mistaken.

Please join us next week, when a Zen Buddhist nun joins us to share with us her life in a monastery.

PROGRAM 18
Second Mark of Existence: Life of a Zen Nun

How shall we live this fleeting life? Merely acquiring or having wealth is not a life.

(*Mutually Sustaining Life, p. 22*)

Hello, it's a great pleasure to have you join us. What did you think of today's passage? "*How shall we live this fleeting life? Merely acquiring or having wealth is not a life.*" For me, I see it as challenging us to seek for meaning beyond just the material or the ordinary. The passage encourages us to make basic decisions about how we lead our lives. Unfortunately, there are many among us who have no clear answer to this question.

This reminds me of a humorous story told by a famous Zen master, Kosho Uchiyama. A fellow, I shall call him "Richard," had just begun to learn horseback riding, and as of yet the horse was not under his control. As he passed along a busy street, the horse began to eat carrots at a vegetable stand. The shopkeeper got angry and hit the horse with a stick. The horse was surprised and started to gallop. Richard desperately held onto the mane of the horse, just trying not to be thrown off. A friend happened to be walking down the same street. The friend called out, "Hey Richard, where are you going?" Richard managed to answer, "I don't know. Ask the horse!"

Well I know one person who is not like Richard. She is our guest today, Rev. Wako Ishikawa, who made the choice in her life to answer the question, "How shall we live this fleeting life?" And that choice was to become a Buddhist nun in the Soto Zen tradition. She currently resides in a monastery in Sapporo, Japan, but, interestingly, it was while she was living in California that she became seriously interested in Buddhism. We would like to take this wonderful opportunity to ask Rev. Ishikawa about the reasons that led her to make the choices that she has made as well as the daily life of a Buddhist nun.

Interview

KT: So, Rev. Ishikawa, thank you for joining us and to share your thoughts and experiences with us

Rev. Ishikawa: Thank you, too.

KT: My first question for you is, "When did you first become seriously interested in Buddhism?"

Rev. Ishikawa: Well, I was born and grown up in Japan but did not have any special belief for me. It was a kind of our daily life and a part of culture. However, when I was a college student in San Francisco, my American friends were interested in Japanese Buddhism. And they were practicing *zazen*, sit to meditate, seriously. That made me surprised and made me [motivated and be] interested in Buddhism.

KT: I see. So you studied in California, and you were exposed to Buddhism in San Francisco. Then, you went back to Japan. And how did you feel about Japan, then?

Rev. Ishikawa: I felt freer than what I expected. I expected Japanese society [to be] more tightened and strict than American society. However, Japan was already modern country, and Tokyo was a cosmopolitan city already.

KT: And you said that you were surprised. Then you thought about how Americans, young Americans, especially were interested in Japanese Buddhism.

Rev. Ishikawa: Yes. So in Japanese society they, American young men, were looking for something for themselves in Japanese tradition now, Buddhism, which existed already 1,500 years in Japan. So, that made me more [motivated] to be interested in Buddhism.

KT: So, what did you do?

Rev. Ishikawa: I became to want to know that actual figure or how Japanese Buddhism is practiced in Japan. So, I visited Eihei-ji Temple, which is in Fukui Prefecture in Japan.

KT: And Eihei-ji is ...?

Rev. Ishikawa: ... is the head temple of our Soto [Zen] School. Three hundred monks and priests are living in the mountain. So, I visited and practiced *zazen*, siting meditation, there.

KT: I see. So, you became inspired by Buddhism and became a lay Buddhist. How and when did that happen?

Rev. Ishikawa: When I was in San Francisco, I received a telegram which said that my father was critical and come back to Japan immediately. And he passed away before long. Then I felt something, a kind of suffering. And Buddhism says Bodhisattva mind is promoted by suffering or difficulties. Well, I think, at that time, I felt something like that. So, I received lay precepts, precepts as a lay Buddhist in 1987 at Eihei-ji.

KT: I see. And what were you doing at that time?

Rev. Ishikawa: I was a computer programmer.

KT: Computer programmer? I see.

Rev. Ishikawa: And I worked in Tokyo and California and [would] fly and go back and forth. And Buddha's teaching was living as best way in my work and in my daily life at that time.

KT: So, it came alive in your work.

Rev. Ishikawa: Hai (Yes). My college major was computer information science. So, I was a lay Buddhist as a computer programmer.

KT: I see. Then, you made this big jump to become an ordained priest. Can you tell us more about that?

Rev. Ishikawa: Well, I climbed up my career ladder, and I was hired by American Embassy in Tokyo. So I became a Federal government officer and worked in the Department of Commerce. So, it was a very difficult, busy job. I went to Washington D.C. Then, I came across an accident.

KT: Accident?

Rev. Ishikawa: That became my turning point.

KT: What happened?

Rev. Ishikawa: Well, after work, I was walking toward a subway station after work. And I was walking [on a] sidewalk, and an iron chair fell down on my head. It [had] come from the second floor balcony. And I fainted.

KT: Fainted? And you went to a hospital?

Rev. Ishikawa: And an ambulance came. Well, I thought, I could die, but I just didn't. Or, if [I were] one step ahead, [when] I was walking, I [would] not [have] come across such an accident.

KT: You would not have been hit by the chair. Or, if you were one step back, you would [also have avoided the accident].

Rev. Ishikawa: Exactly.

KT: So, this kind of became the event that made you think seriously about becoming a priest?

Rev. Ishikawa: That was a big turning point of my life. Then, I started to think to devote my life, [the] rest [of my] life, to Buddha's life.

KT: So, you left your work as a government officer and devoted your time to Buddhism, to become a priest?

Rev. Ishikawa: Hai. I became a priest 1996.

KT: So, what are your main activities at the monastery?

Rev. Ishikawa: First of all, [I do] *zazen*, sit to meditate, sutra chanting and also *samu* which means work, mainly cleaning the temple in and out of the temple. And also [I engage in] the work [of doing things] for my master, a venerable priest, [who is] 78 years old.

KT: I see. So, you help him?

Rev. Ishikawa: Hai. Yes.

KT: I see. I see. Can you talk a bit about the role and position of nuns?

Rev. Ishikawa: Well, of course people expect a kind of compassion, compassionate [behavior from the] nuns. However, I could say that the importance as a nun is just [to] live as a nun, which is quite independent economically and spiritually. And life is very basic and simple, and [it is] without compromise with anybody so that Japanese women can seek very fundamental help, spiritual help [in] the nun's life when they come across various difficulties.

KT: I see. There are, I am sure, difficulties in the institution itself.

Rev. Ishikawa: Yes, compared to the men.

KT: I see. So, you think it is harder to be a nun than being a monk?

Rev. Ishikawa: I think so.

KT: I see. So, how do you understand the teaching of interdependence?

Rev. Ishikawa: Well, we can say, it's mutual respect.

KT: Mutual respect? I like that, "mutual respect," to explain interdependence.

Rev. Ishikawa: Yes.

KT: Well, I think we are just about out of time. But I believe we are able to catch a glimpse into your life as a Buddhist nun and the choices you made in answering the question posed in today's passage, "How shall we live this fleeting life?" Thank you very much.

Rev. Ishikawa: Thank you very much, too.

I hope that you found the interview with Rev. Ishikawa as interesting and intriguing as I did, and that it may give some pause for thought in enhancing the quality of your life. You are, of course, not being asked or expected to become a nun or a monk. There have always been far more lay Buddhists than monks and nuns. Simply, our show today will have served its purpose if it helped you to reflect on your own life.

Thanks for watching. And I hope you can join us next week when we explore the social dimension of the Second Mark of Existence, that is, Life is Interdependent.

PROGRAM 19
Second Mark of Existence: Societal Dimension

At one time there lived in the Himalayas a bird with one body and two heads. Once one of the heads noticed the other head eating some sweet fruit and felt jealous. The second head said to itself, "I will then eat poison." So it ate the poison, but the whole bird then died.

(The Teaching of Buddha, p. 274)

Today, I would like to continue our discussion on the Second Mark of Existence, "Life is interdependent," but with a focus on the social dimension of our experience.

The Two-headed Bird

What is the message being conveyed in today's opening passage about a bird with two heads and one body? Well, deep in the mountains of the Himalayas there lived a rare two-headed bird. One of the heads saw that the other head was eating a lot of sweet fruits. Presumably because the first head had only a little or none of the delicious fruit, it felt jealous of the other head. And out of jealousy, this first head wanted to harm the other head by taking poison.

It can be said that this is a case where one party feels *jealousy and hatred* toward the other and reacts by hurting the other. However, since the two [heads] share the same body this action led to the death of not only the second head but also the perpetrator. Given the interdependent and interconnected nature of their relationship, any attempt to hurt the other ultimately harms the whole.

I believe that same principle applies to our society and our world, for the members are interdependent, interconnected and interrelated. However, we often divide the groups, align ourselves with one of them, and fall into the *"us"* and *"them"* mentality. We then claim, "They are they and we are we, and we have little or nothing in common."

However, not only do the various groups have a lot more in common, but they are, in fact, interconnected on a fundamental level. This was aptly expressed by using *iceberg* as a *metaphor* by Rev. Matsunami in an earlier show (Program 12). He said that on the surface of the ocean, we see a group of separate icebergs, but under the surface they are all connected and form one giant block of ice.

So, when one is harmed then the entirety is damaged, which is what happened with the two-headed bird. But the first head did not realize that truth when it tried to hurt the other, for it ended up hurting the entire bird, including itself.

Conflicts Based on the Spirit of the Two-headed Bird

When we apply this to our world, we find many disturbing examples of the plight of the two-headed bird, found in numerous parts of the globe between tribes with centuries-old rivalry and among unforgiving neighboring countries. These conflicts have led to the loss of numerous lives, often those of innocent children.

One poignant example stands out in my mind from a scene shown on a newscast some years back. Caught in a crossfire, a volley of gunfire pins down a young boy of about eight behind a fence of some sort. His father is with him. The boy squats behind the father as he clings to him with all his might. You can see the sense of terror in his face and hear the sound of gunfire and see the bullets shower all around them. And I find myself rooting the boy and his father on. I can feel my heart pumping harder. It's almost surreal that such a scene is being televised at all, but it is definitely real. Then, the camera scene abruptly shifts away from the boy and his father to spare us from the ensuing gruesome scene. Then the reporter announces in an agonizing tone that they have both been hit. My heart sinks in cold despair and soon turns to a burning anger as it is reported that both were killed.

My anger is at the death of the innocent boy and father whose lives were senselessly snatched away. The anger is directed at the people on both sides who continue to perpetrate the conflict with no effort to reconcile. They are like *the two-headed bird*.

I realize that such conflicts are extremely complicated with long histories with implications of geopolitical nature, and that my view may be too simplistic and idealistic. However, it's my hope that sharing with you the lessons of the two-headed bird can have some positive impact in uniting the forces of people of various countries and religions, and to steering more people in the world toward regarding one another as being fundamentally *interdependent, interconnected and interrelated*.

Interdependency of a Community

While the truth of interdependence can have positive impact on a global scale, it also describes the way our communities actually function, even though we are often not aware of it. A community in which we live, be it a town or a city or county, provides services that we often take for granted, such as *public schools, police, fire departments, and hospitals*. Especially, the latter three do not truly concern us until we are in actual need of their services. Allow me to share my personal account of such an experience.

When our daughter, Serena, was one and a half years old, she suddenly developed flu-like symptoms but with a slight difference. She had an extremely high temperature and swollen hands rarely found when experiencing the flu. Soon she broke out in a rash all over her body, with the lymph node under her jaw growing to a size of a golf ball. We rushed her to her pediatrician. The doctor wasn't sure but suspected she had contracted *Kawasaki Disease*. Its cause is not clearly known, but this illness leads to the coagulation or the thickening of the blood, which can lead to a rupture of the blood vessels to the heart and sudden death.

As we rushed her to the Children's Hospital nearby, my wife and I were in state of disbelief that there was a chance that our daughter had come down with such a serious illness. We both prayed that it wasn't so, but after a series of tests, our family doctor's diagnosis was confirmed. Our hearts sank to the floor, but soon we were more preoccupied with making sure that she was getting the right treatment.

Well, even after the treatment started, my daughter cried throughout the evening, as her lips bled from the thickening of the blood. Even as we wiped her lips clean of blood every ten minutes, the bleeding continued and *smeared the pillow bright red* so that we had to change the pillow case every hour or so. It was a harrowing night.

Around 3 a.m., she finally fell asleep. So I went to the cafeteria for a cup of coffee. As I entered the cafeteria, I was struck with an *amazing sight*. There were about forty hospital staff, doctors, nurses and others, in their white uniforms, taking time off from their midnight shifts. All of a sudden, tears welled up, and I had to rush to a nearby table to grab a bunch of napkins to wipe them away.

My surprising reaction caught me off-guard. It stemmed from my realization that there were so many people working throughout the night to attend to patients like my daughter. I was struck by an overwhelming sense of gratitude for the fact that the hospital existed at all. Without it, we are helpless, but the staff has the knowledge and the experience to diagnose such illnesses and the capacity to treat them. This is obvious, but I had not truly appreciated a hospital's value until we needed its services. As I wiped away my tears with the hospital cafeteria napkins, I experienced firsthand the interconnectedness of our community.

Serena ended up being hospitalized for a week and recuperated for another month at home. Though she lost a third of her weight and stopped walking temporarily, fortunately, she has made a full recovery without any damage to her heart and now leads a normal life.

Interconnectedness of Community

I am sure that many of you have had similar experiences. We take hospitals and other public institutions for granted, but only realize their real value when we are *in dire need* of their services. Moreover, the State of California provided generous financial assistance to our family to cover much of the enormous medical costs.

So, to this day, I automatically bow my head whenever I pass by the Children's Hospital. I also am deeply grateful to the State of California and, therefore, can't help but to feel an attachment and fondness for the California flag, and especially to the Grizzly Bear that's emblazoned on its state flag as the state animal.

Given my feelings for these public institutions, I now do what I can to repay them for their generosity, for example, in the form of a donation to their annual fundraising efforts. Fortunately, there is no spirit of the double-headed bird at work here. There is, instead, an abiding sense that the community is interconnected and cannot afford to ignore each other, let alone attack one another.

In our next show, a Zen priest will demonstrate the basics of Zen Meditation. Please join us.

PROGRAM 20
Second Mark of Existence: Zazen Meditation

Do not become attached to the things you like; do not maintain aversion to things you dislike. Sorrow, fear and bondage come from one's likes and dislikes.

(*The Teaching of Buddha, p. 372*)

Hi. It's nice to have you join us. How did your week go? If you answered that your week was just too busy and went by too quickly, then you might be interested in meditation, which is the topic of today's show.

As mentioned in previous shows, one of the reasons for the growing popularity of Buddhism in this country has to do with many people being attracted by meditation, which comes mostly in three forms, Vipassana, Tibetan and Zen. In earlier shows, we have discussed *Vipassana meditation*, which comes to us from the Theravada tradition of Southeast Asia. Another style is found in the *Tibetan tradition*, which has yet to be discussed in our program but is a form that we would like to take up in one of our future shows.

Then, there is *Zen meditation*. Zen meditation has flourished in China and subsequently in Korea, Vietnam and Japan. "Zen" is the Japanese pronunciation of the original Chinese word, which is "*Chan*." To help us gain a better understanding of Zen meditation, Rev. Wakō Ishikawa, who joined us previously, has kindly agreed to demonstrate the basics of Zen meditation.

Interview

KT: Well, it's great to have you back. We're looking forward to having you share how you practice Zen meditation. If it is okay with you, I would like to serve as your student.

Rev. Ishikawa: Sure.

KT: Thank you. Well, let's get started.

Rev. Ishikawa: First of all, I introduce you [to the gesture of] *gasshō* (*holding the palms and fingers of both hands together*). *Gasshō* is an expression of respect and faith. Palm and palm touch each other. And height is nose height, and one fist away from the nose, the distance. *Gasshō* is expression of respect and faith. Whenever greeting others, we use *gasshō*, and when you face the Buddha.

Next, I introduce you to [the way of carrying yourself called] *shashu*. *Shashu* is [carried out] when we walk in the meditation hall, get into meditation hall and get out meditation hall; [those are the times] you make *shashu*. The thumb [on your left hand] is held [covered] by four fingers. Press [the left fist] on your chest and hold it by right hand. [This is] *shashu*.

We are going into meditation hall by *shashu*. [Face] toward the cushion, [then] *gassho* [or] bow. Clockwise turn your body to the other side; *gassho* [or] bow. And sit on a (*meditation*) *cushion* (*Zafu*) and face the wall. [To] sit to meditate, we face the wall.

I [shall now] introduce legs' posture. Make sure that your foot is bare foot. Right foot, put [it] on your left thigh; left foot, put [it] on your right thigh. This is the full lotus position. If you cannot do it, the half lotus position is [fine; take] whichever foot and put [it] on the other thigh.

And next is *hokkai-join*. Right hand place here [below your navel], and the left hand four fingers touch each other [and are placed on top of the right hand], and [both] thumbs slightly touch [each other]. Place [the hands] two to three inches [below your] navel, [as if] holding an egg or a Ping-Pong ball.

Next is [the body] trunk position. You sit straight. The top of your head [points] to the heaven, and slightly you pull your chin [in]. You can make your back straight. And [your body] does not become forward or backward, and does not lean to the right side or to the left side. We make *sayu-yoshin* (*centering your body*) like [the motion of] a metronome. You make your gravity toward the center of the earth. Make straight your [body] trunk.

Your nose and navel are [in a] straight [line, and] your ear and shoulder are [in a] straight [line]. The trunk [of your body is] straight up. Next [are the] *eyes*. Eyes are always open but *half open*. We see [at an angle of] *45 degree* [gazing] beneath. The eyes are half open.

Next [is the] tongue. You attach your tongue to the roof of the *mouth*. Mouth is closed all the time. Inhale and exhale [are] done by nose only. Exhale is important. If you *exhale completely, inhale is produced naturally (kanki-issoku)*, automatically. You exhale [the air completely] from the bottom of [your] abdomen [out of your] nose.

Meditation is started by *hitting the bell three times (shijosho)*. After you've started meditation, various thoughts [will] come up (*kakusoku* awareness). Do not escape or pursue them. Just let it alone.

(Script appears on the screen: *For beginners, try to extend the time you meditate to 25 minutes. Once you reach a certain stage, meditation is generally practiced each time for an average of 40 minutes.*)

Meditation is ended by hitting one bell (chukaisho).[1] You, then, relax your body. You wave (sway) your body left to right slowly and gradually [move more] widely. And [then] release your legs. And turn [back] to the front by [turning] clockwise. And correct (straighten out) the cushion to [what it was] before.

And *gassho* bow. [Then face] the other side and *gassho* bow. And [by carrying yourself in] *shashu* and get out [from the meditation hall].

KT: So, Rev. Ishikawa, there are some people who are not accustomed to siting on the floor. And can they do this by sitting in a chair? And pretend this is a chair; can you show us how to do that?

Rev. Ishikawa: Of course, we can do sitting to meditate with chair. Don't sit deeply. Just slightly sit shallower. And your knees are naturally outside, and the rest of all [the instructions] are the same. Zazen, sitting meditation, is a great gate of peacefulness. Please try.

KT: Okay, I shall. It's a great message, "Great gate of peacefulness." Well, thank you for this great session. We learned a lot.

We hope that you will apply even a tiny bit of what Rev. Ishikawa showed us concerning meditation to enhance and improve the quality of your life. The one important lesson we can learn from today's show is to maintain a more even-keeled outlook in our lives so as not to be swayed by the violent waves of our likes and dislikes. Meditation helps us in this regard, and it is the point of today's passage.

Do not become attached to the things you like; do not maintain aversion to things you dislike. Sorrow, fear and bondage come from one's likes and dislikes.

Please watch us again next week, when we continue to explore new and exciting aspects of the Second Mark of Existence, which is "Life is interdependent."

PROGRAM 21
Second Mark of Existence: The Sacred Self

There is a passage in The Smaller Sūtra on Amitāyus, which goes as follows:

> The color of blue radiates a blue light,
> the yellow a yellow light,
> the red a red light,
> and the white a white light.
> Each color radiates its own light.
> Therein lies the ideal of life and true hope.
>
> (Mutually Sustaining Life, p. 66)

The Sacred Self

Hello and welcome to our show. I hope you had a meaningful and enjoyable week. I'd like to begin with a joke. "Why aren't there any Buddhist rhythm and blues musicians?" Give up? Are you ready for this? It's because Buddhists got no soul! Well, if you didn't get it—and probably many of you didn't—I will explain soon, for the answer goes to the heart of today's topic.

Specifically, as we continue our discussion on the Second Mark of Existence, which is that "Life is Interdependent," I would like to concentrate on a dimension of this mark, which is rarely talked about. And I shall call this dimension or quality, "the sacred self."

This "sacred self" is talked about, for example, in the Nirvāna Sūtra as the "Great Self." And this "great self" is none other than the "awakened self" or how an awakened person sees oneself and others. For one who has realized nirvana, each person, living beings and inanimate things are inherently sacred. And they are sacred since they have intrinsic worth and are unique unto themselves.

Neglected and Misconstrued

Normally, when the Second Mark of Existence is discussed, people pay most of the attention to the interdependent and interconnected dimension, as they should. We, too, did that in our previous shows on our *cosmic and societal connections*. In other words, between the whole and its parts, the whole tends to get much more attention than each of the parts.

Why is this emphasis a problem? When those cosmic and societal dimensions of this mark are applied to people, they can be misconstrued as denying the sacred qualities and even the very existence of the individual person. Perhaps, this is easy to do since, as I explained previously, this mark carries the meaning of *"non-self"* or *"no soul."*

These translations can be confusing. What the correct teaching of "non-self" or "no soul" means is that there is nothing in myself that doesn't change and exist *completely independent* of anything else.

In Buddhism, the self at any given time is viewed as being comprised of *five physico-psychological elements*, which are *senses[1], feelings, thoughts, volition and consciousness.* However, in this context, there is no soul or any other unchanging, independently existing entity over and beyond these five elements. This is why Buddhists are labelled with the phrase, "no soul." Going back to our joke, hopefully you can better appreciate the double meaning or play on words for "soul."

In continuing today's main discussion, let's examine how terms such as "no soul" and "non-self" can diminish the sacred quality of a person and even be misconstrued to deny one's very existence. I, too, was confused for a long time when I first learned about this mark back when I was a student in the seminary. I went around saying to myself, "I don't exist" or "Ken Tanaka is not real." I thought this teaching denied my very existence, but, of course, I existed as breathing, thinking, living individual with an address in California and a Social Security number!

I eventually came to realize that we had to make a distinction between *religious truth* and *mundane truth*. The teaching of "non-self" was on the level of religious truth, but on the mundane level my very existence was real.

---

[1] By "senses" here includes the element of the "physical."

Historical Consequence

This confusion has contributed to the denying of not only one's existence but also one's worth. A good example was the case in Japan before and during the Second World War. During that period of oppressive military regime, this Buddhist teaching of "non-self" was incorrectly interpreted and applied to benefit the state and its military objectives.

It contributed to the undermining of the sacred qualities of the individual and fostered the sacrificing of personal rights and freedom in service of the state, which included the ultimate sacrifice of one's life. I wonder how many people, both ordinary soldiers and civilians in Japan and elsewhere, lost their lives unnecessarily in the belief that the state was more important than individual lives?

Regrettably, some Buddhist leaders, consciously or unconsciously, supported the military state by perpetrating this misguided interpretation of the Buddhist truth. However, many Buddhist institutions since have taken steps to self-reflect and atone for their past mistakes.

Expanded Indra's Net of Jewels

Let's refer back to the metaphor of the Indra's Net of Jewels, which I cited in an earlier show on the "cosmic" dimension of the Second Mark of Existence. Traditionally, this metaphor does not explicitly express the sacred self or *sacred dimension* of the individual parts. However, if we were to do so, I think we can paint the following image in imparting a visual expression to a dimension of the sacred self.

Despite the immeasurable number of illuminating jewels, each jewel is reflected in every other jewel. No jewel is left out. Every jewel is counted and recognized. Every jewel is valued and needed for the totality to function. Hence, every jewel has *inherent worth*.

Also, no jewel or a group of jewels is more dominant or considered superior to others. No hierarchy exists, for all the jewels have *equal value*.

Further, despite the immeasurable number of jewels, no two are the same, for every jewel is unique in its shape, size, color and texture. Even the illumination of each jewel differs in its hue, sheen and brightness. Every jewel is unique.

Application in Society

Hence, when this vision of the sacred self is applied to the human world, particularly to contemporary American society, it shows that each person has worth and makes a valuable contribution to the whole.

In real life, we sometimes feel as though we have no influence in society and nothing we do will be of any consequence, particularly with regard to issues of a global scale, such as global warming. However, as the jeweled net shows, the effort and contribution of *each person has value and real impact*. No matter how miniscule it may seem, the effects of our efforts are not lost. This gives a sense of worth and value to our very existence and effort.

Also, this Buddhist vision affirms the inherent worth of each person, regardless of one's race, religion or economic standing. However, the reality is, of course, different. For example, people of color are still often referred to as "the *minority*," as distinct from people of European descent who make up "the majority."

For myself as an American of Japanese descent and a Buddhist, I had to work myself out of the emotional and psychological "hole" of regarding myself as a "minority," with its subtle, suggestive message of not being fully equal. And I am sure that other "minorities" are able to identify with my experience.

Uplifting Message of the Indra's Net

What helped me out of this mental dilemma was the Indra's Net of Jewels. It painted a vision of what is true and real, and thereby helped me to overcome the effects of how society saw me or labelled me.

Of course, what is great about America is that it continues to evolve toward an ideal society, spurred on by the spirit of expanding opportunity as reflected in the founding principles of democracy and justice. Over the span of this evolutionary process, more and more minorities than ever before are valued for their abilities and accomplishments. As a Buddhist, this political and social progress simply reinforces my religious vision as expressed by the Indra's Net of Jewels.

And most of all, one's unique qualities, even if they are not part of the majority, are affirmed. It is this spirit that is expressed in today's passage, which describes the lotus flowers in the lakes of the *Pure Land* or the realm of awakening or nirvana. In that environment, each flower is affirmed to be true to itself, without being pressured to be something else:

> *The color of blue radiates a blue light,*
> *the yellow a yellow light,*
> *the red a red light,*
> *and the white a white light.*

On a familiar note, doesn't this remind many of you of Mr. Rogers' famous line from his TV show, *Mr. Rogers' Neighborhood*? "There is no one like you in the whole wide world. You are fine just the way you are." Does this mean Mr. Rogers was a Buddhist? … I'm kidding, of course, for he was a Presbyterian minister. My point is that many religions arrive at similar conclusions, for instance, about the sacredness of each person. When we experience what is real, we *all* acquire "soul"… even Buddhists!

Thank you for being with us. See you next week, when we discuss an optimistic teaching of the "Buddha nature" with an interesting guest affiliated with the Rissho Kosei-kai denomination of Buddhism.

PROGRAM 22
Buddha Nature: Interview

However unconscious people may be of the fact that everyone has within his possession this supreme nature, and however degraded and ignorant they may be, Buddha never loses faith in them for he knows that even in the least of them there are, potentially, all the virtues of Buddhahood.

(The Teaching of Buddha, p. 146)

Last week we talked about a dimension of interdependence, which we are calling the "sacred self." Well today, I wish to focus our attention on a related teaching called the *Buddha nature*. Buddha nature is the potentiality to become a Buddha that dwells in all sentient or living beings. This means that Buddha nature is found in humans as well as in non-humans.

As today's message points out, people are often not aware that they have this Buddha nature within. They are not aware, for the Buddha nature is covered over by greed, hatred and ignorance.

Buddha nature is also expressed as *Buddha-womb* (tathāgata-garbha), where the potentiality is compared to a womb that encloses a potential Buddha. A *sutra* (sūtra) typically refers to a text regarded as a discourse of the Buddha, and a sutra called the *Buddha-womb Sutra* focuses on Buddha nature, in which we find ingenious metaphors employed. For example, the Buddha womb is likened to a golden Buddha image wrapped in a dirty rag, or an unborn baby destined to be a prince in the womb of an indigent woman.

In all of these descriptions, undesirable outer layers representing our greed, hatred and ignorance conceal Buddha nature or the Buddha-womb. Yet simultaneously the teaching of Buddha nature promotes a message of hope and inclusion, since all human and living beings are endowed with it.

To help us deepen our understanding, we are fortunate to have with us as our guest, Professor Gene Reeves. Professor Reeves serves as international adviser to Rissho Kosei-kai denomination of

Buddhism and serves on the faculty of its seminary. Among his recent publications is the translation of the *Lotus Sutra,* one of the most important sutras in Mahayana (*Mahāyāna*) Buddhism.

Interview

KT: Well, Gene, thank you very much for taking time from your busy schedule to be with us.

Prof. Gene Reeves: My pleasure.

KT: May I ask you your thoughts, your personal understanding of Buddha nature?

Prof. Gene Reeves: Well, in your introduction, you mentioned an earlier program about *interdependence.* I like to emphasize interdependence in relation to Buddha nature as well. So, for me Buddha nature has to do with a kind of *potential* or even *power* [that] every living being has within themselves *to become a Buddha for **someone else**.*

KT: For someone else?

Prof. Gene Reeves: As you know, the *Lotus Sutra* is very famous for its parables. In all but one case, its parables are basically about relationships, relationships between someone who is a kind of stand-in for the Buddha and someone a kind of stand-in for us, for you and me. And in all of these cases, it's a relationship of interdependence.

So, one of the most famous of those stories is the one in Chapter Four. This is a story about a father who has become very rich in business and whose son ran away as a teenager and has been missing for forty or fifty years. And the father is longing for the son. And quite suddenly, unexpectedly, the son shows up in front of the gate of the father's house. The son doesn't know it's his father and is frightened. The father realizes it's his long lost son and is overjoyed.

I won't tell the whole story, but there's a good part of it where the father finds a way to get the son to work for him, not knowing that it's his father that he's working for. The father finds a way to gradually encourage the son to develop his self-confidence, his sense of self, his ability to deal with his own life and his ability to deal with his father's business.

So, at the end of the story, the father can reveal to the officials and people who work for him and everybody, "This is my real son, and everything I own belongs to him. It's his inheritance." So, it's a kind of story about disclosing the Buddha nature or developing the Buddha nature in the son. But the point that I would like to emphasize is that the father needs the son in order for his life to be complete. And the son needs the father for his life to be complete.

KT: So it's a mutual...

Prof. Gene Reeves: It's a *mutual interdependence* going on. I think it's very important for understanding what Buddha nature is.

KT: Okay, that's very interesting. Usually we think of Buddha nature as something for yourself, but here it's more of [it being] for yourself in *relationship to others*.

Prof. Gene Reeves: Yes, we really teach that one can only discover, in a sense, realize one's own Buddha nature through *seeing the Buddha nature in others*. So, in Rissho Kosei-kai, for example, there is great deal of effort put into trying to help others realize *their* Buddha nature as a way of realizing *our* Buddha nature. So, that means, for example, one of the things interesting about this is that not only other human beings, not only other living beings, but even mountains, rivers, grasses can be revelations of Buddha nature for us.

KT: So, as we mentioned, the *Lotus Sutra* includes some parables that illustrate the teaching of Buddha nature. So, what is your favorite?

Prof. Gene Reeves: Well, you have three children, I think. Which is your favorite? It's a little bit like asking that. I like them all. But rather than a parable, I'd just like to say a few words about a story. It is not a parable. It is found in Chapter 15 of the *Lotus Sutra*. It's kind of a long story, but I'll try to make it short. This is a story in which, earlier in Chapter 11, Buddhas have been assembled from all over the universe in order to see the body of this voice that's coming out of a stupa (stūpa).

KT: What is a stupa?

Prof. Gene Reeves: This is the stupa of a past Buddha called "Many Treasures," who's suddenly appeared.

KT: But it's a monument?

Prof. Gene Reeves: A stupa is basically a depository for the remains, crematory remains of bodies. So, everybody was shocked that a voice comes out of the stupa because it should only be ashes and bones in there. But this voice comes out of the stupa praising Shakyamuni (Śākyamuni) Buddha for preaching the *Lotus Sutra*. And everybody wants to see this body inside.

Well, Shakyamuni explains that the same Buddha said many, many years ago that whenever someone is praising the *Lotus Sutra* he would come to the stupa to praise that person, that Buddha. But he also said that if people wanted to see his whole body it would be necessary to assemble the Buddhas from all over the universe of ten directions. So, everybody says, "Let's do it!" And, anyway, they get assembled.

KT: They all come together?

Prof. Gene Reeves: They all come together. As I said, it's a long story but the part I want to get to actually comes up later. They all get assembled and various things happen. Stories are told and later, in Chapter 15, it's time to think about going back to where they came from. And some of these Bodhisattvas who come from other places, other worlds, go over to Shakyamuni Buddha and they say, "It must be tough. You've got a really difficult job, being the Buddha of this world." People are kind of slow and caught up in desires and things, this and that. So, we would like to volunteer to stay and help you out. And Shakyamuni Buddha basically said, "Well, thank you very much for offering, but no thanks. We have plenty of Bodhisattvas of our own."

And suddenly out of the earth, spring up like water out of a well, come zillions of zillions of zillions of Bodhisattvas. And of course, Maitreya and others are shocked, "Who are these guys? Who taught them? Where did they come from?" And Shakyamuni Buddha explains that he taught them. And these are his followers.

And the point of this story is these Bodhisattvas, these multitude of people who can help others are we ourselves. *We are the Bodhisattvas* who emerged from the earth. And the point of the story is partly to emphasize our responsibilities as Bodhisattvas for carrying on the Buddha's work. But it's also a *powerful affirmation of the importance of life in this world*, as opposed to wanting to go to some other world to escape the troubles of this world. *This* is *our* world. And because it is

Shakyamuni Buddha's world, it's our responsibility.

KT: So, what are some of the implications for those of us living in modern society, especially in the U.S.?

Prof. Gene Reeves: My fear is that in America today, there's a very strong tendency to demonize people, to divide people into the good and the bad, the true and the false. I think that what the *Lotus Sutra* teaches us, above all else, is to *respect other people*. To try to find in everyone, no matter how bad they may appear to us, but try to *find in everyone the good side*, good quality and try to grow that and help to try to develop that. And I think that could be a very important lesson for, especially, for people in the West, who have grown up with a tendency to want to divide people into two kinds. We think that, in everybody, in any living being, there is something good to be nourished.

KT: So, your points are well taken. Thank you very much for joining us.

Prof. Gene Reeves: Thank you for having me.

I hope that you could not only gain a better understanding but be moved and inspired by the presence of Buddha nature in each of you. It's a teaching that gives us hope and a sense of great optimism. We also need to remember that other people and other living beings are all endowed with Buddha nature, thus, encouraging us to regard all living entities, whether animals, birds, fish and even plants, with a deep and abiding respect.

Next week, we'll take a final look at the teaching of the Second Mark of Existence with a focus on the dimension of "emptiness," a mysterious yet alluring Buddhist word. We hope to see you then.

PROGRAM 23
Second Mark of Existence: Emptiness and Letting Go

People naturally fear misfortune and long for good fortune; but if the distinction is carefully studied, misfortune often turns out to be good fortune and good fortune to be misfortune. The wise person learns to meet the changing circumstances of life with an equitable spirit, being neither elated by success nor depressed by failure. Thus, one realizes the truth of non-duality.

(*The Teaching of Buddha, p. 122*)

Hi, how are you today? Hopefully you have been encouraged by the upbeat messages of the sacred self and the Buddha nature in the past two shows.

Four Dimensions of Interdependence

Today, we wish to explore another dimension of the teaching of the Second Mark of Existence, "Life is Interdependent." So far we have discussed three dimensions of this mark, which I am calling cosmic, societal and sacred.

In the *cosmic dimension*, we learned how each of us is part of a supportive interconnected cosmic net. Second, in the *societal dimension*, we saw that our failure or success in fostering the spirit of interdependence within global and local communities can, respectively, lead to conflict or cooperation. Third, in the *sacred dimension*, we realized that interdependence does not mean the loss of the individual but is rather an affirmation of the sacred nature of all living beings.

I would like to refer to the fourth dimension we are exploring today as *"emptiness."* It needs to be emphasized again that "emptiness" does not mean that things do not exist but rather that things are "empty" of substantial entity. Any substantial entity is anything that emerged or exists all by itself, *without depending* on anything else.

Then, as we understand and apply the teachings of this mark, we will inevitably develop an approach to life of *"letting go."* "Letting go" does not mean to be indifferent, uncaring, or have no opinion at all. Instead, "letting go" means not to be too attached or cling so hard to your opinion that you lose sight of the bigger picture or to believe that your view is the only correct one. Just as when you hold a new-born baby, you need to hold gently but not cling so hard as to crush the baby.

Nagarjuna (*Nāgārjuna*)

This concept of "emptiness" was made famous by an eminent Buddhist thinker, whom many, particularly the Mahayana (Mahāyāna) Buddhists (who are found today mostly in China, Korea, Vietnam, Japan and Tibet), consider to be the most important figure after the Buddha. His name is Nagarjuna, who lived in Southern India around the year 200 of the Common Era.

Despite his later fame, in his younger years before he became a Buddhist, Nagarjuna sometimes got himself into trouble. On one occasion, he and three of his close friends sneaked into the female quarters of the royal palace in hopes of seducing the women. They also wanted to test their magical skill by making themselves invisible.

But unfortunately, they quickly learned that their magical abilities failed miserably. Nagarjuna managed to escape, but the guards killed the other three. Though he escaped unharmed, the experience had a deep impact on him. He began to understand that selfish desire is the root of suffering and magical feats are useless. This understanding helped Nagarjuna to turn to the Buddhist teachings of the Buddhist path.

Emptiness (*shunyata - śūnyatā*)

Among Nagarjuna's many writings, the *Commentary on the Middle Way* contains the following famous passage

"Interdependent phenomena are called 'emptiness.'"

The meaning of this statement is essentially the same as the Second Mark of Existence, "All phenomena lack substantial entity." What Nagarjuna did was to point out the relative nature of our experience. In other words, how I experience things is not absolute. For example, the same objects can be experienced differently over time or the same object can be understood differently by different people.

Demonstrating this point is the well-known story of the *"The Blind Men and the Elephant"* from ancient India. Once upon a time, six blind men wanted to know what an elephant looked like. Each felt different parts of the mighty beast. The first man who felt the side of the elephant's body said that it was like a *wall*. The second man grabbed the lower end of the tusk, and said it was like a *spear*. The third man who felt the trunk reported that the elephant was like a *snake*. The fourth man upon touching a leg claimed it was like a *tree trunk*. The fifth man feeling the ear said it was surely like a *fan*. And the last man who grabbed the tail thought it was like a *rope*. So we have the same animal but six different perceptions and opinions.

Such is the nature of our experiences. Due to our three poisons of greed, hatred and ignorance, we are not able to see things as they really are.

Letting Go and Being Open

How are we to apply the truth of emptiness to our lives? Nagarjuna's answer was "don't be attached but instead be open." He cautioned us against making hard and fast judgments to decide your likes and dislikes, and then basing your sense of happiness and unhappiness on them.

Of course, as members of today's modern society with families to raise and jobs to maintain, we can't help but make judgments that are good and bad, and right and wrong in nature. For instance, we need to make judgments about the daycare center and its teachers for our child. Nevertheless, Nagarjuna's message calls for us to be aware of the nature of our perceptions and judgments, realizing that what we experience is not the entire picture, as in the case of the elephant and the blind men.

However, that does not mean that we need to be uncertain and lack confidence when we make judgments and decisions. Hence, as mentioned earlier, our attitude and action should be like *holding the baby gently but not too tightly*.

We should not be overly and unduly attached to our beliefs as the one and only possibility. Instead, we ought to be always open to other possibilities, much like another of my favorite lines, "The mind is like a parachute, for it works best when it's open!"

Story of a Lost Horse

Allow me now to tell you a story from ancient China, which comes to us from the Taoist tradition (translated by Phil Newall).

Near the Great Wall lived an old man, who had a fine horse. One day the horse ran away to the barbarian territory. When his friends and relatives heard the tale, they all came to comfort him. They never expected the old man to say, "Who knows, having my horse run away might bring me luck!"

Several months later, the old man's horse returned, bringing back a horse of the barbarians. Again his friends and neighbors all came, this time to congratulate him. But he responded that even if something went right, the end result could still go wrong.

Regrettably, the old man's words were right on the mark. His son tried to ride the untamed horse, and it threw him off, breaking his leg. Again family and neighbors arrived to express their sympathy. The old man told them, "Although it's too bad that my son broke his leg, it may turn out to be for the best."

A year later, the barbarians attacked and broke through the Great Wall in force. All the healthy young men were called to war, and the vast majority was killed. The old man's son, on the other hand, was spared, because his bad leg kept him out of the military service.

This story points out that in all good fortune there may lurk bad, and vice versa, expressing the truth that *good and bad fortunes are relative*, interdependent, and ever-changing.

Hardship of Breaking Up

I am sure that most everyone has experienced breaking up. Breaking up is, indeed, hard to do, especially when you still wanted the relationship to continue. It's hard to accept the fact that the person you still care for, no longer feels the same about you. In such a situation, the break up causes sheer pain, and you wonder what you did to deserve the suffering.

Well, almost all of us with the experience of breaking up have found that we were wrong, for we have met someone else who is just as right for us. And in hindsight, we come to see that there were many problems in our former relationship that no amount of effort would have overcome.

So, breaking up was best for us, for not only did we learn about our mistakes and our shortcomings, but it also freed us to meet our current partner. For many of us our greatest regret is that we were so attached to our former partner and suffered far more than we should have.

I am sure that many of you can identify with all this. The implications of the points are aptly captured in today's opening passage:

> *People naturally fear misfortune and long for good fortune; but if the distinction is carefully studied, misfortune often turns out to be good fortune and good fortune to be misfortune. The wise person learns to meet the changing circumstances of life with an equitable spirit, being neither elated by success nor depressed by failure. Thus, one realizes the truth of non-duality.*

Well, I hope that you gained something worthwhile from today's show that you can learn from and apply to your own life.

Please tune in next week, for I am sure that our returning guest, Professor Gene Reeves, will have something worthwhile to share when we discuss Guanyin, the Bodhisattva of Compassion.

PROGRAM 24
Guanyin: Bodhisattva of Compassion for the People

Always be mindful and at no moment harbor any
doubts of the virtue of Avalokiteshvara.
He is our strength in suffering, danger, and death.
Avalokiteshvara is replete with all virtues;
He perceives mankind with the eye of compassion;
He is the limitless ocean of happiness.
For this reason let us revere him
                            (Buddha-Dharma, pp. 539-540)

We are pleased to have Professor Gene Reeves with us once again, this time to discuss the role of *Guanyin, the Bodhisattva of Compassion*. Bodhisattvas are awakened beings and are often regarded like the saints are by many Catholics. In the original Sanskrit teachings, Guanyin is known as *Avalokiteshvara* (Avalokiteśvara), and is immensely popular in China, Korea, Vietnam, Japan, Tibet and other countries where Mahayana (Mahāyāna) Buddhism is dominant.

In our earlier shows, we discussed the images and learned of the enormous popularity of Bodhisattva, particularly among the common people. This concern for the ordinary people is reflected in the name Avalokiteshvara, which means the "lord who looks down on the world from on high." In China, Guanyin came to be understood as, *"one who listens to the cries of the world."*

Guanyin responds not only to calls of a religious nature but also to people seeking protection from misfortune, cures from illness, assurances of longevity, and bestowing of material benefits and worldly success. It is for this reason that the *Thousand-armed Guanyin* is popular, for he is able to exhibit a thousand different ways to respond to a vast array of needs.

Interview

KT: Well, Gene, great to have you back.

Prof. Gene Reeves: Thank you.

KT: And let me begin by asking you what you think about Guanyin. Here we have an image of Guanyin.

Prof. Gene Reeves: Well, at least two things.

KT: Two things? Okay.

Prof. Gene Reeves: One is that Guanyin brings Buddhism to the common ordinary people. This Guanyin is sitting on a rock, not a lord that looks down from on high but a Bodhisattva of compassion who is down to earth. You know, I visited hundreds and hundreds of temples and homes in China, Taiwan, Hong Kong and Singapore. Everywhere you go, it doesn't matter if it's a Buddhist temple or a Taoist temple or what kind of home, everywhere you go, there are statues of Guanyin.

And it's because there are two reasons. One is that Guanyin is understood to be a kind of a *savior*, one who can help others. But more importantly, Guanyin is also understood to be a *model* for us, as someone who can engender compassion in us and be a kind of model.

You know it's quite common for people to think that religion is like climbing to a mountain top. But Guanyin teaches us the opposite. Guanyin teaches us that as Buddhists we don't belong on mountain tops but belong in the low places, in the low and dirty, dark places where people are suffering, with people who are suffering.

So, as Buddhists, I think, we really shouldn't be climbing mountain tops unless it's to be like Martin Luther King, Jr. You remember that famous Washington speech. He said, "I've been to the mountain top and I've seen the other side." There is no suggestion that he should stay on the mountain top. The mountain top is merely a kind of outlook for seeing what might be. And that's what Guanyin really teaches us. That is we should be with people who are suffering in the low places of this world.

You know, in the *Lotus Sutra*, it says that Guanyin can take on 32 or 33 different forms. It says if someone needs the body of a Buddha or to see someone in the body of a Buddha in order to be saved, Guanyin takes on the body of Buddha. And it goes on, and I won't tell you the whole thirty-three, but it comes down to the wife of a peasant, or to a boy, or to a girl, or to a common ordinary person.

Well, of course, you can see in China even to this day depictions of these thirty-three forms of the Guanyin. But the point is, the point is a very interesting one. The point is this means not only Guanyin can take various forms, but we can see Guanyin in all kinds of people, in our boss, in our unruly teenage child, in the guy who lives across the street and doesn't behave the way we think he ought to.

KT: Awfully hard.

Prof. Gene Reeves: Awfully hard. It's difficult, but that's the point of the Guanyin devotion. It's to help us see Guanyin in anyone we meet.

KT: You know, Gene, one of the fascinating things about the development of Guanyin in China over time was that he underwent *gender transformation*. Didn't it go from being a male to female?

Prof. Gene Reeves: Well, yes and no. I would say basically "No."

KT: No?

Prof. Gene Reeves: In China, Guanyin became *male and female*.

KT: And female. Both?

Prof. Gene Reeves: Both. And I think, just last week actually, I was in Hong Kong and was talking with a woman at a beautiful big temple the Japanese call Myohoji. And I asked her about Guanyin. There was a statue of Guanyin, and we were talking about it. She said, at some point in the conversation, "We don't know whether to call her or him. We don't know whether to say her or him." I think that is correct because it is both. I think this is important because it not only means that Guanyin opens up Buddha Dharma or teachings to women but also opens Buddha Dharma to *the woman who is in each of us*, maybe somewhere hidden behind our hearts.

KT: "Each of us" means each of us *men*? Woman in men.

Prof. Gene Reeves: Men. That's right. So that Guanyin opens up the possibility of men recognizing the woman in themselves.

KT: An interesting perspective.

Prof. Gene Reeves: And it's made an enormous difference. Guanyin devotion has made an enormous difference in contemporary Buddhism. I frankly am inspired by the nuns at Fo Guang Shan in Taiwan. And at that temple, the master is a man, a male monk, but there are about twelve hundred or fourteen hundred nuns there. And the kind of work they are doing with poor people and other kinds of problematic situations all over the world is truly inspiring!

KT: Do you think that what we just talked about, does this go to demonstrate that Buddhism is not just a philosophy as some people say but that it's, indeed, a religion.

Prof. Gene Reeves: Yeah, I don't know really what would lead people to think Buddhism is just a philosophy.

KT: Well, there are a lot of people who say that.

Prof. Gene Reeves: I guess that's right. I don't happen to know any of them. But in any case, at least it seems to me that there would be at least two reasons why it would not be appropriate to think of it as merely a philosophy. Of course there are philosophies within Buddhism. Make no mistake about it. There are some very significant philosophy and philosophical ideas.

But Buddhism primarily is aimed at inspiring people. It's not merely giving people something to think about. It's giving something to live by. And at least in my understanding of these terms of philosophy and religion, that would make Buddhism a kind of religion. It's kind of something *to inspire people, to give them hope*, to give them reason to carry on, to develop themselves even in very difficult situations.

The second thing I would want to just mention is that Buddhism, at least in East Asia, I don't know as much about the situation in the States, but in East Asia Buddhism has a great variety of dimensions. It has monks and nuns, temples, and it has rituals, it has sutras, it has all of the kinds of things that, at least in my understanding of it, go to make up a religion, including philosophical ideas and highly developed systems of thought. But it's not *merely* a system of thought. It's really, at least in my way of thinking, it's really a *way of life*.

KT: Yes, yes. Perhaps one of the reasons of this is when it first came in to the West, it tended to be very intellectual. And intellectuals in the West adopted Buddhism and so we still see that legacy.

Prof. Gene Reeves: Yes. Well, of course, you also can see it a little bit in [the Japanese word] *Bukkyo*. *Bukkyo* is "Buddhist teachings," and there has been an awful a lot of emphasis in Buddhism also in Asia on teachings. But the point that people miss is that in Buddhism, teaching means teaching people how to live. It's not merely conveying ideas and information. It's a matter of, in a variety of ways, both through doctrines but also through examples, through stories, a wide variety of ways, teaching people how to live.

KT: Actually, I think in the U.S. or at least in the West, you have two groups of people. There are those who primarily study, but there are those who now do primarily practice. And there is some gap there between the two groups.

Prof. Gene Reeves: Yeah, I actually would want to make an argument for saying that study can be a kind of practice.

KT: Okay.

Prof. Gene Reeves: But I don't know if you would agree with that.

KT: So in the end, I think we would agree that, in the end, the teaching needs to lead to practice and to people being inspired and inspiring other people.

Prof. Gene Reeves: Yeah, I think we need to be little bit careful about that though, because very often in the West, at least in my understanding, the word practice has come to mean meditation. And I wouldn't want to say that.

KT: I'm not saying that either. I would include other forms.

Prof. Gene Reeves: That's right. So, for us, I think that the important form of practice, as we agree, the important form of practice is what we call the *Bodhisattva Way*. It's the way of developing our Buddha nature through helping others. And it's a matter of how we live our lives, not just how we think about the world but how we live in the world.

KT: Well, Gene, it was very fascinating. And I think you helped to fill out the picture of Buddhism in ways that we haven't been able to do so far. So, thank you very much for joining us again.

Prof. Gene Reeves: Thank you, my friend.

Well, we hope that you enjoyed today's discussion and, as a result, will be even more attuned to the spirit of compassion that embraces all of our lives in many different ways.

Next week our theme moves to the topic of impermanence or change, the Third Mark of Existence. See you then.

CHAPTER SIX:
Teachings of the Third Mark of Existence

◆ ◆ ◆

PROGRAM 25

Third Mark of Existence:
Truly Understand that Life Is Impermanent

*This life is impermanent. In an ever-changing world, we are living
a new life every day.*

(*Mutually Sustaining Life, p. 56*)

Hello. How are you? I hope we find you in the best of spirit and
health.

Third Mark of Existence

Today, I would like to begin by looking at the Third Mark of
Existence, *"All Conditioned Phenomena are impermanent,"* or rephrased,
"Life is impermanent." This means that everything in our life is subject
to change.

What can we do as ordinary persons living in today's modern
society to apply the lessons drawn from the truth of impermanence
in our lives? Well, from my viewpoint, there are three things: First, to
fully understand the truth of impermanence; second, to focus on the
now and *live fully in the present*; and third, to *be open to changes* that
unfold in our lives.

I want to stress the fact that these lessons are oriented more toward lay persons living in contemporary society; whereas monks and
nuns, on the other hand, have different priorities and, therefore, place
more emphasis on not being attached to things because of their impermanence. The ultimate goal is the same, however, and the difference is merely a matter of degree.

Today, I will be concentrating on the first of three lessons, which
is the call for us to truly understand the truth of impermanence with
our total being. Most of us know with our head that things change, but
it's extremely difficult to accept change when it hits home, especially
in the form of the loss of a loved one.

Kisagotami (Kisāgotamī)and the Mustard Seed

To illustrate this point there is a well-known parable of "Kisagotami and the Mustard Seed."

Once there lived a woman named *Kisagotami*, who married a wealthy man and soon had a child. Her life was going very well. However, just as her son was about to walk, the child suddenly died of unknown causes. In great shock and disbelief, frantically holding the dead child in her arms, Kisagotami sought help from anyone she met in the town, pleading "Please save my child!"

A follower of the Buddha was moved by Kisagotami's plight and told her, "Your child's ailment is too serious for any doctor to cure. There is only one person who can save him, and that is the Buddha, who happens to be visiting our town and residing at *Jetavana Park* at the outskirts of town."

Kisagotami immediately went to the park and requested the Buddha to save her son. After listening intently, the Buddha told her, "To cure this child we need several *grains of mustard seed*. So, please go gather them in town." Buoyed by this, Kisagotami started off without delay, at which time, the Buddha added, "Those mustard seeds must come from a *household that has never experienced death*." However, Kisagotami was too excited to fully comprehend the meaning of the Buddha's words.

She went to the first house and sought the mustard seed, but the house had just recently experienced a death of an elder member of the family. The second house, too, had lost a member of their family a few years earlier, and the third household had also lost a small child. Despite these setbacks, Kisagotami continued to knock on the door of the neighboring houses, spurred on by the hope of saving her child. She visited many more houses, only to be told that each house had experienced death.

At the end of the day as the sun began to set, Kisagotami felt utterly despondent and hopeless. Then in the midst of her despair, her mind suddenly opened up in the realization of what the Buddha was trying to teach her: that death was universal and *no household was exempt* from the pain of losing their loved ones. Kisagotami, then, understood that she was not alone.

She, thus, abandoned her efforts to gather the mustard seeds, and instead went to give her child a proper funeral, and then returned to Jetavana Park to see the Buddha. The Buddha asked her, "Were you able to get those mustard seeds?" Kisagotami confided in the Buddha of her realization and her acceptance of the loss of her child. She then sought to become a disciple of the Buddha by joining the order of nuns.

What the Story is Telling Us

The most important point of this story is that although many of us know about the truth of impermanence with our mind, we must make a greater effort to understand fully with our total being, just as Kisagotami came to do by the end of the story

In order to appreciate the truth of impermanence, let's look at how changes are taking place all around us. Some changes are obvious, while others are not.

On the *cosmic plane*, nothing remains constant, for astrophysicists tell us that the universe continues to expand at astronomical speeds. We don't really feel or notice this motion because everything else around us—including the sun, the solar system and our galaxy—are all moving together.

On *our earth* as well, the changes are unceasing. The very ground that we stand on is moving, though very slowly, so that geologists tell us that North America will eventually merge with the Asian continent.

Our body is also constantly changing. Physiologists tell us that the cells in our body completely renew themselves within a period of three months. In other words, the cells that make up our body now are completely different from the ones that we had three months ago. The cells are dying and renewing themselves constantly.

Leaving the physical realm for the *social realm*, we notice that changes are ongoing. Language is one of the best barometers of social change. The same word carries different meaning, reflecting change. For example, 50 years ago, when we said *"chip,"* it meant a piece of wood, not a component of computer hardware; *"hardware"* back then was identified with a store that sold nails, garbage cans and shovels, and "*software*" was not even a word. In those days, "*coke*" was a cold drink, "*pot*" was something you cooked in, and "*grass*" was a lawn that we mowed.

Changes are also apparent in moral values. For instance, *living together* before marriage used to be hotly debated, but today it has largely become a non-issue for many people.

Our human relationships are also subject to change. This becomes apparent if you look at your personal address book 15 years ago or even 5 years ago. You will notice many people who are no longer in your life. Among them are those with whom you had a falling out, those who moved far away, and those who have passed on. And the older we get, the more the last group grows in size. I think it's safe to say that the changes in our relationships with others are the source of our greatest joys as well as the most painful heartaches, as we saw in Kisagotami's plight of losing her son.

Impermanence is everywhere, from the cosmic realm to our social values as well as our personal relationships. This is what the Third Mark of Existence is all about, "All Conditioned Phenomena are impermanent," or "Life is impermanent."

Impermanence Is Also Too Fast and Sudden

What's more, don't you agree that these changes seem to start to *speed* up with age? I recall when I was 12 years old; I wanted so badly to be 13 so that I could be a "teenager." However, one year seemed so long, and I could hardly wait for the time to pass. Now, one year goes by much too quickly and much too fast to keep up mentally. For instance, when our birthday approaches, we utter to ourselves, "already!" Thus, the truth of impermanence doesn't only mean that things are constantly changing, but rather that they *change a little too fast*!

Calm Waters Amid Rough Seas

How are we to deal or react to the fact that things in our lives are in constant flux as we have discussed? Well, today, I have been stressing the importance of understanding this truth with our total being. To do so, we must keep reminding ourselves in our readings and practice for this teaching to be internalized. The more we internalize, a mental space is formed within ourselves wherein we can find the strength and the tranquility for dealing effectively with the changes that we experience in our lives.

The Dalai Lama explains this process using a *metaphor of the ocean*. He speaks of the *topsy-turvy world on the surface* of the ocean, but when a person has cultivated understanding, he or she can always go beneath the surface of the mind to experience the *area of calm and peace*. One way to nurture such a space within each of us is for us to truly understand the truth of impermanence with our total being as expressed in today's passage:

> *This life is impermanent. In an ever-changing world, we are living a new life every day.*

Thanks for being with us. In our next show, a Tibetan Buddhist monk will join us to share his thoughts on the truth of impermanence. See you then.

PROGRAM 26
Third Mark of Existence: A Tibetan Lama's View of Impermanence

It is worthy to perform the present duty well and without failure; do not seek to avoid or postpone it till tomorrow. By acting now, one can live a good day.

(*The Teaching of Buddha, p. 378*)

Spiritual Dimension of Impermanence

Today, we have with us a *Tibetan Lama* as our guest to discuss the ongoing theme of impermanence, which is the third of the Four Marks of Existence. As I mentioned last time, impermanence means that all things—from our human body to our physical surroundings and our relationships with others—are constantly changing.

Together with our guest, we will be focusing on the spiritual dimension of impermanence. For example, how do we regard the changes we encounter, especially the difficult ones, in the context of our spiritual lives? In other words, do we simply accept painful changes fatalistically or do we turn them into a power for looking deeper into our lives and cultivating wisdom?

Traditional Buddhist Worldview

In connection, it's helpful to know something about the traditional Buddhist worldview of what is called *samsara* (saṃsāra) in Sanskrit, and translated as "*the cycle of birth and death*" or "*transmigration*." This idea is also found in other religions such as Hinduism and Jainism that originated in India. In the West, it is most often referred to as "*reincarnation*" or "*rebirth*."

In traditional Buddhism, it is thought that there are *six realms of existence*. The six realms are those of *gods or heavenly beings, demigods* or *titans, humans, animals, hungry ghosts* and *hell beings*. The gods are the highest, while the *hell beings* are the lowest. And it's our *action or karma* that determines into which realm we are born. Also, in accordance with this worldview, we have been transmigrating in the various realms for an immeasurable [number of] lives

In this life, you and I happen to be born as human beings. This is something to celebrate, for we are in the best realm, as compared to the other five, from which to aspire to become Buddhas or to be fully awakened.

Two Interpretations of the Six Realms

There are many Buddhists today who understand these six realms *not* as actual *realms of existence* but more as *psychological states*. In other words, we experience these different states in the daily course of our lives. For example, when we are extremely happy, we are gods, and when we feel jealous toward others, we are demi-gods. When we are caught up only in our own concerns, we are in the realm of animals. When we are obsessed in satisfying our desires, we are like the hungry ghosts. And when we are in the depths of our agony and pain, we are in the hellish realm.

Now, let's explore this and the concept of impermanence further in our discussion with today's guest, *Venerable Geshe Sonam Gyaltsen Gonta*. Venerable Gonta belongs to the *Gelukpa school*, which is the same as that of the Dalai Lama. By the way, Dalai means "Great Ocean [of Wisdom]" and Lama means "Teacher," or in other words, "*The Teacher of Great Ocean [of Wisdom]*."[1] So, we are pleased to have with us Venerable Gonta, who is part of this [Gelugpa] tradition.

Interview

KT: So, Venerable Gonta, thank you for being with us. We have been discussing impermanence and wondering what your thoughts are on the teaching of impermanence.

Ven. Gonta: Yes, impermanence is very important, and it's a reality.

KT: Reality?

Ven. Gonta: Reality. Yes, it's a reality whether you think about

---

[1] The TV script contains an error regarding this passage, for it had reversed the meanings of "Dalai" and "Lama." Also the "Dalai" means "Great Ocean," not just "Great Wisdom."

impermanence or permanence, it (*impermanence*) *is a reality*. But the thing is that we should *be aware of impermanence*.

KT: [We] should be aware [of it].

Ven. Gonta: Be aware of impermanence. And [what] I can say is that impermanence can be divided into two that can be *subtle impermanence and gross impermanence*.

KT: Subtle and gross?

Ven. Gonta: Yes. About gross impermanence, this is actually easy [to understand, for example,] I should say death.

KT: Death?

Ven. Gonta: Since we are born, we have to die. This is reality. But again, if I give example of myself, I was born, and I am subject to death; but I am not very aware [of it]. That's why the big problem is that I always *think [only] about this life*, for livelihood of this life. [And we] don't think about the next life or for the future lives.

KT: So, most people are not thinking beyond this life.

Ven. Gonta: Yes, that's the big problem.

KT: They're focused too much on desire and getting [material] things.

Ven. Gonta: Right.

KT: So, if we think about impermanence more fully, then we'll have bigger heart and we think about bigger things.

Ven. Gonta: Yes, that's right. We can think, you see, we think human beings versus animal beings. We human beings think that they (animals) have dull intelligence and less wisdom. Human beings have more intelligence. They can see further and look further.

KT: Human beings, as opposed to animals, have greater capacity.

Ven. Gonta: Yes, capacity.

KT: In a way, you are saying [that] it's rare to be a human being?

Ven. Gonta: That's right.

KT: It's *precious to be a human being*.

Ven. Gonta: Very very important.

KT: So, we can do practice and cultivate [ourselves]?

Ven. Gonta: Yes, that's true. In Buddhism, we believe in the six realms.

KT: Six realms?

Ven. Gonta: Yes, six realms. Especially for the practice of Dharma (the teachings), being human being is very rare and very precious. It's precious in the sense that we can practice Dharma by especially thinking about impermanence. And that means, it can broaden our minds. It can see not only this life but see the next life and many more lives after that. We can attain Nirvana-hood and Buddha-hood. That [becomes possible precisely] because [we become aware] of impermanence.

KT: Now, you have emphasized the next life and looking at things in a bigger context. As part of that, some Buddhists, especially, "more modern" Buddhists, talk about impermanence [in the sense that] because of impermanence, you focus more on the *now*, [for] every moment is precious. That's why even [if] our loved ones may not be with us all the time, but, therefore, we really [want to] spend quality time with each person that we care about. What do you think about *that* approach, that way of responding to impermanence?

Ven. Gonta: Yes, yes, that's great. We say, of course, "The past is past."

KT: The past is past.

Ven. Gonta: [The important] thing is *now. Now is important.* We say death [can come] sudden. But we don't know when we will die. The thing is that when we die, we don't even know whether we will die tomorrow. There is no guarantee that we will live tomorrow, you see. That's why, *practice now for the betterment of future*, for the betterment of future lives. And when you talk about Buddhahood, we have [to think about] not only for oneself but for all sentient beings.

KT: All sentient beings?

Ven. Gonta: [Yes,] all sentient beings. Like me, others, too, are subject to death.

KT: So, the teaching of impermanence helps us to open up and to think about the bigger issues. So, how about Six Realms? How does it relate to impermanence, to *impermanence and Six Realms and to Buddha-hood*?

Ven. Gonta: You know, *samsara*.

KT: *Samsara* is the realm of rebirth.

Ven. Gonta: Yes, rebirth. That means "birth death," "birth death."

This means impermanence. So, we should have *love for [other] sentient beings*.

KT: Love for sentient beings, living beings?

Ven. Gonta: [Yes,] sentient beings. And one thing, we can have [is the] *"bodhi-citta mind"*; that means *"altruistic mind."*

KT: Altruistic? *Bodhi-citta.*

Ven. Gonta: Yes, *bodhi-citta* mind. That's why by remembering, by being aware, and by meditating not only on this samsara, but we should also be aware of Nirvana-hood or Buddha-hood.

KT: Nirvana-hood and Buddha-hood, which is beyond...

Ven. Gonta: Beyond *samsara.*

KT: *Samsara,* or cycle of birth and death.

Ven. Gonta: We can be freed from this chain of birth and death.

KT: Be liberated.

Ven. Gonta: Yes, be liberated: liberation. Nirvana means liberation from delusion and karmic action.

KT: So, in Nirvana and Buddha-hood you find peace, tranquility?

Ven. Gonta: Yes.

KT: So, Venerable Gonta, thank you very much for your insightful remarks, especially from a Tibetan Buddhist perspective. We really appreciate it very much.

Ven. Gonta: Thank you.

Well, I hope that our discussion has encouraged you to think a little more deeply about dealing with the changes in your life. It is our hope that you look at such changes not as reasons to feel depressed or sad about life, but rather as an opportunity to practice virtues and to cultivate love and compassion for others.

Whether you believe in the teachings of transmigration through the six realms as actual existences or see the six realms as psychological states in this life, our belief should not detract from us practicing and cultivating virtues right now in this life, keeping in mind the spirit as expressed in today's opening passage:

> It is worthy to perform the present duty well and without failure;
> do not seek to avoid or postpone it till tomorrow. By acting now,
> one can live a good day.

PROGRAM 25

Third Mark of Existence:
Truly Understand that Life Is Impermanent

This life is impermanent. In an ever-changing world, we are living a new life every day.

(*Mutually Sustaining Life, p. 56*)

Hello. How are you? I hope we find you in the best of spirit and health.

Third Mark of Existence

Today, I would like to begin by looking at the Third Mark of Existence, "*All Conditioned Phenomena are impermanent,*" or rephrased, "*Life is impermanent.*" This means that everything in our life is subject to change.

What can we do as ordinary persons living in today's modern society to apply the lessons drawn from the truth of impermanence in our lives? Well, from my viewpoint, there are three things: First, to *fully understand* the truth of impermanence; second, to focus on the now and *live fully in the present*; and third, to *be open to changes* that unfold in our lives.

I want to stress the fact that these lessons are oriented more toward lay persons living in contemporary society; whereas monks and nuns, on the other hand, have different priorities and, therefore, place more emphasis on not being attached to things because of their impermanence. The ultimate goal is the same, however, and the difference is merely a matter of degree.

Today, I will be concentrating on the first of three lessons, which is the call for us to truly understand the truth of impermanence with *our total being*. Most of us know with our head that things change, but it's extremely difficult to accept change when it hits home, especially in the form of the loss of a loved one.

strated earlier by various traditions all stressed mindfulness, or the ability to be in the present moment. As another example, I'd like to cite a popular line that I see quoted in many places, but for which the author is unknown. You may have already heard it:

"Yesterday is history. Tomorrow is a mystery, but this moment is a gift. That is why it's called the 'present.'"

It's all too true that we cannot forget the past, since it is because of the past that we have the present. And we cannot ignore tomorrow, since we must often plan for and anticipate it. However, we often find ourselves unduly dwelling in the past or overly anticipating tomorrow so that we forget about what lies right in front of us. As the passage reminds us, yesterday is history and tomorrow remains unknown, but the present is real. Actually life is none other than the present. And when we open our mind and heart to the present moment, we are able to see, hear, smell, taste and feel many of the myriad manifestations of life and receive them as gifts.

Practice for Living in the Present

Traditional Buddhist practice encourages one to live in the present. One prime example is the way monks and nuns are trained to eat their meals. Allow me to share my experience of how I took my meals when I lived a life of a novice monk in Thailand many years ago. First of all, the monks only eat two meals a day, breakfast and lunch.

In the morning, we partake of the food that we have received during our neighborhood begging or alms-collecting rounds. We place the bowl before us. Then we look at the food carefully and take a morsel of food with our hand in a very deliberate manner. We try to feel the texture of the food with our fingers, and then bring the food slowly to our mouth. After placing the food in our mouth, we chew very slowly and savor the food. Breakfast usually takes about half an hour, concentrating on the act of eating and nothing else. Consequently, I remember exactly what I was eating and felt satisfied both in mind and body.

The practice of living in the moment also extended to other facets of monastic life, which are carried out with *mindfulness*. The one lesson I remember very well was when I was hanging my wet towel in a usual manner like this (hanging it over the clothes line from the front to back). However, my master reprimanded me for not being mindful. He then showed me his way of hanging the towel, which was to do it backwards (hanging it over the clothes line from the back to the front by going under the clothes line). I then asked him why he did it in what seemed to me to be a rather awkward and unusual way. He explained that his way makes us be much more mindful and be in the present [precisely because it's physically the more difficult and awkward way]. And I found that my teacher was right.

Dr. Yutang Lin

What is the relationship between the truth of impermanence and being focused fully in the present? Well, when a person truly comes to understand the impermanent nature of life, he or she paradoxically comes to feel "how precious the 'now' really is" and seeks to live each moment as deeply and fully as possible.

To illustrate this point, I'd like to tell you about a remarkable contemporary Buddhist teacher, Dr. Yutang Lin. He came from Taiwan to study chemistry in the United States, and eventually earned a Ph.D. in chemistry from the University of California at Berkeley. Soon after, he met a Buddhist teacher, who impressed him immensely. He was so taken by the teacher and his teaching that he gave away all of his books on chemistry to concentrate on studying and practicing Buddhism. Of course, he gave up a potentially promising career in the field of chemistry. Without holding any professional position in any Buddhist institution, Dr. Lin has since dedicated his life to promoting Buddhism out of his own home through numerous publications and teachings to anyone interested.

He enjoys his daily walks, especially the part that takes him through the nearby cemetery. I asked him why he enjoyed and found meaning in walking through a cemetery, for most people would find that a little odd. He answered that the cemetery put things in perspective. Life is ever changing and is so unpredictable, and we never know what lies ahead. Therefore, his walks through the cemetery remind him of what is important and what is not. The following is a poem he wrote, perhaps written after one of his walks through the cemetery, which aptly expresses his outlook:

Suddenly I see that life could end at any moment!
Once I realize that I am so close to death, I am instantly free in life.
Why bother to criticize or fight with others?
Let me just be pure in mind and enjoy living!

For Dr. Lin, when he squarely faces the fact of impermanence, he feels in actual fact, "instantly free in life." His sense of freedom comes from realizing that in this world of shifting and changing conditions, he needs to be focused in the now and in what is truly important.

Don't Get Hung Up

In my view, to be focused in the present helps a person to be clearer on what is important and what is not, what are the big things and what are the small things. A person comes to realize that certain things are not worth all the fuss. Dr. Lin realized that, when he cannot and should not be *hung up* on the small things of life, as seen in the line in his poem, "Why bother to criticize or fight with others?"

Nevertheless, to some degree or another, many of us get caught up in criticizing and fighting others. Sometimes the stakes are high and the issues are important, so we need to hold our ground and assert our position. However, many times, won't you agree that the issues are not worth getting all worked up over? For instance, I recall once in the office I was working in, my co-workers argued intensely over where to place the new copying machine. After a while it turned into a battle of egos. It was quite ridiculous and a real waste of energy!

And how often do we as employees criticize and complain about our boss? In that same office just mentioned, certain people complained all the time about our boss and the administration that he represented. Certainly, constructive criticism is needed, but these co-workers complained endlessly about things that could not be changed or about things in the company that were far from being as bad as they saw them. In fact, it dawned on me that their idle complaining was the common denominator that galvanized the group.

Without it, they would have little else to talk about.

Impermanence and Daily Inspiration

I find that these examples of unnecessary arguments and complaining are prime examples of the small things, which Dr. Lin would not get caught up in. He would, instead, direct that energy more constructively, for instance, toward cultivating his mind, as he says in the poem, *"Let me just be pure in mind and enjoy living."*[1]

It is this awareness about impermanence and the urge to live fully in the present moment with the implied sense of appreciation and inspiration that today's opening passage expresses.

> *Do not dwell in the past, do not dream of*[2] *the future, and, instead, concentrate the mind on the present moment.*

Well, we look forward to seeing you next time, when Venerable Gonta, a Tibetan Lama, rejoins us to share his thoughts on meditation and show us a basic meditation posture. See you then, and have a great week.

---

[1] In the TV program I say, "enjoy life," but it should be "enjoy living" in keeping with his poem.

[2] In the TV program I say, "do not wait for," but it should be "do not dream of" in keeping with today's opening passage.

PROGRAM 28
Tibetan Buddhist Meditation

*The secret of health for both mind and body is not to mourn for the
past, not to worry about the future, or not to anticipate troubles,
but to live wisely and earnestly for the present.*

(The Teaching of Buddha, p. 378)

Hello. Thanks for tuning in.

So far in our program, we have looked at meditation from the
Theravada and Zen traditions. By covering *Tibetan meditation* today,
we will have taken a look at all of the three major styles of Buddhist
meditation that are popular today in the United States.

Needless to say, there are numerous kinds and levels of meditation within Tibetan Buddhism. Today, we are fortunate to have back
with us *Venerable Geshe Sonam Gyaltsen Gonta* of the *Gelukpa denomination,* of which the Dalai Lama is the head. Venerable Gonta was with
us two shows ago when we discussed the teaching of impermanence.

Interview

KT: Well, Venerable Gonta, it's great to have you back. Today we
are talking about meditation. You know meditation is part of overall
practice. So, my question is, "Why do we practice in the first place?"

Ven. Gonta: Practice is important because everyone wants happiness and doesn't want suffering. That's why meditation is [impor-
tant.] [It is] because through meditation, we can accumulate virtuous
action.

KT: Virtuous action?

Ven. Gonta: Virtuous action. Through virtuous action, we can be
a happy person. [*Be happy*]

KT: So, if we practice virtuous action, we can be happy. That's
the assumption?

Ven. Gonta: Happy, yes. Secondly, I can [ask and] say, "Can you
practice?" Yes, right now, *we can practice* because we are born *as a human being.*

KT: As a human being?

Ven. Gonta: Yes, human being. As we talked last time, it is very precious [to be born as a human being for we have] very deep intelligence unlike [other] animals. That's why we can practice. That's one thing. And secondly, we have the external teachers. [Having teachers] *"Internally" means we were born as human beings. "Externally," spiritual masters are there [as our] Dharma teachers.*

KT: Externally, we have teachers to help us?

Ven. Gonta: Yes, in other words, Dharma teachings are there.

KT: Dharma teachings, and then internally, we have the ...?

Ven. Gonta: Human mind.

KT: Human mind. Okay.

Ven. Gonta: Yes, this is the second, you see. Thirdly, I want to say [that] you *can't wait* for next life. You have to *practice now in this life.*

KT: This life?

Ven. Gonta: This life. [It is] because if you don't practice in this life, we don't know ... we can't say if we will be born as a same human being. Okay [that's the] third thing. Lastly, some people say, "Oh, I have time. Maybe I'll practice the last ten years [of my life], after retiring, or next year, or next month, or tomorrow." But this, we can't say because the *time of death is uncertain.*

KT: Time of death is uncertain?

Ven. Gonta: That's right. That's why we have to practice now for the betterment of the future.

KT: Now, part of practice is meditation.

Ven. Gonta: Yes, it's an important part.

KT: So, why do we practice meditation? [*Why should we meditate?*] We talked about why we do practice in general. But why do we practice ... why do you suggest that we meditate?

Ven. Gonta: Yes, this is important. Meditation means, to *be familiar [with or] be accustomed to be happy.* That's why by practicing meditation, we can [become more] familiar with renunciation, Bodhicitta (aspiration for enlightenment) mind, altruistic mind, [thinking about] the well-being of other beings, unlike attachment or [things] like that.

KT: So, meditation makes us familiar with the mind of . . .

Ven. Gonta: Good things.

KT: Good things. Altruistic mind, you said? Bodhi-citta means the mind of aspiring to become enlightened or awakened. And thinking of other people; these are the good things.

Ven. Gonta: Yes.

KT: So, meditation helps us cultivate those qualities? I see. Okay.

Ven. Gonta: Right now, one thing I should say is that right now, you see, as a common human being, we are so much familiar with attachment, anger, and all these things. Even if these are not taught by others, since we are familiar with them from the beginning-less time till now, we are accustomed to and are habituated to them. That's why we soon [right away] get angry.

KT: So, anger and attachment are more natural for us?

Ven. Gonta: Yes. We are accustomed [to them].

KT: You're saying that we are accustomed to or familiar with them (anger and attachment), but we are not familiar with the [Dharma] teachings.

Ven. Gonta: Yes, the good things.

KT: So, we have to cultivate the good things. So, in a way, negative things are easy because it is natural, but the positive things, we have to work at?

Ven. Gonta: That's why we have to practice. We have to meditate purposely with some effort.

KT: Okay. Now, let me ask you, "what are the *benefits of meditation?*" You know there are 10 million people in the United States who do some kind of meditation a day, every day. Ten million people, that's a lot of people! I am sure there are people who find meditation to be beneficial. In your view, what are the benefits of meditation?

Ven. Gonta: There are a lot of benefits, you see. Any way, concisely speaking, we can have positive virtuous action.

KT: Positive virtuous . . . ?

Ven. Gonta: *Positive virtuous action.*

KT: Action

Ven. Gonta: Action. That means we can have passion, generosity, good effort.

KT: So, passion, generosity, good effort.

Ven. Gonta: [These are the] things we can develop from meditating. These are the benefits, you see. In other words, we can be mentally rich; be physically and mentally rich.

KT: Okay. So, we are talking about in this life, right?

Ven. Gonta: Even in this life. Of course, especially from the Buddhist point of view, our aim or end is not this life but future life or enlightenment. But even if you don't think about this life [as the ultimate aim], we can *physically or mentally be enriched and happy* [*in this life*].

KT: So, I think you have convinced me meditation is good. So, we have looked at Zen and Theravada kinds of meditation. So, could you show us one form of meditation that you've practiced in your tradition? I know there are many. You can just show us one form or one slice of your meditative tradition?

Ven. Gonta: Okay.

KT: Okay!

Tibetan Meditation

Ven. Gonta: Here we have *Seven Vairocana Postures*. I will try to demonstrate to you.

1) First, your *legs* should be crossed. [This is] what we call *"Vairocana Posture"* or, in other word, we have the [full] *lotus posture or half lotus posture*. If it's uneasy for you, you can even sit in a chair.

2) Secondly, you have your *hands* or palms under the navel like this. This is [what] we call "meditational equipoise."

3) Thirdly, your back [*spine*] should be straight so that your channels and blood circulation are good.

4) Then, your *shoulders* should be straight.

5) Then, your *mouth* should be closed.

6) And your *tongue* should just touch the backside of [your] teeth.

7) Then, you shouldn't close your *eyes*, just half closed.

Okay, these are the Seven Vairocana Postures that you can do.

You can then *visualize all sentient beings around you*, [for example,] your father of this life at the right hand [side] of you (*right side: father*). You can visualize your mother at the left [-hand side] (*left side: mother*). And in front of you, if you have an enemy, you can visualize your enemy. If you don't have [enemies, then visualize] any persons you don't like (*front: enemy or person you dislike*). On the backside of you, you can visualize the friends or persons you like so that you won't get attached to them (*behind: friend or person you like*). Then, all around them, [visualize] all sentient beings as [being] born as hell beings. So, thinking that they're all suffering, you can develop love and compassion. And [visualize that] they're in the form of human beings like you, because human beings are in the best [condition] to do Dharma practice.

Then, the most important thing when doing meditation is your motivation. Your motivation should be: *for the well-being of all sentient beings, I should attain enlightenment*. You see, this is very important. This is how you begin meditation. Then, after that you can do the actual meditation.

Conclusion

So, there you have it. You have witnessed a form of Tibetan meditation demonstrated to us by Venerable Gonta. One of the most important lessons that we can draw from this is that the real enemy is often our own ignorance and delusion within, rather than actual persons out there. To help us conquer this enemy within, we should constantly keep in mind the meaning of today's opening passage:

> *The secret of health for both mind and body is not to mourn for the past, not to worry about the future, or not to anticipate troubles, but to live wisely and earnestly for the present.*

In our next show, we will look at another dimension of the teaching of impermanence, where we are inspired to be open to changes without resisting. See you then.

PROGRAM 29
Third Mark of Existence: Be Open to Change

To worry in anticipation or to cherish regret for the past is like the reeds that are cut and wither away.

(The Teaching of Buddha, p. 378)

Hi, how are you doing today? For our regular viewers, we hope that our program is making a difference in your lives. And if you have joined us for the first time, welcome!

Being Open to Change

In today's show, we wish to continue with our discussion of the Third Mark of Existence, that is, All Conditioned Phenomena are Impermanent, or simply, *Life is Impermanent.*

As I mentioned previously, we are able to understand this truth with our head, but are not often able to fully put this concept into practice in our lives. As today's opening passage tells us, we often worry about the future or hold onto regrets from the past. Let me recite the passage again:

To worry in anticipation or to cherish regret for the past is like the reeds that are cut and wither away.

In other words, we are encouraged not to be overly attached to the past or worry about the future, for if we do, we are like a lifeless reed.

In today's show, I wish to emphasize the need for us to *be open to change*, which is the third of three dimensions of the Third Mark of Existence. The other two dimensions that we discussed in two previous shows were to *fully understand* the truth with our total being, and to *live fully in the present.*

We are stressing this need to be *open, not closed*, to change, for it is often more difficult to practice than we anticipate. This is due, in part, to our human nature to cling to what is familiar, especially when we are happy with the situation we are in.

A Parable

This characteristic or trait is perhaps nowhere better exemplified than by a couple of characters from a popular book called *Who Moved My Cheese?* by Dr. Spencer Johnson. I am sure some of you have read it.

Although it is not a Buddhist book per se, I found the story to be extremely effective in conveying many of the valuable points I wish to make in relation to the Buddhist teaching, Life is Impermanent.

Well, once upon a time in a land far away, there lived four little characters who ran through a maze looking for cheese to nourish them and make them happy. Two were mice named *"Sniff"* and *"Scurry"* and two were Little people named *"Hem"* and *"Haw,"* who were as small as mice but looked and acted a lot like people today.

One day, they found a huge cheese near Cheese Station C at the end of one of the corridors in the Maze. They were naturally overjoyed with this find. Every morning, the two mice, Sniff and Scurry, went to Cheese Station C to nibble at the delicious cheese. When they got there they took off their running shoes, then tied them together and hung them around their necks so that they could get to their shoes when needed.

In contrast, Hem and Haw settled in and made themselves at home at Station C. They took off their shoes and changed into their comfortable slippers. They felt secure and proud of their huge cheese, so much so that they soon moved their home nearby.

One day, when they arrived at Cheese Station C, the cheese had *disappeared completely*! Hem and Haw couldn't believe it, and Hem hollered out in anger and disbelief, "Who moved my cheese?" In contrast, Sniff and Scurry weren't surprised, for they had noticed that the cheese was growing smaller and were prepared for the inevitable. They simply looked at each other, removed their shoes hung conveniently around their necks, put them on, and were quickly off in search of the next cheese.

Hem and Haw ranted and raved. They felt it was *their* cheese, and that their rights were violated. "It's not fair!" they cried out. Then they began to blame others, who were now seen to be responsible for the disappearance of the cheese. And they chose to wait at Cheese

Station C for it to reappear. However, day after day, the two Little people were disappointed, for the cheese did not return. Hem and Haw became weary and exhausted.

Soon Haw began to have second thoughts about their response, and suggested that they begin looking for a new cheese like Sniff and Scurry. However, Hem scoffed at the mice, who were only responding instinctively. Surely *they* were smarter than the mice and would figure out a way for the cheese to reappear again.

But as they became physically weaker and failed to figure out what to do, Haw stepped out of Station C in search of new cheese, while Hem continued to resist change and cling to the past.

Haw felt better and liberated to be looking rather than merely doing nothing. Of course, he was not without anxiety. He was afraid to leave the comfortable environment of Cheese Station C, and yet at the same time, he was afraid that he would not find a new cheese. But it soon dawned on him that between the two fears, he felt *more empowered* to move forward to take on the fear and anxiety of what uncertainties lie ahead than remain afraid and just wait and hope for the cheese to reappear.

And as he moved forward into the Maze he felt more invigorated by the anticipation of where the path would take him. He also realized that things were not as bad as he had imagined (on screen: *Things are never as bad as we imagine*). In fact, what he had imagined was far worse than the actual reality. He regretted all the time he wasted on thinking negative thoughts and being gripped by the fear of the unknown. Instead, he began to think in a more positive manner, seeing himself finding and savoring the new cheese.

Then, as he turned one corner he came upon a huge cheese that filled an entire cavern at Cheese Station N. It was the biggest supply of cheese he had ever seen, certainly much larger than the one that had disappeared. For a moment, he thought it was just his imagination, but he knew it wasn't when he saw Sniff and Scurry, already there with their fat little bellies, welcoming Haw to the new cheese!

Message of the Parable

This parable is highly instructive and conveys a number of vital points for us to keep in mind about the truth of impermanence and how we can respond to changes in our life.

First, undesirable changes often seem to take place unexpectedly without warning, but under closer scrutiny we learn that many *changes are foreseeable*. The two mice anticipated the inevitable change. They were always ready to respond quickly. In stark contrast, Hem and Haw were not. As a result, they were unwilling to look at the reality, even as the size of the cheese began to dwindle.

Second, in an ever-changing world, we cannot claim things as *"mine,"* as a child often does with his toys. As Hem and Haw experienced, we are bound to be disappointed if we feel we are entitled to things, for changes are often the result of numerous conditions and forces that are far beyond our control. *There is nothing that we can own permanently.*

Also, our reluctance to move with the changes is often rooted in our anxiety about the future and fear of failure. It often feels more secure to stay with the familiar, but here as well lurks the uneasiness or apprehension of clinging to the past. So, either way, one experiences fear and anxiety. As Haw learned, when faced with two choices, it is often *better to take on the anxiety of the future* than to remain entrenched with the anxiety of the past.

At the same time, *the reality is often better than what we had imagined.* We have a strong tendency to imagine the worst, and thereby resist any proactive responses to change. Yes, there are obstacles to overcome and challenges to be met in adapting to changes, but the situation is often not as dire as one had thought.

Last, but not least, it is important to remember that while things are going badly now, this *negative situation will eventually pass*, for that is the nature of impermanence. There will be bumps at times, but our lives will not always be rocky and unsure. The truth of impermanence helps us to be optimistic when things are not going well because they *will* and *do* change for the better.

A Sense of Humor

Traditionally, the Buddhist teaching has encouraged non-attachment because all things change, and certainly that is important to keep in our minds. (*Humor as a form of non-attachment*) As contemporary lay Buddhists, we can practice non-attachment to an extent in the form of maintaining a sense of levity, lightheartedness and humor about ourselves. Haw realized this when he saw how silly they both looked. He felt more alive as he was finally able to laugh at himself and announce, "It's ... Maze ... time!" Then, he started off in search of new cheese. On the other hand, Hem didn't laugh or try to see a brighter side, and continued to be miserable.

I hope that in the event that *our* cheese disappears, we would respond like the two mice, but if we cannot, we would at least be like Haw. Otherwise, we would be miserable and afraid like Hem.

Well, please join us next week, when we interview Professor Jidong Chen, whose involvement in the Tiananmen Square incident in 1989 sparked his dedication to Buddhism.

PROGRAM 30
From Tiananmen Square to Dharma

Better than a hundred verses is one single Dharma statement that gives the hearer calmness of mind.
(Dhammapada 102, Buddha-Dharma, p. 433)

Hello, it's truly a pleasure to be with you again.

In our recent shows, we have been pursuing the topic of *impermanence*, the third of the Four Marks of Existence. As I have said previously, this truth is relatively easy for us to understand and accept, especially since we all experience anticipated as well as unexpected, changes in our lives. It was so for Hem, Haw, Scurry and Sniff in the best-selling book, *Who Moved My Cheese?*, which we talked about in our last show.

In that story, two Little people, Hem and Haw, had difficulty adjusting to the sudden disappearance of their beloved cheese, and as a consequence suffered enormously. On the other hand, the two mice Scurry and Sniff, responded well to such unexpected change.

Each and every one of us has or will come face to face with changes in our lives that are unforeseen and also undesirable. However, how we *deal with them* can be the event that impacts the rest of our lives.

Our guest today, Professor Jidong Chen, experienced such change soon after graduating from college. Professor Chen currently specializes in modern Chinese Buddhist thought. He is also a practicing Buddhist.

He attended Peking University, where he majored in philosophy. Upon graduation, Professor Chen was asked to stay on to teach. As a junior faculty member, he was enjoying his work. Shortly thereafter, the campus of Peking University became the center of a student movement for democratic reform, which culminated in the well-known *Tiananmen Square Incident* in 1989. As the whole world watched the turmoil unfold, Professor Chen found himself as one of the participants as the tanks rolled onto the streets of Beijing.

Now, let's find out what happened and how this life-changing event contributed to Professor Chen becoming a committed Buddhist.

Interview

KT: Professor Chen, thank you very much for coming to talk with us. Before we inquire about the turmoil of the democratic reform movement, I'd like to ask you about your earlier life. Did you grow up in a Buddhist family?

Prof. Chen: No, my father was a Communist and also a factory manager. On religious belief, he was an atheist. However, my mother and my grandmother liked Buddhism and Daoism, but they couldn't teach me anything about the teachings. In other words, my family was not very religious.

KT: When did you begin to take an interest in Buddhism?

Prof. Chen: In my third year at Peking University, I took a class called "social survey." As part of my class, I went to *Mount Le Shan* in Sichuan Province for one month. I was deeply affected by its grandeur. The great Buddha statues on that mountain are very famous in China. There, I met an older Buddhist *Chan master*, who was so kind and had both wisdom and virtue. In that discussion with him, I really became very curious about Buddhism.

KT: What made you become interested in *studying* Buddhism?

Prof. Chen: When I was a graduate student, I really began to be interested in Buddhism. I read a biography about *Kumarajiva* (*Kumārajīva*). He was a famous Buddhist and a great translator from Central Asia. He came to China around the year 400.

KT: About 1,600 years ago.

Prof. Chen: Yes. I was really deeply affected by his lifetime of frustration and genuine Buddhist belief. From that time I read many, many books on Buddhism.

KT: Around that time, I understand you met a teacher.

Prof. Chen: Yes. Meanwhile, I began to visit a Chan Master named Jinghui. He showed me how to do *meditation* (*chan*), and he also told me a lot of knowledge about Buddhism.

KT: What did you study in graduate school?

Prof. Chen: Well, I wrote my master's thesis about a modern Chinese philosopher, named *Xiong Shili*. His philosophy was a new interpretation of the traditional Buddhist *Consciousness-only School*. In Chinese, we call it "Weishi." My general interest in studying Buddhism was to explain the Buddhist influence on Chinese thought and culture. Second, I tried to answer what made Buddhism fascinating especially to the Chinese. Third, I wanted to understand the relationship between Buddhism and traditional Chinese culture.

KT: What then made you become more seriously interested as a Buddhist? It's different from being a student studying Buddhism, for you became a more committed Buddhist.

Prof. Chen: In June, 1989, there was the "Tiananmen Incident." (*on screen: *Tiananmen Square Incident*) At that time, I was teaching as a lecturer in the Department of Philosophy at Peking University. Many of my students took active part in the democratic movement. I was also a supporter of the student movement. On the evening of June 3rd, when the soldiers appeared in the streets of the capital, I escaped to a Buddhist temple. There, my Buddhist master Jinghui and other Buddhists helped me to stay overnight. I really hoped that the Chinese government would put the political reform in practice, but the "Tiananmen Massacre" made me very, very disappointed and very angry.

KT: It must have been a very difficult and a harrowing time for you. What happened after that?

Prof. Chen: After June 4th, all the young teachers of Peking University were forced to go to rural areas to undergo brainwashing. I was among them. I was really disgusted with our government. Fortunately, I got the chance to study Buddhism in Japan. For this reason, in September, 1991, I resigned from the teaching profession.

KT: We discussed the *teaching of impermanence* last time in our program. So, I am very curious as to what you think about that teaching of impermanence. Can you comment on that?

Prof. Chen: It's a difficult question, I think. When I escaped from the capital during the Tiananmen Incident, I met with my master, Jinghui. He talked to me about "impermanence." In my understanding, there are two meanings of "impermanence." One is the usual meaning that all things change and reform.

KT: Yes, all things change, and we have talked about that in our previous programs, but you mentioned a second one. So what's the second meaning?

Prof. Chen: The second meaning is *"being open to all possibilities."* For example, I was involved in the democratic movement. It taught me that we may not be able to achieve our goal for a long time or, perhaps, we may not be able to achieve it at all. But there is meaning in everything that happens to us. I feel that the teaching helped me to be more *patient* and to see things more clearly with all the confusion around me.

KT: There was a lot of confusion, but it gave you patience. So, it was your teacher Jinghui's explanation on impermanence that helped you to get you through those difficult times?

Prof. Chen: Yes, his explanation was simple and direct. It still helps me today in many ways.

KT: So, your teacher's words must have had a great impact on you as they continue to live in you even today.
Well, it looks like we are out of time. I like to thank you for being with us to share your fascinating story with us. I appreciate it very much.

We hope that you enjoyed the personal journey of Professor Chen, who overcame a number of obstacles to become a dedicated Buddhist. In that process, we should not forget that a teacher offered words of light on impermanence that helped Professor Chen to gather himself amidst the confusion and uncertainty of the time, which is aptly captured in today's passage:

> *Better than a hundred verses is one single Dharma statement that gives the hearer calmness of mind.*

May you, too, find such words of light and inspiration in the course of your spiritual path.

Thank you for joining us, and we hope you will tune in next week when we move on to the Fourth Mark of Existence, Nirvana is Peaceful and Tranquil.

CHAPTER SEVEN:
Teachings of the Fourth Mark of Existence

PROGRAM 31
Fourth Mark of Existence: Nirvana is Peaceful and Tranquil

For one who has completed the journey, for one who is free from
sorrow, for one who is free from all fetters, there are no anxieties.
(Dhammapada 90, Buddha-Dharma, p. 433)

Hi, I trust you're having a good day. And it's our hope that you will find something worthwhile in this program to add further meaning to your day and beyond.

Fourth Mark of Existence

Let's begin by discussing the fourth of the Four Marks of Existence, which is, "*Nirvana* (Nirvāna) *is peaceful and tranquil*," or rephrased, "*Life can be great*." To review, the first three of the Four Marks of Existence, rephrased in colloquial terms, are: **1)** *Life is a bumpy road*, **2)** *Life is interdependent*, and **3)** *Life is impermanent*.

This fourth mark, which is "*Nirvana is peaceful and tranquil*" or "*Life can be great*," differs from the first three as it refers to the realm of awakening. It is the state attained by Shakyamuni (Śākyamuni) Buddha when he realized awakening under the Bodhi tree at the age of thirty-five. This transformed him as the Buddha, which literally means "the awakened one." And all Buddhists ever since have regarded it as their cherished goal. Hence, awakening is the essence of the Buddhist religion.

Here, this awakening is referred to as "Nirvana is peaceful and tranquil." "*Nirvana*" literally means "*blown out*," or pointing to the state where one's fire of greed, hatred and ignorance is *extinguished*. And such a state is, indeed, "peaceful and tranquil."

Four Stages of Awakening

It should be pointed out that Buddhism has always recognized various stages of awakening, with Shakyamuni Buddha as having realized the ultimate stage.

According to one standard teaching, there are four stages of awakening. At each stage, the fetters or blind passions such as greed, hatred and ignorance are gradually extinguished.

At the first stage, a person extinguishes three fetters, which are **1)** the false view that sees the self as having a separate and unconnected existence (*false view of self*), **2)** any doubt about the Buddhist teachings and practices as having any efficacy (*doubt concerning the teachings*), and **3)** the belief that rituals and ethical actions *alone* can lead to awakening (*belief that rituals alone are enough*).

At the second stage, the fetters of greed and hatred weaken. At the third stage, these fetters are extinguished. And at the fourth or final stage of awakening, all other fetters are extinguished, which include "*self-pride.*" Pride is very subtle and is the most tenacious of the fetters to extinguish.

Some of you may now be feeling quite intimidated by what is expected for Buddhist awakening, saying to yourself, "No way, I can't do that!" However, the first stage is within the reach of many people who make a serious and conscientious effort. Plus, even if the first stage is not reached, any sincere effort to practice and understand the teachings can make a huge positive difference in your life. That has been the case for millions of ordinary people throughout the centuries.

Dipa Ma (Dīpa Mā, 1911-1989)

I would like to share with you a description of an awakened person as given to us by Jack Engler in a recent issue of *Tricycle: A Buddhist Review*, an informative quarterly Buddhist magazine published in New York.

The awakened person is an Indian woman named Dipa Ma, who lived and taught in Calcutta, India. Jack, an American, describes Dipa Ma, who served as his teacher, as follows: "Dipa Ma was without any of the outward trappings or symbols of recognized teachers; just a tiny woman in a tiny room in an impoverished neighborhood of old Calcutta, unknown outside her circle of friends and students, teaching in the traditional Indian way, at home all day, every day, for anyone who wanted to come by and talk about dharma."

Dipa Ma is impressive, for she was a lay woman and teacher in a tradition where virtually all of the teachers have been monks. Further, she was a widow in a society where widows normally stay confined to home. She overcame extreme personal difficulties. For instance, when she turned 41, her loving husband suddenly died; she had experienced two stillbirths and was enduring a number of life-threatening physical ailments, and the doctors told her she would die soon. Out of desperation, she began to practice Buddhism.

Overcoming all of these obstacles, Dipa Ma had gone very far in her practice and is considered to have achieved the higher stages of awakening described earlier.

Where is the Pizzazz?

Once Jack told Dipa Ma that he felt that the awakened state seemed kind of gray and dull, for once a person eliminated desire, anger and passion there seemed to be no juice! Jack asked, "*Where is the pizzazz? Where is the chutzpah?*"

Dipa Ma immediately broke out laughing and responded, "Oh, you don't understand! Life was dull and boring *before*; always the same routine, nothing new. Once you get rid of all that stale stuff you've been carrying around, every moment is fresh and new, interesting and alive. Now everything has zest and taste. No two moments are ever the same."

And her words are supported by the traditional explanation of the qualities of an awakened mind, which are *joy, generosity, compassion, curiosity, truthfulness, serenity, equanimity, wakefulness, one-pointedness and impeccability*. There is definitely no lack of pizzazz or chutzpah here!

Benefits of Awakening

Dipa Ma used to worry a lot about the future, for example, how she would live, what would happen to her, and how she would take care of her daughter. She also felt enormous suffering over the sudden death of her husband. She was "burning" day and night with grief. However, the burning grief cooled down and left her, and she was able to accept the truth that *wherever there is birth, there is death*.

As for desire, Dipa Ma made a distinction between *sense-pleasure and sense-desire*. Sense-pleasure, like pain, is part of normal human experience. Sense-desire, on the other hand, creates suffering. It is the grasping at pleasure and the avoidance of pain. What is called for, however, is for lay persons to train themselves not to go to the extremes or cling to these sense-pleasures; otherwise they will turn into sense-desires, thereby leading to unnecessary suffering.

One such example is sexuality. It can be the most satisfying and precious act within a loving, committed relationship, but can wreak havoc in the relationship when trust is broken as sexuality turns, in Dipa Ma's words, from sense-pleasure into sense-desire in an act of adultery.

Human Relationships

In terms of relationships, Dipa Ma no longer divided and categorized people, saying to herself, "These are my friends, and they are not." She saw that there was much attachment in such dichotomy, and, in turn, felt a *loving kindness (mettā) toward everyone*.

She still enjoyed being around people who talked about the teachings, the mind or their spiritual life, and wanted to help if she felt she could. However, she had no interest in ordinary or useless talk or going somewhere to visit someone just to visit. She *never felt lonely (even) when she was alone*. Dipa Ma felt that her practice of Buddhism made her more certain of her responsibilities toward her family. She became *more confident as a mother*. For example, she was asked to stay in Burma to serve as a meditation teacher, but decided to return to India in order that her daughter would not lose touch with her Indian roots.

Life in General

Dipa Ma's life changed greatly as a result of her practice, for before she was attached to everything. She wanted do so much. Now, she *felt free, not bound.* She no longer wanted anything for herself. In her words, "I'm living, that's all. That's enough."

Also for her, there was nothing ultimately desirable or to cling to in this world. However, she felt that we can make good use of everything in this world, for all experiences can be used for personal learning, betterment and for helping others. Dipa Ma said that she was *no longer afraid of death.* She understood that dying is natural and is part and parcel of life.

So, you might ask, "What is there for her to live for?" Well, Dipa Ma said that she would like to be *completely* free from her attachments and fetters, and so, would continue to practice to cultivate herself. And she would also share her wisdom and compassion freely with anyone who seeks awakening.

This remarkable human being and Buddhist teacher, Dipa Ma, certainly exemplifies today's opening passage:

> For one who has completed the journey, for one who is free from sorrow, for one who is free from all fetters, there are no anxieties.

In our next show, Professor Jidong Chen, representing the Chinese Buddhist tradition, will be back with us as we explore the qualities of awakened persons who are within our midst.

PROGRAM 32
Qualities of Awakened People

Hard rock is not shaken by wind; likewise the wise are not disturbed by praise or blame.

Today's passage encourages us to be mindful of one of the important characteristics of an awakened person. Let us work toward making this quality, even in some small way, come alive in our lives.
(Buddha-Dharma, p. 432)

Hello. We hope you've been looking forward to watching our program as much we have been to presenting the program to you.

Today, we are pleased to have Professor Jidong Chen back with us to share his views based on his experience and knowledge of the Chinese Buddhist tradition. Two shows ago, we learned about Professor Chen's fascinating personal journey from growing up in a non-religious family to his involvement in the Tiananmen Square incident and becoming a Buddhist scholar and practitioner.

Today, we would like to direct our focus on one person who's considered to be awakened or enlightened.

Interview

KT: Well, Professor Chen, thank you for being with us again. We enjoyed your visit the last time. Today's opening passage reads as follows:

"Hard rock is not shaken by wind; likewise the wise are not disturbed by praise or blame."

This refers to a quality of an awakened person, or someone close to that state. Do you think this is an accurate description?

Prof. Chen: Yes, I think so, but I also think that it does not mean that an awakened person ignores people's opinion. He is interested in what others say, but they *do not easily sway* his *core views*.

KT: I see. Now, do you know anyone whom you consider to be awakened or at least close to that state?

Prof. Chen: Perhaps, I can think of one person. He is my teacher who helped me during the democratic reform and Tiananmen Incident in 1989. His name is *Jinghui* and he is a monk living in a city not too far from Beijing.

KT: I see. Previously when you appeared on our show, you talked about Tiananmen Square and how much turmoil and difficulties that caused you. But it was at that time that you were able to talk to your teacher, Master Jinghui, and get some advice from him that helped you greatly; isn't that right?

Professor Chen: Yes. He strongly supported the democratic movement. He was quite critical of the government. So, Master Jinghui was sympathetic to what the young people were feeling and experiencing. He was very helpful to others and me. Because of his support, the government also criticized him.

KT: Oh, I see. Now, how was he helpful to you during that time?

Professor Chen: He listened very well. He paid attention to what we had to say. He also gave us much advice on how to think about our situation. And all during this time, Master Jinghui had *calmness of mind*, which was very soothing for me. He made me feel settled and calm, too.

KT: You said that he helped you by showing how to think. Can you tell us about that?

Prof. Chen: Master Jinghui stressed the importance of having what can best be described as a *"Big Mind."*

KT: "Big Mind"? Big?

Prof. Chen: It's difficult to explain easily, but it means *"not to come to conclusions."* Master Jinghui once asked me, "What is Buddhism?" So, I said something like, "It's a way to become awakened." I thought it was a good answer, but he wasn't satisfied. So, I tried, "Buddhism is to see things as they really are." I thought he would be pleased, but again he wasn't. It turned out that he didn't like my answers because they sounded like *conclusions*. It was too set and sounded too absolute. He was looking for me to have a Big Mind, where I would be *open to more possibilities*.

KT: I see. What did he mean by "being more open to possibilities"?

Prof. Chen: Well, let me use an example of the game Go, an East Asian game similar to chess.

KT: Do you play that?

Prof. Chen: I love to play Go. When I play Go, I make my moves. When I make my moves, I do not think that the move is the one and only one I can make. It is *not absolute*. Instead, I try to be aware of the other possibilities, not only of my move but also my opponent's moves. And I must anticipate my opponent's many possible moves. By being open to all the possibilities, I am ready to respond better.

KT: Is that what your master, Jinghui meant by "Big Mind"?

Prof. Chen: Yes, I believe so.

The Qualities of an Awakened or Enlightened Person

KT: Can I ask a little more about your teacher? I know that he achieved a rather high level of wisdom and compassion. So spiritually he had achieved a higher level, but in terms of his involvement in society — as a member of the society — how was he in that regard?

Prof. Chen: He was always teaching the Dharma and sharing his experiences with many people within and outside the temple. Among them were university students who, like me, sought his help during the democratic reform movement. In fact, some of them became monks and nuns. And one of them has now become the head of the temple where Master Jinghui continues to live.

KT: So, he was active in the world, not just confined to personal meditation and studies.

Prof. Chen: That's right. So, he *practiced the "Big Mind"* and was not limited to one or the other. I would like to mention that he was also *thoughtful*. During my long stay at the temple, life was hard. But Master Jinghui gave me extra sweets and drinks that I love. He sometimes gave me extra servings of food. He said that I was young, so I needed extra.

KT: I see. But wasn't that breaking the precepts or the rules of the monastery?

Prof. Chen: Yes, but he understood that he needed to be *flexible with rules and precepts*. They can be bent if those rules caused someone to be too weak and even get sick. Maybe, you can say that this, too, was an example of his Big Mind!

KT: Ah, I see! So this is an example of an enlightened mind, where one is open to possibilities yet not be very fixed, and based on his practice and cultivation of wisdom and compassion. And I think that makes him very human, truly human, [which is] a real quality of an awakened mind.

Well, thank you very much for your time and sharing your teacher with us. And that has helped us to give us a better idea of what to seek as we aspire to attain the goals of Buddhism. Thank you for being with us.

An enlightened mind is not absolutely fixed and is open to possibilities based on a deep cultivation of wisdom and compassion. It is such qualities that make awakened people truly human.

Conclusion

As we saw in the case of Professor Chen's teacher, awakened persons are not necessarily confined to monasteries and nunneries away from society. In fact, a truly awakened person would be eager to relate to people in today's world with the intent to be of service to them. In Buddhism such people are referred to as *Bodhisattvas*, who dedicate their lives to guiding others to awakening.

Also, they are not necessarily "saint-like" or persons who never make mistakes or who are always abiding by the rules. As we saw with Professor Chen's teacher, these persons are sometimes willing to break the rules if he can help to liberate or awaken others. There is even a mischievous quality about them. That is why I said earlier that awakened people become truly human. But most of all, they inspire as well as offer solace to people because of their nature, which is grounded in wisdom and compassion.

Once again, this is reflected in today's passage:

Hard rock is not shaken by wind;
likewise the wise are not disturbed by praise or blame.

In our next show, we will continue to explore even more qualities of awakening and awakened people. Won't you join us?

PROGRAM 33

Fourth Mark of Existence:
Change Comes From Within

To conquer oneself is a greater victory than to conquer thousands in battle.

(The Teaching of Buddha, p. 370)

Hello, and it's a pleasure to have you join us for today's show.

Life Can be Great

Today, we are continuing our discussion on the Fourth Mark of Existence, which is *"Nirvana is Peaceful and Tranquil,"* or rephrased, *"Life can be Great."* In this show, I will use a more colloquial expression, Life can be Great.

The expression "Life can be Great" reveals two things. First, it tells us that when this state is realized, one experiences far less suffering and far more happiness than previously experienced, for his or her life becomes imbued with the qualities, as discussed in our previous show, of *joy, generosity, compassion, curiosity, truthfulness, serenity, equanimity, wakefulness, one-pointedness and impeccability.* This is what is meant by "Great."

Secondly, we have phrased it, *"Life can be Great"* and not *"Life is Great."* The reason goes to the heart of Buddhist awakening, which calls for individuals to take the initiative *"to change from within."* With this internal change or transformation, a person experiences his or her life as being "Great." So, we are not making a blanket statement about *all* life for *all* people, since we are not in a position to speak for others. That is why I have stressed the "can" in "Life *can* be Great," and have tried not to be presumptuous to say, "Life *is* Great."

Today's Theme: "To Change From Within"

This leads me to the point, which I wish to emphasize today, that is, the change must come from *within*. Buddhism helps us to change the way we see the world and ourselves. When we change within, it changes the way we see the outside world and how we act in it.

A Monk and a Hot Dog

In one of the earlier shows, I shared a joke about a monk and a hot dog, and today I'd like to complete the second half, which pertains to today's topic. I'll start from the beginning.

Well, a Buddhist monk wanted a hot dog. So he walked over to a hot dog vender on a busy street corner. The vender asked, "What would you like, sir?" The monk answered, *"Make me ONE with EVERYTHING!"* Just to make sure you got it, let me explain. The conventional meaning is that he wanted one hot dog with all the condiments, for example, mustard, ketchup, diced onion, relish, and sauerkraut: in other words, "make me *one* [hot dog] with everything [on it]."

But the deeper meaning points to a religious experience where a person feels at *one* with the universe, in a peak religious experience associated with the state of awakening in Buddhism: so in other words, "make me *one* with everything."

Now, let me tell you the second half of the joke that I didn't talk about before. Well, after getting the hot dog, the monk gives the vender a $20 bill, but even after a while he didn't get his change back. The monk waited patiently a little longer, but finally a bit flustered, he asked, "What about my change?" The vender faced the monk and replied, *"Sir, the change must come from within."*!

The joke about a monk and a hot dog is a reminder that spiritual transformation or *change* must come from within, the heart of today's topic.

A Parable of a Drowning Sailor

To illustrate this point, there is a wonderful story about a sailor lost at sea. I grew up hearing this story being told in our temples in California. No one seems to know when or where it came from, but it's had an enormous influence on my personal understanding.

At night a ship leaves the port of a tropical island. After many hours on the high seas a *sailor falls overboard.* No one on the ship notices that the man is missing, and the ship sails on its way. The water is chilly, and the waves are choppy. It is hauntingly dark. The sailor paddles frantically to keep afloat.

He then starts to swim toward an island he saw before he fell overboard. He soon loses all sense of direction. So he is not sure if he's even heading in the right direction. Although he is a good swimmer, his arms and legs soon grow weary. His breathing becomes labored, and he gasps for air. The sailor feels lost and totally alone in the middle of the ocean. He realizes that this could be the end for him. *Despair overcomes him,* and his energy begins to drain from him like sand from an hourglass. He begins to choke on the water hitting his face, and he can feel his body being dragged under.

At this instant he recalls the teaching of non-attachment, which calls for the act of *"letting go."* He then ceases his striving to swim on his own power. Instead, he turns over on his back with his limbs outstretched as if he were in a backyard hammock on a lazy summer afternoon.

As he does so, the ocean holds him afloat without any effort on his part! The ocean that was ready to drag him under now caresses him. The sailor is overjoyed! He is also grateful to know that he is all right.

He soon realizes that *he was fine all along.* He just didn't know it. The ocean had not changed at all. But rather, by changing his thinking, the sailor's relationship with the ocean has changed. The sea changed from being a dangerous and frightening enemy to a friend who embraced and supported him.

The sailor knows that he cannot stay afloat forever in the middle of the ocean. If he had no obligations in the world, maybe he could afford to stay and rest in this joyful calm. But the image of his wife and small children waiting anxiously at home inspires him to try to reach the shore.

He begins to swim as before but with one important difference. *He now trusts the ocean* as he would a caring and protective loved one. He knows that whenever he becomes tired, he can let go, and the ocean will support him. More importantly, he now knows that while he swims, it is the power of the ocean, not his own power that keeps him afloat. Yes, he moves his limbs to swim, but he has learned he can stay afloat by not struggling to do so.

Now that he feels safe in the arms of the sea, the sailor can think about finding the island. He studies the positions of the stars and the moon and the direction of the wind. Using his nautical training, he imagines where the island might be and moves toward it. He has no absolute guarantee that he is swimming in the right direction, but the sailor is now sure that the ocean will not let him drown and that eventually he will reach the island.

Change from Within

So what are the main points of this parable? First of all, what saved the sailor from drowning was not some outside divine help. We don't find him looking beyond himself for an answer to his dilemma. As he recalls the teaching of non-attachment, he remembers to abandon the notion that he had to be in total control. It was then that he relaxed and let go of his striving. And when he let go of his reliance on his own power, he discovered the supportive power of the ocean. So, it was the *"change from within"* that saved him.

Then, he discovers that the ocean had transformed from an enemy to a friend. Before his "change from within" the ocean seemed ready to pull him under, but after the change he found the ocean to be supportive and caring. The interesting point is that *the ocean had not changed at all*. It was the same ocean, but because he had changed, the ocean had also changed.

Now this change gave the sailor a very important gift: *confidence*. So when he started to swim back home, he now had the confidence in the ocean that it would not fail him. Whenever he got tired, he would simply let go and relax. This assurance gave him more space in his heart and mind, allowing him to fully exercise all his knowledge and ability to find his way home. He was able to see more, listen fully and think better.

Application to Our Life

If you are now confronted by a difficulty in your life, please see if you could apply the teaching of "changing from within." Sometimes we take on so much and get overwhelmed by all the expectations. In such a case, perhaps, we sometimes need to "let go" like the drowning sailor. And we'll probably find that an organization or a cause you are so involved in will go on just fine.

If you are having difficulties with a relationship, perhaps, it might be good for you to look within and see if there are attitudes or opinions that you could change. By so changing, you will probably find some opening in the other person for reconciliation.

If life is not offering what you expected, then let go of your striving and turn over on your back like the sailor. You are bound to discover people and things that are physically and spiritually supporting your very existence: from the air that we breathe, to breathtaking beauty of nature, as well as the people who care about you. Then, for you, *life becomes a friend and not an enemy*. You can then resume your swim with greater confidence and creativity.

Next week, we're planning an exciting show featuring Buddhist children's songs. Please tune in, and have a great week.

PROGRAM 34

Dharma School Songs from the U.S.: Jōdo Shinshū Children's Songs

To make a Buddhist community complete, there must be perfect harmony among the members. The teachers teach the members, and the members honor the teachers so that there can be harmony between them.

(Mutually Sustaining Life, p. 228)

It's great to have you join us for today's show. I'm sure you won't regret that you tuned in, as we are especially pleased to present a performance of Buddhist children's music for your enjoyment.

Buddhism and Music

Traditionally, monks and nuns are not allowed to listen to or play music. Music is seen to be a distraction to mental concentration and to overall practice. This is especially true in the Theravada tradition centered in Southeast Asia.

And when musical instruments such as bells, drums, and horns are used—especially among the Mahayana Buddhists in Tibet, China, Korea, Vietnam and Japan—they are primarily for enhancing the quality of the rituals and not meant as entertainment. For example, drums are used to signify the beginning of a daily service, and bells are rung at the beginning and the end of sutra chanting. Other percussion instruments, such as the wooden gong, are struck for purposes of keeping the rhythm of sutra chanting. Variations depend on the practices of respective denominations.

Now I am going to show you an example of how a bell is used to signal the start and the end of chanting.

(Demonstration by Ken Tanaka: Chanting in the Jodo Shinshu Buddhist tradition. The bell is hit twice at the beginning of a sutra chanting. Then the bell is struck three times at the end.)

When Buddhism arrived in North America, songs were composed and written in keeping with the modern Western style. The lay people accustomed to the religious practices in North America expected and wanted songs to be part of religious services. Particularly in the Jodo Shinshu temples of the Japanese Pure Land tradition, children at *Sunday School or Dharma School* enjoyed singing songs, referred to as *gathas*. Gatha is an Americanized pronunciation of the Sanskrit word *gātha*, meaning poetic verses.

These gathas form an important and enjoyable part of the services for the children at Dharma schools on Sundays. As is well known, songs sung together have the power to bring the group together. And these *gathas* have played a vital role in helping to create harmony among the temple members as encouraged in today's opening passage:

> *To make a Buddhist community complete, there must be perfect harmony among the members. The teachers teach the members, and the members honor the teachers so that there can be harmony between them.*

Today's Songs

Today, we would like to present to you three songs. All three pieces were composed by *Jane Imamura* with lyrics by *Kimi Hisatsune*. Both are daughters of priests and have devoted their lives to the promotion of Dharma in North America, particularly in the area of Buddhist music. The three songs have provided comfort and inspiration for many children for decades and continue to do so today.

The high school music group called *Samurai River* will perform the songs. We have Brian Hettrick on drums, Kenta Shimizu on base, Gino Melillo on guitar and Nathan Nishikawa also on guitar. Serena Nishikawa will join in to recite the middle four verses.

The first song, entitled "Long Ago in India," captures some of the major events from the first half of the Buddha's life.

Okay, take it away, guys.

"Long Ago in India"

1) *Long ago in India, a little babe was born. And all around were pretty flowers to greet the glorious morn.*

2) *Far away in India, this babe began to grow. And all around were happy sights, so pain he did not know.*

3) *Long ago in India, he studied hard from all. He learned so well he soon became the greatest Prince of all.*

4) *Far away in India, the Prince went out to see the city and its habitants. And felt deep sympathy.*

5) *Long ago in India, the prince decided to go. And seek the way to save us all from pain of birth and death.*

6) *Far away in India, the Prince had found the truth. And now he's Buddha wise and kind, who shows the way to peace.*

(2 minutes)

How did you like it? I hope you enjoyed it. I personally like the melody but also the phrases "Long ago in India" and "Far away in India"; they both convey a sense of great distance in time and space, but ironically the Buddha also feels very close to home. He is far yet near. Further, the prince conveys a deep sense of caring for humanity as well as living creatures, for he embarked on his search, as the song says, "to save *us* all from pain."

The second song to be performed is called "It's Raining" and is often sung on a rainy or overcast Sunday.

"It's Raining"

It's raining and raining outside today, But it's so nice inside. The ground is too wet for us to play, but indoors we keep very warm. Keep very warm, keep very warm, keep very warm. We can keep very warm.

People may trick us and be very mean, but we must keep in mind. To Buddha's great love we can always lean. And so keep our hearts very warm. Keep very warm, keep very warm, keep very warm. Keep our hearts very warm.

(1:30)

Despite the threatening weather outside, this song reinforces the sense of well-being of going to and being in the temple. In the temple where the Buddha and the Dharma dwell, the children are protected and can maintain their hope and vitality.

The third and the last song is appropriately called "Farewell." The song is sung at the end of the service as children bid farewell, with the hope of seeing each other again the following Sunday, in the "presence" of the Buddha.

"Farewell"

Dharma School is over for another day, Let us gather around the shrine, bow our heads and say, Thank you, teacher, for your help, Thank you, every one, Buddha's love will keep us safe, 'till our work is done.

So we'll meet again next week, won't you take good care? Let us try to do what's right, always kind and fair, We shall spread the happiness faith in Buddha brings, Now it's time to say good bye, till we meet again.

Namu Amida Butsu sing this fine refrain, Namu Amida Butsu, sunny day or rain, Namu Amida Butsu, strong in faith remain, Namu Amida Butsu, till we meet again.

(1:30)

As we bid *you* farewell here, we hope that you enjoyed the songs and got a glimpse into a slice of contemporary American Buddhist songs for children.

In our next show, we shall return to the ongoing topic of the Fourth Mark of Existence, Nirvana is Tranquil and Peaceful, with a focus on the theme of "seeing things as they truly are." Please join us.

PROGRAM 35

Fourth Mark of Existence: Seeing Things as They Truly Are

An arrow-maker tries to make his arrows straight; so a wise man tries to keep his mind straight.

(The Teaching of Buddha, p. 364)

Hi, how are you doing? Today, we want to pursue another dimension of the Fourth Mark of Existence, "*Nirvana is Tranquil and Peaceful*" or "*Life can be Great.*" And *that* dimension is the quality of "*seeing things as they truly are*" and not "*how I want to see things.*"

The Crooked Tree

I like to demonstrate this point with a riddle of sorts. Here you see a model of a crooked tree. (A piece of bent wire coat hanger.) Well, in any case, please pretend that this is a crooked tree. I would now like you to concentrate on it, so that you will "*see the tree straight.*" Please go ahead.

Okay, unfortunately our time is limited, so that at this time I'd like to ask, "how many of you saw the tree straight?" When I do this with school children, including those from junior high school, there are always some who enthusiastically raise their hands, claiming, "Yeah, the tree trunk got straight; it wasn't crooked any more."

Well, I praise them for sharing their views with the class, but I then have to tell them that their answers are wrong. Of course, it is possible that they actually saw the tree trunk straighten out, but that is not the aim of Buddhism. The aim is not to perform some miraculous feat by making the tree trunk become straight.

Instead, the aim in Buddhism is to *see the crooked tree as a **crooked tree**!* That's what I meant by "Seeing the tree straight." And this is an example of "seeing things as they truly are," and not "how I want to see things." It is exactly the message being encouraged in today's opening passage:

An arrow-maker tries to make his arrows straight; so a wise man tries to keep his mind straight.

In another words, a fully awakened person would see things as they truly are, while others are in the habit of seeing how *they* want to see things.

My Child and the Blanket

As an example of the latter, the misguided habit of seeing things in a self-centered way, let me share an episode from my life that's left a deep impression on me even though it happened over ten years ago.

One day as I returned home from work totally exhausted from a demanding day, I slumped down flat on my back on the living room couch. Lying comfortably, almost asleep, I felt a tug on my left sleeve and murmuring voice, calling, "Daddy, Daddy." It was my two-year-old son, Nathan.

I said to myself, "Oh no, he wants to wrestle with me again. I am in no shape, mentally or physically, to wrestle with him. Doesn't he see how tired I am? I guess not, and explaining to him won't help." So, I pretended to be asleep.

But my son continued to tug at my sleeve, calling, "Daddy, Daddy!" I became more irritated and began conjuring up all kinds of unkind thoughts about my two-year-old, saying to myself, "All he thinks about is *himself*. Doesn't he understand I'm sleeping? His stubbornness in not giving up in bothering me must come from my wife's side!"

But he kept tugging, "Daddy, Daddy." Finally, totally frustrated, I opened my eyes ready to scold him.

But as I opened my eyes, what I saw completely surprised and caught me totally off guard. Well, there stood my two-year-old *holding a blanket in his left hand*, and I realized that all that time he was trying to call my attention to the fact that he had brought a blanket for *me*. He wanted me to wake up to put the blanket on myself.

He had dragged the blanket all the way from my bedroom by himself. And his mother and I had never even taught him to do this. He did it completely on his own. I felt about two inches tall.

Even today I still recall the negative thoughts *I* had harbored about my two-year-old son with a sense of shame and embarrassment. At the same time, I could not but be amazed by my son's caring act, despite my self-centered thoughts. I felt so grateful and lucky. This was clearly a case of "seeing how I wanted to see things," and a complete failure "to see things as they truly are."

Have you had any similar experience? If you have, I am sure you can sympathize and understand the feeling that you get after realizing that you had completely missed the boat, as you say to yourself, "How could I have been so off base?!"

Well, an awakened person would have little or no such projections and be able to experience things as they truly are.

Piling On

The Buddhist teaching has long regarded the cause for the failure to see things as they truly are to lie in our act of *"imposing" or "piling on"* (adhyāropa in Sanskrit). Perhaps, "projection"—a psychological term—captures a similar meaning.

Let me use the more casual of the terms, "piling on," for now. When we experience things in our daily lives, we are aware of the stimuli from the outside world through the five senses of seeing, hearing, smelling, tasting and touching. From a Buddhist perspective, we then feel them as pleasant, unpleasant or neutral. We also interpret or try to make conceptual sense, followed by our volition or response to the stimuli.

The less awakened we are, we tend to over-interpret or pile on more of our own thoughts onto what we are sensing. Instead of allowing the stimuli from the senses to filter directly in, our likes and dislikes are piled on through our thoughts and feelings. So we don't see how things truly are but more as how I want to see things.

Stereotypes as Piling On

This act of "piling on" describes the mechanism of our stereotypes that we hold about people who are different from us. That difference can be in terms of race, ethnicity, gender, religion, sexual orientation or class.

If a person is a member of a particular race, an awakened person would not "pile on" any stereotypical descriptions about that race and, instead, would see any person as a human being first and foremost. Unfortunately, as all of us know too well, many of these stereotypes tend to be quite negative and demeaning. For example, they can be expressed by such adjectives as lazy, shrewd, smelly, sneaky, bossy, talkative and clannish.

Those who are prone to stereotyping people take these descriptions and *automatically pile them (labels) on* to a member of a particular race. These so-called "labels" cover over the person, so that they fail to see that person as he or she truly is.

On the other hand, awakened people would not participate in such stereotyping. They know about these stereotypes, but they would not pile them on or make automatic association.

I believe it's important to keep in mind that we live in a society where such stereotypes abound; none of us are immune from knowing about them and sometimes even coming to believe they are true. It's very easy to fall into the trap of "piling on." So, we must constantly be on our guard against automatically imposing these demeaning characteristics onto any person.

Mental Awareness and Cultivation

I believe that the Buddhist practice of mental cultivation can make a valuable contribution toward helping people not to automatically pile on stereotypes. With more calm and space in their hearts and mind through awareness and cultivation, people would be better able to catch themselves from falling into the trap of "piling on."

There is nothing new about my message to combat stereotypes and discrimination. However, Buddhism is especially strong in helping us to see how these stereotypes are fictions of our imagination. They are merely a notion, or are constructs and, therefore, are not real!

Buddhist awareness and cultivation further clarify for us the mental mechanism of how stereotyping occurs, and also offer practical ways to minimize and prevent us from making stereotypes. Ideals are important, but they must be translated into practical results in the real world. For this, each person must make a concerted effort.

Beyond these personal efforts, we must further work *to improve society as a whole*, for social systems have much to do with how people see and relate to each other. Extreme inequity and excessive competition create conditions for promoting greater stereotyping and discrimination. Such social conditions must be minimized as much as possible. And as we know, change does not happen automatically.

Crooked Tree

Remember the crooked tree mentioned at the top of today's show? Piling on or discriminating against people is like those who try to make the crooked tree become straight. They want to see the tree in accordance from their own self-centered perspective. To the contrary, if they are able to see others for who they truly are, then it would be like seeing the *crooked tree as a crooked tree*, as described in today's opening passage:

> An arrow-maker tries to make his arrows straight; so a wise man
> tries to keep his mind straight.

In our next show, we take a closer look at the inspirational utterances of awakened people, which include those of the Buddha and his disciples. We look forward to you joining us then. Have a great week.

PROGRAM 36
Utterances of the Awakened

*To live a single day and hear a good teaching is better than to live
a hundred years without knowing such teaching.*

(The Teaching of Buddha, p. 370)

Utterances of Awakening

Hello. I hope your week went well and that you are having a good day.

As part of our continuous learning, let's explore and listen to the utterances of awakened people. Such utterances go to the heart of awakening, the topic we have been exploring during the past several shows, and are perceived to be the most direct and purest expression of awakening.

The Buddha's Utterances

Let's begin with those of the Buddha himself.

We have invited Mr. Bholanath Ghosh to recite the passage for us. Mr. Ghosh teaches comparative religions in high school, and his family roots are in India, where the Buddha attained awakening some 2,500 years ago.

> *I have conquered and I know all,*
> *I am enlightened quite by myself and have none as teacher.*
> *There is no one that is the same as I in the whole world*
> *where there are many deities.*
> *I am the one who is of real worth,*
> *I am the most supreme teacher.*
> *I am the only one who is fully enlightened.*
> *I am tranquil.*
> *I am now in Nirvana.*

This set of utterances probably requires an explanation, for it can be misconstrued as being a bit self-centered and egotistical. However, these words are meant to convey the unique and transcendent nature of the Buddha's awakening. For example, the Buddha realized awakening without a teacher to guide him, one of the hallmarks of his accomplishments. Also, the Buddha claims that his awakening experience is of a different order from that of the established religions of his time where gods abound. Rather than worshipping deities, the Buddha's awakening involved inner transformation.

The next set of utterances provides us with a basis for a deeper understanding of the nature of the Buddha's awakening. Though its full meaning is beyond the comprehension of the ordinary mind, it provides us with a glimpse into the nature of awakening and a firm direction for our spiritual quest.

> *Looking for the builder of this house*
> *Through the rounds of many births,*
> *It was to no avail, and wearisome is birth again and again.*
> *But now, I have seen you, the maker of the house.*
> *You shall not build this house again.*
> *All the rafters are broken,*
> *Thy ridge-pole is shattered;*
> *The mind released from its binding conditions,*
> *Has attained to the extinction of all ego-centric desires.*
>
> *(Suzuki 44)*

This is not easy to comprehend. As for "the builder of this house," "the builder" is a metaphor for the "ego" (ātman), and the "house" refers to one's fears, worries and all the negative thoughts and feelings. A "house" normally carries a positive image, but in this context, it is seen as a source of worries and anxieties of paying for it, maintaining it and protecting it. An owner becomes burdened by it. Moreover, from the Indian cosmological worldview, the ego is the cause for one's transmigration thorough the endless cycle of birth and death, which is undesirable.

However, the Buddha has now come face to face with this ego and has conquered it, so that "he will not build this house again." Both the ego and the undesirable conditions have been eliminated, allowing for the person's mind to be free from the bondage, both mentally and spiritually.

Women Disciples

At this time, I would like to turn our attention to the utterances by the Buddha's women disciples, as found in a canonical text called, *The Psalms of the Sisters*. All three of the women become Arhats or those who attain the highest level of awakening.

To recite their words, we have asked Ms. Serena Nishikawa, who is one of Mr. Ghosh's students and a Buddhist herself.

The first of the women disciples is Mutta, a daughter of a poor family of Brahmins—a member of a Hindu priestly cast—who was sent to marry a hunchbacked Brahmin. However, Mutta felt she could not continue her life as it was and was given permission to become a nun. After much practice, she realized joyous awakening:

> *O free, indeed! O gloriously free*
> *Am I in freedom from three crooked things:*
> *From mill, from mortar, from my crookbacked lord!*
> *Ay, but I'm free from rebirth and from death,*
> *And all that dragged me back is hurled way.*

She speaks of her freedom from mundane restrictions, including the daily household chores as represented by the word "mortar," and from her marriage to a "crookbacked lord." However, she is most elated and proud of her spiritual attainment of being released from "all that [which] dragged me back."

The second of the female disciples is Mettika, an elderly nun. She climbed the famed Vulture's Peak to carry out her practice, where the Buddha had delivered many of his sermons. Despite the hardship of the climb in her old age, Mettika reflects upon her accomplishments with joy:

> *Though I be suffering and weak,*
> *and all my youthful spring be gone,*
> *Yet have I come, leaning upon my staff,*
> *and climb aloft the mountain peak.*
> *My cloak thrown off,*
> *My little bowl overturned,*
> *So I sit here upon the rock.*
>   *And over my spirit sweeps*

Now my heart is set free.
I win, I win.
The Triple Lore! The Buddha's will is done!

The third person is Queen Ubbiri, who had suffered a loss of her child. Devastated by the loss of her daughter, Jiva, the queen went to the cemetery every day to mourn for the child. Seeing her in extreme pain, the Buddha approaches her to reminds her that there are 84,000 daughters like Jiva cremated at the cemetery. He then utters the following words to her:

O Ubbiri, who wails in the wood,
Crying "O Jiva! O my daughter dear!"
Come to yourself! Lo, in this burying-ground
Are burnt full many a thousand daughters dear,
And all of them were named like her.
Now for which of all those Jivas do you mourn?

Awakened to her senses and stirred by the truth of the teachings given by the Buddha, Ubbiri soon reaches the highest level of awakening. And she accomplishes this as a lay woman, and there is no mention that she ever becomes a nun. She speaks in delight:

Lo! From my heart the hidden shaft is gone!
The shaft that nestled there has been removed.
And that consuming grief for my dead child
Which poisoned all the life of me is dead.

Today my heart is healed, my yearning stayed,
And all within is purity and peace.
Lo! I go for refuge to the Buddha—the only wise,
the Dharma and the Sangha.

The case of Ubbiri is instructive, for one does not have to become a nun or a monk to realize awakening. Awakening is equally accessible to all.

I hope these recitations have given you a better understanding and appreciation of Buddha's awakening. As the meanings of some of the utterances were unclear, as perhaps they should to us ordinary beings, I would like to cite a description by Venerable Walpola

Rahula, a Thervadin monk from Sri Lanka, from his well-known book, *What the Buddha Taught*. I have taken the liberty of changing the gender in the first paragraph to allow for equal representation of a female voice.

> *She who has realized the Truth, Nirvana, is the happiest being in the world. She is free from all "complexes" and obsessions, the worries and troubles that torment others. Her mental health is perfect. She does not repent the past, nor does she brood over the future. She lives fully in the present. Therefore she appreciates and enjoys things in the purest sense without self-projections. She is joyful, exultant, enjoying the pure life, her faculties pleased, free from anxiety, serene and peaceful.*

> *As he is free from selfish desire, hatred, ignorance, conceit, pride, and all such 'defilements,' he is pure and gentle, full of universal love, compassion, kindness, sympathy, understanding and tolerance. His service to others is the purest, for he has no thought of self. He gains nothing, accumulates nothing, not even anything spiritual, because he is free from the illusion of 'self,' and the 'thirst' for becoming.*

> (*Rahula*, p. 43)

Please join us again next week, when we look at more ways in which we can make awakening become part of our everyday lives. We'll see you then.

PROGRAM 37

Fourth Mark of Existence:
Awaken to Everyday Compassion

*And just like a soft breeze and a few blossoms on a branch that tell
the coming of spring, so when a person attains awakening, grass,
trees, mountains, rivers and all other things begin to throb with
new life.*

(*The Teaching of Buddha,* p. 464)

Hello. I hope that we would find you well and in good spirits.

Awaken to Everyday Compassion

Today, we like to explore another dimension of the Fourth Mark
of Existence, which refers to the state of Buddhist spiritual awakening or enlightenment. This state often refers to the ultimate state that
the Buddha experienced under the Bodhi tree at the age of thirty-five,
but it can also refer to the lower levels of awakening that any of us
can realize today.

And as the degree of awakening deepens, we inevitably come to
experience more and more of what I call, *"everyday compassion."* So,
in today's show, I would like to encourage all of us to awaken our
minds to the everyday compassion that embraces our lives.

Let me now elaborate on what I mean by "everyday compassion."
We can find it, for example, in our daily feelings of awe and gratitude
for the *life-giving forces* that produce, nurture, and sustain our lives,
whether we are aware of them or not. They include, for example, the
DNA molecules, the sunshine, the rain, and the oxygen in the air we
breathe. Then, there are the innumerable plants and animals we have
partaken and will continue to consume to sustain our bodies.

Everyday compassion also includes the *inspirations* that we derive from listening to a truly beautiful piece of music, or seeing an
impressive artistic work, or being part of an unforgettable athletic
performance. For me, I continue to be moved by many of the Beatles
songs, and I shall always remember the 1981 football championship

and the miracle touchdown pass thrown by the San Francisco 49ers quarterback Joe Montana to beat the Dallas Cowboys.

The *deep bonds* that we have with our families and true friends are painfully precious. For many of us with small children, the angelic look on their faces when they are sleeping never fails to make us smile. Our smiles show the joy, pride, and gratitude we feel, because they make up part of the everyday compassion that we experience in our lives

Aesthetic Appreciation of Nature

For me personally, I also find compassion in the beauty and greatness of nature. Nowhere is this fulfilling sense of everyday compassion felt more intensely than during my three-mile walks to or from work. The beauty of the blooming *garden flowers* of all shapes and colors enlivens my spirit. These flowers cheer me on even during times of personal disappointment.

They are joined by the chirping of the *birds*, whose exquisite songs I enjoy and relish as much as I can. Once a *baby squirrel* came out onto the sidewalk, lured by the rattling of my keys, and even perched on my shoes looking for food or, perhaps, its mother.

And most of all, the *trees* are the constant source of my inspiration. The majesty of their silence is combined with their leaves that reach out by providing the source of life, the very air that we breathe. When the cool soothing breeze makes the leaves dance, flutter and shimmer in their shades of green, I experience a sense of inexpressible "oneness"!

Unfortunately, my experiences of everyday compassion are far from being as complete or as frequent as I wish. However, they provide me with a glimpse into what a fully awakened person would experience far more deeply and frequently, as expressed in today's opening passage:

> And just like a soft breeze and a few blossoms on a branch that tell the coming of spring, so when a person attains awakening, grass, trees, mountains, rivers and all other things begin to **throb** with new life.

Everyday Compassion and Awakening

I really like the expression, *"throb with new life."* I think it's true that when a person's awakening deepens, his or her life becomes more imbued with everyday compassion in its various manifestations.

To use an analogy, the initial stage of awakening is like turning on the radio switch, and the everyday compassion is like the radio waves. [*awakening = turning on the radio switch; everyday compassion = radio waves*] Unless we turn on the switch we can't encounter the existence of the radio waves.

And yet, turning on the switch alone will not be enough. So, we need to *turn up the volume.* The more we turn it up, the more we can hear, just as the more our awakening deepens, the more we become aware of the everyday compassion in our lives.

Our Shortcomings

As our awareness of everyday compassion deepens, our recognition of our shortcomings also deepens. In other words, *the greater the compassion, the greater the shortcomings!*

These two seem contradictory, but they actually make up a set, like a sunlight and shade. Imagine sunlight upon a tree. The shade will inevitably fall on the tree. Thus, this light represents the everyday compassion, and the shade represents the shortcomings that we come to realize.

As our awareness of everyday compassion deepens, we feel a profound gratitude to other people, creatures and things that sustain us. And we regret that we had not realized such things earlier in a more intense way. Quite simply, our shortcomings become much more easy to see.

This is especially true about non-human creatures that are sacrificed on our behalf. One poignant example comes to us from a modern Japanese woman poet by the name of *Misuzu Kaneko (1903-1930),* who was strongly influenced by Buddhism. This particular poem is entitled "A Great Catch," in which she describes the boats returning to a fishing village with huge catches. People rush to the harbor to welcome back the boats with joy and excitement, but Ms. Kaneko is aware of their shortcomings. Let's hear what she has to say:

A Great Catch

At dawn with the sky filled
with bright sunrise colors.
It's a large catch!
Truly a large catch of giant sardines!
The harbor is like a festival.
But in the ocean, I wonder
How many sardine funerals
are taking place?

She is painfully aware of the lost lives of the fish. Kaneko sees the fish as she would a human family. Here, it's important to note that she sees herself equally at fault, although as a member of the fishing village she, too, is pleased to some degree with the huge catch. She also finds herself in a dilemma, but what makes her different from others is her awareness of her shortcomings, in other words, the human need to rely on other lives and our failure to fully acknowledge that fact.

Quirks as a Shortcoming:

Let me conclude today's topic on somewhat of a lighter note. This sense of shortcoming is of a different order from the sense of guilt that can be imposed from above by religious hierarchy. Instead, it's an integral part of one's personal awakening.

In most cases, it is tinged with an ability to laugh at one's own limitations. The people that I have known as being awakened are not paragons of perfection. In fact they are quite ordinary in many ways and are able to accept and laugh at their own imperfections, for example, their *quirks* or unusual habits.

Once in a Sunday discussion group at the temple, some members and I shared our own quirks. One person talked about her quirky habit about *cookies and milk*; she has to make sure that when she is done eating the cookie, she needs to have the milk finished at the *same time*. It bugs her to no end, if there is milk still left when she is done with her cookie, or vice versa. So she carefully measures how much milk she drinks and how much of the cookie she eats.

Another person's quirk had to do with *filling up the gas* in his car. In his case, he is compelled to make sure the meter ends up with an *even* number. So, it bothers him if the meter ends at $19.59. If this happens, he will try to pump in more gas so he can get to an even amount.

By now you might be saying to yourself, people are certainly weird and quirky... but *I am* definitely not that way. Well, let's not jump to conclusions, [for] even I have found myself to be wrong.

I was once telling my wife that a friend of ours had a quirky habit of having to keep making *mounds of his fried rice* with his spoon as he ate. As he took a bite or two of the fried rice, he would make the mound again. I was chuckling as I talked about this quirky habit to my wife. Then, she then smiled and said, "*You* do that, too."

I first objected, "That's not true. I don't do that!" Then as I thought about it more, I had to admit that I, *probably*, did that as well. So, it *is* difficult to see yourself objectively, especially at your own shortcomings and quirks!

However, we must remember that we are able to admit to our shortcomings, *precisely* because we are aware of our everyday compassion. Again, there is shade because there is sunlight. So, the two go together to make up a vital element of an awakened person.

As I close today, I hope what I have talked about encourages you to open up your mind to our shortcomings and to the everyday compassion that embraces our lives.

Join us for our next show when one of the foremost experts on the study of Zen Buddhism in Asia and North America will join us.

PROGRAM 38
American Zen Buddhists

Just as rain falls on all vegetation, so Buddha's compassion extends equally to all people.

Just as different plants receive particular benefits from the same rain, so people of different natures and circumstances are blessed in different ways.

(The Teaching of Buddha, p. 40)

Hello. It's truly a pleasure and an honor for us to be able to share our message with you. From a Buddhist standpoint, it's a miracle to be born a human, let alone be able to communicate, albeit through an electronic medium.

To illustrate this point there is a well-known Buddhist parable that goes as follows. There lived a sea turtle in the vast ocean. A piece of wood with a round hole, of about a foot in diameter, was thrown in the ocean. The turtle living in the depth of the sea only comes up to the surface every 1,000 years. And the chance of that turtle coming up to the surface and sticking his head through that hole is the same as that of us being born a human being!

Well, speaking of miracles, we are fortunate to have as our guest a person, whose work keeps him constantly on the go between North America and Asia. Dr. John McRae is a professor of Buddhist Studies at Indiana University, where his primary area of specialization is *Chinese Chan and Japanese Zen* ("Zen" is the Japanese pronunciation of the Chinese original "Chan"), but his recent interests have included a study of American Buddhism, particularly of Zen Buddhism.

In any case, we thought we would take this opportunity to have him share his thoughts on Buddhism in America with a focus on Zen.

KT: Well, John, thanks for coming on our show. I appreciate you being here.

Prof. McRae: I am very happy to be here.

KT: My first question has to do with the *state of Buddhism in America*. What's going on? How do you assess the situation as far as

Buddhism [is concerned]?

Prof. McRae: I think Buddhism is growing pretty well in the United States, perhaps not as rapidly as Islam, for example. I think that Islam benefits from much more organized efforts to propagate religion, whereas Buddhism in the United States is growing up from the grassroots and from, how do we say, from the energy internal to American culture.

KT: Good, so it's growing. How is it when we compared this situation with the one when we were back in our college days? I know we were on the same Stanford [University] campus in the late '60s. I don't recall seeing too much Buddhist presence then.

Prof. McRae: Yeah, but there was around that time, a kind of Zen boom for example. Maybe that was right about at the beginning. I know that you and I graduated … in '63 or '64, I guess.

KT: No, that early? I think it's a little later.

Prof. McRae: No, that's high school. Yes, my memory is fading these days. I actually graduated in '69. I was giving you high school years.

KT: That makes sense. Okay.

Prof. McRae: But around that time Zen started really taking off in the United States. Other forms of Buddhism … I mean, at that point, there was Buddhism and there was Zen. And people thought of them being as quite separate things actually. (*Buddhism separate from Zen*)

KT: Zen as being not even Buddhist sometimes.

Prof. McRae: In a way, yes. And there was a famous book, *Three Ways of Eastern Wisdom* or something, that was Hinduism, Buddhism and Zen.

KT: I see. So, it's been said that those who convert to Buddhism in America become members of *four* schools: Zen, Tibetan, Theravada or Vipassana and Sokagakkai. So, how is Zen Buddhism doing in relation to the other three? (*Zen Buddhism coverts vs. other schools*)

Prof. McRae: I think now Tibetan Buddhism is getting most of the media attention. And there are good reasons for that. The Dalai Lama is a very very impressive figure, and the story of Tibet is compelling. But Zen Buddhism is *expanding at kind of a grassroots level*. And there are practice centers in many many cities and smaller towns. So,

I think Zen is not in its boom years that it once was, but it's growing and maturing very nicely.

KT: I see. Recent shows dealt with awakening. I know you've done some studies on American Zen Buddhists. And so, I'm wondering, how do Zen Buddhists *conceptualize awakening* or think of awakening?

Prof. McRae: Oh, interesting question … because Zen gives people something to do. I mean there is a practice. But what I did was … I've gone to about a dozen American Soto Zen centers, and I talked to students. I talked to teachers also, but I interviewed the students. Within the Dogen tradition of Soto Zen, there is a real … almost prohibition and *self-prohibition against thinking about, talking about awakening*.

KT: Really? That's ironic.

Prof. McRae: It is ironic. It is ironic. So they sit. These are people who are captivated by *zazen* (sitting meditation). They can't always say why they do it, but it's become central to their lives. But there're some questions they won't answer. "What is the nature of awakening" is one of those questions.

KT: So, they are more interested in zazen or sitting meditation than thinking about what is the ultimate goal of Buddhism.

Prof. McRae: For example, this is not exactly what you asked me, but I would ask them, "how does Zen fit in to the rest of your religious life?" and "do you still believe in God, a Christian God some way?" because many of these people were Christians, former Christians or Jews. Or "what happens to you after you die?" which is a big issue for all of us, I think. And mostly they would say, "Gee, I don't know. Ask me after I die." So, they were kind of consciously putting off making decisions in a way that I think of it as "articulate reticence."

KT: Articulate reticence?

Prof. McRae: They're very well spoken, very well educated, but there're certain issues they're just not going to take a stand on. And I think even "awakening" is one of those issues.

KT: Well, you hear a lot about the emphasis on *"living in the moment"* and "in the present." Do you find that kind of talk in your study?

Prof. McRae: Well, in this particular study with this group of re-spondents, I was stunned that it almost never came up. I was stunned because that rhetoric of living in the now or applying Zen in one's daily life [is so prevalent, but] it didn't come out that much.

KT: But you find it a lot in Zen literature and in the culture, so to speak. Anyway, can I move on to asking you a question regard-ing comparing *American Zen experience with contemporary Japanese Zen Buddhists* and how they think about awakening and practice?

Prof. McRae: I think that what's unique in the American situation is that these are *lay people who are creating communities together*.

KT: Yes, that's important: lay people and communal.

Prof. McRae: Exactly.

KT: That's interesting.

Prof. McRae: Exactly. I know Zen people who do Zen practice in Japan. I know both priests and lay people there. But it seems that you go to a temple and go to *zazen-kai* (sitting meditation sessions) and practice.

KT: They are usually priests and have been a part of a long tradi-tion with temples and all of that. If I can move a little bit further to China and maybe back a few centuries. I know you are one of the foremost scholars on Chinese Chan and Buddhism. How would you see American Zen within that context? (*American Zen Buddhism vs. classical Chinese Chan Buddhism*)

Prof. McRae: There is a common point, at least. I think there are probably a lot of differences, but the common point is that some as-pects of Zen were designed in China for people who think too much; people who think too much or study too much, who are overedu-cated. So, it's [a teaching that encourages one to] kind of let go of that nonsense. In a way that was very attractive to a lot of American Zen Buddhists. So putting down those cares and worries and so forth is a strong element in Zen.

KT: Do you think Americans are messing things up? I mean, [in terms of] how they are taking Buddhism?

Prof. McRae: Well, no doubt yes in many many ways. No doubt. But there is one similarity that always strikes me. We think of the American culture as an instant, kind of McDonald's [way of] use it and throw it away. But in 8th century China where Zen really took off, there was a Zen boom in the Chinese capital, the largest city in the world, at that time with population of a million. And the whole emphasis was on, *"Do it now."* Buddhism is not something for way off many life times in the future. This is a rare opportunity to be a human. Grab that opportunity and *get enlightened now.*

KT: And that's similar to American culture?

Prof. McRae: I think there is a similarity. Buddhism or Zen practice is not something you should do in the future or for the future. Do it in the now. Do it for the now.

KT: Well, looks like we are out of time. I appreciate you taking the time to visit us and sharing your thoughts with us. I appreciate it very much.

Prof. McRae: Thank you very much. I appreciate being able to be here.

As we sign off, we've learned that the American experience about awakening differs to some extent from the other parts of the world as we saw in today's opening passage.

> *Just as rain falls on all vegetation, so Buddha's compassion extends equally to all people.*
> *Just as different plants receive particular benefits from the same rain, so people of different natures and circumstances are blessed in different ways.*

In our next show, we will discuss the idea of "Thinking BIIG" and "Not Thinking SMAL," as we conclude the topic of the Four Marks of Existence.

PROGRAM 39

Four Marks of Existence:
"Think BIIG, Don't Think SMAL"

If a man's mind becomes pure, his surroundings will also become pure.

(The Teaching of Buddha, p. 464)

I hope that your past week went well and that you are physically, mentally and spiritually sound. If not, I hope today's program will help you to get you back on track.

"Think BIIG, Don't Think SMAL"

In my previous talk, I concluded our discussion of the fourth of the Four Marks of Existence. What I would like to do today is to address all four of the Four Marks of Existence as a whole to present an outlook that is more in keeping with Buddhist awakening.

As we do so, I would like to once again summarize the Four Marks of Existence. They are *Life is a Bumpy road*, *Life is Interdependent*, *Life is Impermanent* and *Life can be Great*. By taking the first letters of Bumpy, Interdependent, Impermanent and Great, we get "*BIIG*." So, to remember the four, please "*Think BIIG!*"

Oh, and it gets better. Now, the opposite of Thinking BIIG, or the incorrect way to see things is as follows: *Life is Smooth* as opposed to Life is a Bumpy Road, *Life is Mine* as opposed to Life is Interdependent, *Life is Always the Same* as opposed to Life is Impermanent, and *Life is Lousy* as opposed to Life can be Great. And if we take the first letters of Smooth, Mine, Always and Lousy, we get *SMAL*. So, to remember the incorrect four, please "Don't think SMAL!" And put together, "*Think BIIG and don't think SMAL!*"

Pretty clever, huh? Remember that I have a patent out on these phrases, so please don't use them without permission … Just kidding, of course. I would be happy if these light-hearted phrases can help you to remember these basic truths when applying them to your daily lives.

Applying to Our Experiences

Speaking of applying them to our lives, let's see how "Thinking BIIG and not thinking SMAL" can assist us in dealing with difficulties in our lives. To make my point, I like to refer to the four characters from the best-selling book *Who Moved My Cheese?* by Dr. Spencer Johnson, which I talked about in a couple of earlier shows. In a faraway land, there lived two mice named *"Sniff" and "Scurry"* and two Little people named *"Hem" and "Haw,"* who were as small as mice but looked and acted a lot like people today. Each day they ran through a maze looking for cheese to nourish them and make them happy. One day, the four characters found a huge cheese near Cheese Station C. They were naturally overjoyed with the find. Their life was going very well until one day, when they arrived at Cheese Station C, the cheese had *disappeared completely*!

Well, the two groups responded in stark contrast to each other. The mice Sniff and Scurry responded in keeping with "BIIG," while the Little people Hem and Haw in accord with "SMAL." More specifically, when Hem and Haw found their cheese gone, they were completely unprepared. They screamed and yelled, "What! No cheese. It's not fair." For them, "it was not the way things were supposed to be." What they expected was for their lives to be *Smooth*.

On the other hand, the problem was simple for the two mice. They were not surprised that the cheese had disappeared, for they had noticed that it had been getting smaller every day. If you constantly consume something, eventually it will be gone. That's the way things are supposed to be. So for Sniff and Scurry, life was indeed a *Bumpy* road. Now, the two Little people were also deeply upset because they felt that the cheese was theirs. Hem, in particular, felt that way and insisted that the "cheese is *Mine*."

The mice made no such claims. They did not overanalyze things. They assumed nothing. They knew that the cheese which they had enjoyed was the result of numerous *Interdependent* causes and conditions, and that its disappearance, too, was due to the same principle. When the cheese disappeared, the Little people were caught totally off guard, for they had not been paying attention to the small changes taking place each day. They took for granted that the cheese would *Always* be there.

On the other hand, the mice weren't surprised, for they were prepared for the change and wasted no time in looking for the new cheese. Their actions corresponded with the outlook that all things are *Impermanent*.

Transformation

For Hem and Haw, the disappearance of the cheese brought them misery. They refused to accept the situation, and, instead, clung to the way things were. As they waited for the cheese to return, they became mentally and physically weary and exhausted. Their situation was simply *Lousy*.

On the other hand, the mice had *immediately* set out in search of a new cheese. It took them some time, but they did come upon a great supply of new cheese. They squealed with delight when they found what they were looking for, and it was the biggest store of cheese they had ever seen! So, for Sniff and Scurry, their situation was, indeed, *Great*.

The question for all of us is, "Which is the better way to go, thinking SMAL like the Little people or thinking BIIG like the mice?" Well, the answer is obvious, don't you think? So, we need be ready to make that transformation from SMAL to BIIG.

In Our Own Lives

However, we should keep in mind that it's easier to see all this in hindsight and for someone else's situation. When we are in the middle of *our own* situation, we can very easily fall into the trap of "thinking SMAL" and getting stuck there, like Hem and Haw.

Well, I know someone who was quite miserable for about half a year. He was in a graduate Ph.D. program that took on the average about 7 years. The studies of the program were not only very demanding, but even if he were to get the degree the prospects of finding an academic job were very bleak. This was made worse by the difficulties of finding an appropriate dissertation topic in the area that he had originally proposed.

In the meantime, he and his wife had a baby. However, because of their low income they could not afford to live anywhere but in the university housing, which had only showers but no bathtub to bathe the baby. His friends, on the other hand, with their lucrative incomes were purchasing their own homes, and some were even buying their second home.

He felt jealous of his friends and felt guilty for putting his family through the hardships. He even questioned the choices he had made to become a scholar. He knew that the graduate program was less than easy but expected things to go far more smoothly and quickly. But to the contrary, he was now approaching his mid-thirties but could not see the proverbial "light at the end of the tunnel." He felt miserable, and he was definitely "Thinking SMAL."

Then one day, he was able to begin to make the transformation, triggered by what his wife told him. She suggested that he switch his dissertation topic to one that he was really interested in; there was no need to be stuck on the original plan. Further, she reminded him of the reasons for aspiring to become a scholar, which was to become better trained to be more effective in his eventual work.

He had, instead, gotten too bogged down by his self-centered concerns and self-pity, and had lost the initial idealism that included the desire to serve others. Plus, his wife told him that she did not mind the low income, for she was braced for a rough economic ride as a spouse of a Ph.D. student and that he should not be comparing his situation with those of his friends with regular jobs.

The suggestion, the advice, and the reminder triggered a shift, in which he felt a big burden being unloaded. He then saw how he had boxed himself in with his rigid plans, narrow perspective and self-pity. He had lost sight of his original aspirations. He moved from the mode of Thinking SMAL to Thinking BIIG.

Yet undoubtedly we all do this from time to time. Therefore, we find ourselves straying away from our original intent or plans. I am sure that you, too, have had similar experiences in your own lives. None of us are exempt. Such is the nature of human beings. That's why we need religious teachings to help us turn away from Thinking SMAL. Also, we need a good friend or a teacher. In the case of the graduate student, it was his wife.

Well, I know this too well, for that graduate student was me. So, I learned firsthand the meaning of today's passage.

If a man's mind becomes pure, his surroundings will also become pure.

I am not sure how pure my mind became, but definitely my daily life became much more pleasant and meaningful. If you find yourself Thinking SMAL, instead, try to Think BIIG. We all have the capacity to exercise the power of the mind to make a huge difference for ourselves and for others. You owe it to yourself and to your loved ones.

In our next show, we plan to have a little fun as we share some Buddhist humor from the past and present. Till then, have a good week, and see you then.

PROGRAM 40
Humorous and Lighthearted Buddhist Stories

*The eternal Buddha always appears before people in the most
friendly forms and brings to them the wisest methods of relief.*
(*The Teaching of Buddha, p. 30*)

Hi. How are you doing today? We're glad you tuned in because
we are ready to have some fun.

Today, let's explore some of the *humorous and lighthearted* Buddhist
stories from the classical literature from Asia as well as the American
Buddhist experience. "Why?" you might ask. Well, humor is an effective method for conveying the teachings. Also, humor represents
a vital quality of awakened persons, who often reveal an air of levity
and joy.

To help us, Prof. John McRae of Indiana University is, once again,
here as our guest, and [we are] especially with a bit of good luck since
it turns out that he also has a personal interest in Buddhist humor.

KT: Well, John. Thank you for coming back to our show. And I
think we are going to have lots of fun.

Prof. McRae: I'm very glad to be back.

KT: We are talking about humor. And what does humor have to
do with Buddhism, and what does a Buddhist have to do with humor?

Prof. McRae: My first impression is that Buddhists are actually
cheery people. I've known Buddhist monks and nuns from lots of
countries, Taiwan and Southeast Asia. Buddhism might have the
reputation—I think it's unfounded—as a dour religion. Buddhists
are really very happy. I don't know, I think maybe celibacy may be
good for the disposition, don't you think?

KT: I don't know if I have a question on that one. But you may
be right, and you may be wrong. But... well ... in contemporary
American lore and discussions about Buddhism, especially about
Zen, there is one experience I wanted to share with you. Once I went
to pick up my son at his friend's place, and his mother came out,

and she was all sweaty and looking disheveled. So I asked what happened. She said, "I'm zenning out." I said, "What?" I had never heard that term, "zenning out." She said, "Well, I'm cleaning my house, clearing the shelves." So, that's how "Zen" is being brought into American culture and language. So, related to that, I understand that you once made a list of all the books with Zen in the titles. (*Book titles with Zen*) So, can you talk a little bit about that?

Prof. McRae: Zen is used in English to mean, to do things simply, to do things in a kind of unbroken state of concentration, and [being] aesthetically simple. So, your "zenning out" example fits perfectly within that. But as evidence of that, if you look for books with Zen in the titles, you have the old ones [such as], *Zen and the Art of Archery*, *Zen and the Art of Flower Arranging*, *Zen and the Art of Taming the Bull*. A lot of good books on Zen have that kind of title.

But then there are things like *Zen and the Art of Macintosh*, *Zen and the Art of Windsurfing*, *Zen and the Art of Tennis*, *Zen and the Art of Golf*, *Zen and the Art of Driving*. I mean you can go on and on. One that I always found strange was *Zen and the Art of Cubing*, and the subtitle is *In Search of the Seventh Side*. I thought that was quite mysterious. There is one author who wrote two very different books. One was on Zen and computers and the other on Zen and the art of sex. I hope they were different books!

KT: Did they sell?

Prof. McRae: I don't know.

KT: So, that's contemporary American Zen scene. How about in *classical Buddhist literature*? There must be some interesting stories or humorous, lighthearted stories.

Prof. McRae: Oh, there are. There are lots of them. For example, there is the story of a master, a Zen master, and his student who come up to a river, and there is a young lady trying to get across the river. But the current is too strong, [and she] doesn't know quite what to do. And the master just picks her up and puts her on his back and carries her across the river. And they all wade across that way. [At] the other side of the river, he put her down, and they walk on. And after a few minutes, the student asks his teacher "Well, wasn't that a violation of the Vinaya of the monastic regulations, you know [that of] touching a woman?" And the master says something to the effect, "Well, I put her down way back there. Why haven't you put her down yet?"

KT: So, what is the point of that story?

Prof. McRae: It has a serious implication, meaning to it. I mean there is nothing wrong with a beautiful woman. That's a personal *conviction* as well! You can imagine the student walking behind the teacher. And if he's (teacher) carrying her on his back, he's (student) examining with great interest her feet and the beauty of her personal being, and that's what the problem is. It's that he's aroused his own desire, and he can't let go of it. He's supposed to let go of things. If you have feelings, and there is nothing wrong with those feelings, but in Zen training and Buddhist training in general, the problem is *hanging on to them, getting stuck to,* [and] *getting ...*

KT: Attached?

Prof. McRae: ... *attached* to them. Exactly.

KT: Well, I have one. This one I heard from Rev. Mas Kodani, who's a minister in Los Angeles. And he told a story of ... a man hanging on a cliff. And as he's hanging there, the Buddha appears. So the man looks up and says with his last ounce of energy, "Oh Buddha, save me, save me." Then the Buddha says, "I will. ... Let go!"

Prof. McRae: ... Okay? So, he lets go or what?

KT: Well, he lets go and you think he fell down, but this is an illusion or delusion on the man's part. So, he thought he was hanging vertically on a cliff, but actually the Buddha knows that he is lying horizontally, and so that all that fear of falling off or falling down was just an illusion. And, so, what the Buddha is trying to say is that that's how we are. We suffer because we think ... we have illusions or delusions but life is impermanent, but people want to cling on to things. And, so, by clinging on to and fighting change, you're struggling. You know, *life is change and you let go* and you flow. That's the point of the story. I think it's pretty good.

Prof. McRae: So, in both of these stories, Buddhism is saying, "Let go," and the humor is situations where we have to find, "*how* to let go."

KT: That's true. Yes. So, we've been talking about humorous stories from the classical period. So, how about some from the contemporary American scene? And I have one … Why did the Buddha buy a happy meal?

Prof. McRae: I don't know why.

KT: Because he realized that life is suffering.

Prof. McRae: Okay. Okay, now there is a genre of jokes where you have a guy with a long beard and in ragged clothes, and he is carrying a sign saying, "Jesus is coming." And you see all kinds of ones like this, but I saw one where behind the guy with a placard saying "Jesus is coming," there's probably a Chinese or Japanese looking guy with a sign saying, "Buddha here now!"

KT: The "NOW" one! I have heard this other one, that is not specifically Buddhist, but there is a Buddhist in it. He plays a minor role. But anyway, here are three guys fishing in the middle of huge lake, and all of sudden the boat capsizes. They don't know how to swim, and it's just too far [to the shore]. So they were clinging on to the boat in the middle of this huge lake. And the leader says, "Well, I guess the only option we got is to pray. So, you pray." And the first guy says, "No, I'm an atheist, so I don't pray." The second guy, "How about you?" "Well, I'm a Buddhist. So we don't pray in that sense of asking for things." And then, the leader says, "Well then, I don't go to church, but I live next to a church. So, I hear them praying all the time. So, let's bow our heads." So, all three of them bow their heads. And they said … Then he goes, "B-5, I-28, O-64 … You get it?

Prof. McRae: So, it's bingo, right? That reminds me of something that happened, actually happened at the Los Angeles Zen Center many years ago. They were holding a *sesshin*, a meditation retreat, and every day, maybe several times a day, they go to the master. It was Maezumi Roshi at the time. And they tell their *koan*.

KT: And *koan* is?

Prof. McRae: *Koan* is a meditation subject. So, the first thing you do when you go to the teacher is you recite the *koan*. And many of them were reciting "the Mu *koan*." "Mu" is an enigmatic answer that means "nothing" or "non-being" or something. But they go into the teacher and say each time "Mu … ." Well, apparently the building is quite close to other buildings, and there were some people, just ordinary people, living next door. After time and time again someone coming in and going "Mu … ," they yelled, "Kill the cow and get over with it."

KT: Real story?

Prof. McRae: Real story.

KT: That's great. Thank you for sharing that.

Well, that was enjoyable. And it's good to know that in Buddhism there are these stories to convey the teachings. So, thank you for taking your time to share your wisdom about humor.

Prof. McRae: Thank you very much.

KT: Thank you.

As you can see, humor is a way to talk about Buddhism. This is especially true in America where a friendly and humorous approach is appreciated, as reflected in today's passage:

> *The eternal Buddha always appears before people in the most friendly forms and brings to them the wisest methods of relief.*

Starting next week, we shall move to the topic of the Eightfold Noble Path, which places more weight on how we *act* than how we view things. We hope you join us.

CHAPTER EIGHT:
Teachings of the Eightfold Noble Path

PROGRAM 41
Eightfold Noble Path: Conduct

To utter pleasant words without practicing them is like a flower without fragrance.

(The Teaching of Buddha, p. 366)

Hello, and thanks for being with us for today's show.

How did your week go? I hope that things were okay. However, even if things didn't go as expected, I hope you were able to apply the Buddhist teachings to the things that occur in your daily life.

Remember, what is important is not *what life presents us* but *how we experience life*. And how we experience our lives depends on the quality of wisdom we have cultivated within ourselves. This wisdom can also be expressed as understanding, view, or insight.

Concrete Set of Practices

In Buddhism, there are many ways of cultivating wisdom within ourselves, but the most well-known is the *Eightfold Noble Path*. There are eight ways that make up the Eightfold Noble Path. You can think of them as representing each of the eight spokes of the *Wheel of Dharma*. They are *Right View, Right Thought, Right Speech, Right Action, Right Livelihood, Right Effort, Right Mindfulness and Right Concentration*.

However, the eight should not be seen as stages, where each one is completed before moving on to the next. Instead, all eight are practiced together as a unified set that complement and support each other.

Also, the Noble Path is not so much a commandment as it is a set of self-imposed guidelines by those seeking to cultivate themselves. Each of the eight is referred to as "right," but they are not meant to be "right" as opposed to "wrong" in the *moral sense*. Instead, "right" is meant in the sense of being "appropriate" in keeping with truth, which then helps a person to lessen suffering and experience joy.

Three Categories

The eight items of the Eightfold Noble Path are often categorized into *wisdom, conduct and meditation*. Right View and Right Thought constitute wisdom, while Right Speech, Right Action, and Right Livelihood make up conduct. And Right Effort, Right Mindfulness and Right Concentration constitute meditation.

This division into wisdom, conduct and meditation makes sense even when we see how these three categories are necessary in training for success in any endeavor or occupation in today's world, whether as athletes, teachers, office workers, or factory workers.

Practice Cultivates Success

Let's take the case of an athlete, say, Tiger Woods. Yes, I know, his talents and accomplishments are extraordinary, and you may feel that he would not be a good example.

However, even he has to exercise these three categories in order to be at the top of his game. For example, he constantly studies and works on his form, whether it be his drives, approaches or putts. Before any tournament he studies the peculiarities of the course. An understanding is essential, even for someone especially gifted as Tiger Woods. And this is analogous to the *wisdom* dimension of the Eightfold Path.

At the same time, I am sure that Tiger Woods requires a lifestyle that includes a healthy diet, ample sleeping time, and a satisfying relationship with his people. His relationships, for example, would suffer if he were to speak harshly to his family and lie to his business associates. He could not afford the disruptions and upheavals in his personal life that would inevitably result from such behavior. So, proper conduct is necessary for a person to be physically fit and emotionally supported by others to do well in one's work, even Tiger Woods. This corresponds to the *conduct* dimension.

The ability for golfers to concentrate on their game is very important. We have become accustomed to seeing Tiger Woods gaze intently on the ball and the hole. As he does so, thousands in the gallery look on, with millions more doing the same on television. While millions of eyes are on him, Tiger's eyes are on the ball and nothing else. And his ability to focus on the game is truly impressive.

In a TV interview that I once saw, Tiger attributed his ability to concentrate, partly on the values of his Thai mother, for whom Buddhist meditation was a vital part of her Thai heritage. In any event, the ability to focus and concentrate on one's work is essential for success, whether you are Tiger Woods or any person in any line of work. This corresponds to the *meditation* dimension.

So, we can see the importance of cultivating the three categories or dimensions of wisdom, conduct and meditation. The Buddha had recognized this over 2,500 years ago and formulated his teaching into the Eightfold Noble Path. Now, let's take a look at each of the components of this path.

Wisdom: Right View and Right Thought

Right View and Right Thought make up the wisdom dimension of the Eightfold Path. Right View refers to our *understanding* of the Four Noble Truths and other Buddhist principles such as the Four Marks of Existence, which we have focused on over the course of this program series up to now.

And Right Thought points to the *intentions and aspirations* with which we face the world and the way in which we see ourselves, based on Right View.

Now, since we have devoted ample time during our previous shows to these two that make up the wisdom dimension, I won't dwell on them any further. Instead, I would like now to turn our attention on the conduct dimension of the Eightfold Noble Path.

Conduct Dimension of Eightfold Noble Path

The conduct dimension is comprised of Right Speech, Right Action and Right Livelihood. Let's begin with Right Speech.

Right Speech

Right speech calls for us to refrain from four things: false speech, divisive speech, hurtful words and idle chatter.

False speech or lying is denied in virtually all religions. So it requires no detailed explanation. It is simply the act of saying something that is different from the facts or opposite of what is in your heart.

Divisive speech includes slandering, backbiting and talks that can lead to hatred and disunity among individuals or groups of people.

Hurtful words include harsh, rude, malicious and abusive language that is hurtful to others.

Idle chatter refers to the act of talking about things that have very little value, such as gossip, which is based on hearsay and often talked about just to pass the time or to build a false sense of camaraderie in the spirit of self righteousness.

Buddhism has discouraged these four conducts because they are often carried out with greed, hatred, and ignorance. However, when we try to refrain from them, we can naturally choose words and cultivate a manner of speaking that is closer to truth and speak in ways that are more pleasant, considerate and compassionate.

Right Action

Right action calls for us to refrain from killing, stealing and sexual misconduct.

Killing constitutes the act of taking a life, which includes human life, but also in Buddhism it also includes animals, birds, fish and other living creatures. This discouraged Buddhists to stay away from occupations, as we will discuss in a minute, which involve killing such as trading in arms and weapons.

Stealing is simply the act of taking what does not belong to you. This, too, is one of the widely held prohibitions found in virtually all religions.

Sexual misconduct for the monks and nuns means prohibition of any kind of sexual activity, since they have taken vows of celibacy. For lay people, it becomes a little more difficult in defining what constitutes "misconduct" among different cultures and with the passing of time. However, the best way for those of us living today to understand "misconduct" is to take it to mean any action that causes *harm* to others.

Right Livelihood

For monks and nuns, Right Livelihood prohibits them from engaging in activities that are unbecoming of spiritual seekers. For lay Buddhists, it refers to adhering to actions or engaging in related occupations that do not go against basic Buddhist ethical values.

One such value is refraining from killing, as I mentioned before. Such being the case, traditionally there have been occupations that are considered unsuitable. They include occupations that involve trading in arms and lethal weapons, as well as killing animals. Other unsuitable occupations are those that involve slavery, prostitution, and intoxicants.

It's clear from this that Buddhism discouraged professions that bring harm to others. This is in line with the Buddhist position of strongly opposing any kind of war and aggressive acts as reflected in the Buddha's well-known words, *"Hatred is not overcome by hatred, but only by acts of non-hatred." (Dhammapada)*

The Importance of Practice

So, Buddhism has always stressed the importance of putting our ideals into practice, as seen in today's opening passage:

"To utter pleasant words without practicing them is like a flower without fragrance."

Maybe it can be said that by practicing, you will be "smelling like a rose"! In any event, by practicing the Eightfold Noble Path diligently I cannot guarantee that you will become another Tiger Woods! However, I can say with confidence that your life and the lives of those around you will be better for it, and that you will probably start wearing some of his infectious *smiles*!

In our next show, we will be visiting with a Korean Buddhist monk. Please join us, and have a great week.

PROGRAM 42
Korean Buddhism

Thousands of candles can be lighted from a single candle, and the life of that one candle will not be shortened. Happiness never decreases by being shared.

(*The Teaching of Buddha, p. 260*)

Hi, I hope we find you in good health and good spirits, after a meaningful week.

Today, we are pleased to have with us a guest representing the Korean Buddhist tradition.

In my recent visits to Korea, I have been impressed by the vitality of Buddhism. For example, I visited a huge hospital newly built by Dongguk University, one of the major Buddhist universities in Korea. The mission of the hospital is to integrate the latest Western medical methods with the wisdom of Eastern medicine, in which patients are cared for and supported by Buddhist spiritual counseling.

The hospital even has a hall for conducting funerals! I haven't seen this in any other country that I have visited. However, this should not be so surprising if we take seriously the Buddhist teaching that both birth and death are natural elements of life.

Now it's time to present our guest today, Venerable Seok Ohjin. His name means the "Thunder of Awakening," and he is a member of Chogye-jong, the largest school of Buddhism in Korea.

KT: Welcome to our show and thank you very much for joining us. Let me begin by asking you, "how old were you when you were ordained as a monk?"

Ven. Seok Ohjin : I became ordained when I was 13 years old at *Haeinsa Buddhist Monastery*.

KT: Isn't Haein Monastery famous for its *wood block prints* of the Buddhist canon or the sacred books? (Ven. Seok Ohjin agrees) I actually have visited the monastery, which is located way up in the mountains. I was so impressed by the thousands of these huge wood block prints stored in buildings that must have covered at least half an acre. I understand the wood blocks are about a thousand years old.

Ven. Seok Ohjin: Yes, they are. They are a national treasure. They have also made a great *contribution to the spreading of Buddhism*. The scriptures printed with these blocks greatly influenced the studies of Buddhism in Japan and in other countries.

KT: Yes, I certainly agree. Actually, we don't hear enough about Korean Buddhism and the vital role that it has played and continues to play today. I was personally impressed by the energy and the vitality of the monks and nuns I have met.

And if you don't mind I would like to ask you some personal questions. You said that you were ordained at the age of 13. Isn't that very young? And didn't your parents object?

Ven. Seok Ohjin: Yes, they did object, especially because my family was a strong *Confucian family*. My family taught me to read the *sacred Confucian texts* from a very young age. My father was especially against my becoming a monk. To become a monk means to leave one's family and society. This is one of the worst things you can do as a Confucian.

KT: So, didn't your father try to stop you from becoming a Buddhist monk?

Ven. Seok Ohjin: Yes, he tried, especially because I was the oldest son, but I had made up my mind. In fact, my father came to the temple to take me back home, but I refused the first time. Then he came back the second time begging me to return, but I told him, "Father, you can come to see me as a lay Buddhist but not as my father." *My father went home in tears* and never returned to the temple. I felt very bad, but my mind was made up.

KT: I can understand that. So, you must have been strongly attracted to Buddhism?

Ven. Seok Ohjin: Even as a child, I especially liked going to the temple.

KT: But usually that alone doesn't lead someone to go so far as to become a monk. What other points attracted you to Buddhism?

Ven. Seok Ohjin: I really liked the *teaching of compassion*, and there are two meanings to compassion.

The first meaning is to *care about all living beings*. As you know in

Buddhism, living beings include insects, fish, birds, animals, and all non-human creatures. Of course, people are included, but we also think about other non-human beings as well.

The second meaning is to *respect all individuals* because each person is sacred. In Buddhism, each person has *Buddha nature*, which is the potential to become a Buddha. We respect each person as a *future Buddha*!

That is one of the reasons why the Buddhists *greet each other* by putting their palms together as a show of respect to the other person.

KT: So were there events in your life when your Buddhist value was really tested?

Ven. Seok Ohjin: Yes, there have been many, but the one that I recall the most was during the *Vietnam War*. In Korea, we have a draft system even for monks. So I ended up being sent to Vietnam War.

KT: It must have been hard for you to become a soldier.

Ven. Seok Ohjin: Of course, I felt a big conflict between being a soldier and practicing compassion.

KT: Did that conflict come up in Vietnam?

Ven. Seok Ohjin: Yes, often. But the one experience I recall the most was when I was *serving in the general headquarters with the officers*. One late evening we got a call for help from a group of soldiers who were *surrounded by the enemy*. There was *little we could do* because it was in the middle of the night, giving us no way to reach them.

KT: So what happened?

Ven. Seok Ohjin: Well, it was so painful to learn in the morning that almost everyone was killed.

At a meeting that afternoon, *an officer said that at least the soldiers killed were not officers!* Well, I could not believe what I had heard. I told him that *life is equally precious*, whether it was the life of a [regular] soldier or of an officer. I demanded an apology. His attitude went *completely against the teaching of compassion*, the very teaching that attracted me to Buddhism.

KT: You know our recent programs have dealt with the Eightfold Noble Path. Can you comment on that?

Ven. Seok Ohjin: All of the eight are important to put into practice, but they don't have any real meaning without compassion as the source and motivation for practicing them.

KT: So, if we are motivated by compassion, then how about the aim of practicing the Eightfold Path?

Ven. Seok Ohjin: It's the same. We practice Eightfold Noble Path, not because we want to be *morally* right but because we want to become more compassionate.

KT: Very well put! I also believe that the heart of Buddhism is compassion. I think that *you* have exemplified that by how you have led your life and by your actions, of which we got a small glimpse.

Before we wrap up, I would like to ask you to do us the honor of demonstrating a short chanting in Korean.

Ven. Seok Ohjin: (Chanting for about a minute.)

KT: Well, that was wonderful. Thank you so much. We really appreciate your joining us for today's show.

In my view, Ven. Seok Ohjin exemplifies the candle that shares the light and happiness through his practice of compassion as found in today's opening passage:

> *Thousands of candles can be lighted from a single candle, and the life of that one candle will not be shortened. Happiness never decreases by being shared.*

Well, we're glad you joined us. Be sure to join us next week, when we explore the topic of right action in our daily lives. May you have a meaningful and enjoyable week!

PROGRAM 43
Eightfold Noble Path: Meditation

Right Mindfulness is applying one's thinking at all times with a clear mind, observing the body, the senses, the mind, and the elements, and overcoming greed and that which arises from it.

(Buddha-Dharma, p. 87)

Hi, we are glad you could join us.

In our recent shows, we have been focusing on the *Eightfold Noble Path*, which constitutes the basic set of practices or self-imposed guidelines that help us to put into practice the principles that we have been discussing.

In a previous show, we noted that there are three categories or dimensions to the Eightfold Noble Path, specifically, *wisdom, conduct and meditation*. We have already talked about the wisdom and conduct categories. So today, we shall focus on the meditation dimension.

The meditation dimension refers to *Right Effort, Right Mindfulness and Right Concentration of the Eightfold Noble Path.*

Right Effort

Right effort is the *focused, energetic will* to foster positive and wholesome states of mind. The four ways of accomplishing this as explained traditionally are, **1)** *to prevent negative and unwholesome states of mind from arising,* **2)** *to prevent negative and unwholesome states of mind that have already arisen,* **3)** *to produce positive and wholesome states of mind that have not yet arisen,* and **4)** *to foster and bring to perfection the positive and wholesome states of mind that have already arisen.*

Right Mindfulness

In my view, Right Mindfulness is the most useful and accessible practice for lay people living in today's society. Mindfulness practice calls for four so-called objects, which are, **1)** *the activities of the body,* **2)** *sensations or feelings,* **3)** *activities of the mind,* and **4)** *"objects" of the mind such as ideas, thoughts, and conceptions.*

Mindfulness of the Body

Mindfulness of the first [object], the activities of the body, is the most accessible to beginners among the four. So today, I will concentrate on this and leave the other three for discussion at a later time.

This mindfulness practice of the body can be further divided into three types: **1)** *breathing,* **2)** *bodily activities,* and **3)** *elements of our body.*

Breathing

I will begin by explaining the mindfulness of breathing. I am certainly not an expert on this form of meditation, but I did undergo some formal training years ago as a Theravada monk in Thailand. Plus, in preparing for this show, I received some guidance from *Gil Frondsal,* a well-respected teacher at *Insight Meditation Center* of Menlo Park in Northern California.

Traditionally, you sit with your legs crossed on the floor as you see here with this image of the Buddha. Your hands are placed naturally and comfortably on your lap. And your back is kept straight.

However, in order to make it possible for more people to practice this, I am going to break from the tradition by sitting in a chair. We can practice mindfulness whenever you have a little time, for example, while waiting for your plane at the airport, just before going to bed, or waiting in the car to pick up your children or grandchildren, but … not *while* driving!

Your *head should be cast downward* generally about 45 degrees. As for your eyes, you can keep them *half-opened or fully closed,* whichever is more comfortable for you. You then *breathe naturally* through your *nose,* not your mouth. Breathing should also be very natural.

Now, as for your thoughts, some people *mistakenly* think, "we should not think of anything" or "empty our minds." Instead, you should *pay full attention to your breathing.* This can be done in a number of ways.

One way is to silently say *"in"* when you breathe in, and *"out"* when you breathe out. Or the other method is to direct your atten-

229

tion to the spot under your nostrils to bring attention to the fact that it feels *cool* when you breathe in, and it's *warm* when you breathe out. Or you can focus your attention to the slight rise and fall of your abdomen; as you breathe in, your abdomen rises, at which time you can say silently to yourself, "*rising*"; and as you breathe out, your abdomen falls, at which time you can say "*falling.*"

Especially in the beginning, your mind will wander; various feelings and thoughts will crop up, making it extremely difficult to concentrate on your breathing. Actually, you cannot prevent such distractions from coming up, for the seeds have been planted through your past actions, and they are the inevitable fruit. So, the objective is *not* to prevent them or to think of nothing.

What you must do is to allow those feelings and thoughts to emerge and then let them go. Let them come and go, but you should not cling and get entangled in them. As you let your thoughts come and go, you return to paying attention to your breathing, just as a spider eventually returns to the center of its web. *Breathing is the center of the web.*

However, if the emotions or thoughts are just too intense to ignore, you can pay attention to them in order to see them clearly and then to see them with awareness that is independent of how you are thinking about them. When this is accomplished, then you return to breathing or, metaphorically speaking, to the center of the web.

Benefits

The well-known Vietnamese monk, Thich Nhat Hanh, says that many people hate their bodies, but breathing helps them to become more acquainted with their bodies. He knows a meditation teacher who begins her practice session by telling her students, "Let us be aware of our bodies. Breathing in, I know I am standing here in my body. Breathing out, I smile to my body." She encourages us to make peace with our body.

In any case, when you are practicing the mindfulness of breathing, you can do this for several minutes or for however long you wish. I have found that even a few minutes will leave you feeling a little more settled and physically refreshed.

Mindfulness of Bodily Activities

The second category of mindfulness on the body calls for us to *pay full attention* to our bodily activities, such as putting on our clothes, listening to others, and eating your meals. Let's take the example of *listening to someone* else talk. As we all know, listening with undivided attention is not an easy task. However, with mindfulness practice, we can be trained to listen more fully and deeply.

The same goes for *eating*. Often at times we are not even aware of what we are eating, because we may be eating while watching television, reading a magazine or while being too absorbed in a conversation. If we are not aware of what we are eating, then we certainly would not be savoring the food; this very frequently leaves us feeling emotionally unfulfilled.

However, this mindfulness helps to ease this unsatisfactory feeling, while leading you to experience greater contentment. This sense of fulfillment cannot be explained logically. You simply need to practice and experience it!

Mindfulness on the Elements of Our Body

The Buddha taught that our body is comprised of the elements of earth, water, fire and wind.

First, we become mindful of the *earth element* in us, which refers to that which is solid. So, there are earth elements within you as well as outside of you. When we realize that we are comprised of the same elements as those outside us, then we see that there is no real boundary between us and the rest of the universe.

Next, we pay attention to the *water element* within us, which makes up over seventy-five percent of our body. When we do, we realize that we are, again, deeply connected to the water that is outside us, be it as rain or water in the rivers and the oceans.

The same is true for the *heat element* that is within us. Heat is found in the various bodily processes that manifest themselves in the warmth of our body. And this is intimately connected to the heat outside of us, which ultimately is based on the sun, which is some 93 million miles away.

The fourth is the *wind element*. This exists as air within us and as wind outside of us, as previously discussed in connection with mindfulness of breathing.

So, in meditating on the four elements, we become more aware of the components that make up our body as well as its essential connection to the world outside, helping us to realize with our body that we are, indeed, *one* with the universe!

Right Concentration

The last or the eighth on the list of the Eightfold Noble Path is Right Concentration; its original Sanskrit is *dhyana* from which we get the word *Zen*. As concentration entails quite an advanced set of practices that go beyond the aim of this program, I will leave this discussion for another day. Instead, it would be great if you are able to walk away with something beneficial from our discussion on mindfulness, to which we have devoted today's show.

As we close, I would like to point out that we have now completed our discussion on the *meditation* dimension, which together with *wisdom* and *conduct* dimensions rounds out the *Eightfold Noble Path*. Again, if you can put into practice some of these principles, I am sure that there will be changes for the better in your spiritual and mental life.

In our next show, we will be discussing the growing opportunity for studying Buddhism in American colleges. We hope to see you then.

CHAPTER NINE:
Cultural and Societal Manifestations

PROGRAM 44
Studying Buddhism in American Colleges

*As the light of a small candle spreads from one to another in suc-
cession, so the light of Buddha's compassion passes from one mind
to another endlessly.*

(*The Teaching of Buddha,* p. 470)

Hello. And thanks for joining us.

Professor Charles Prebish of Pennsylvania State University, one of
the foremost specialists on American Buddhism, coined a term, "*Silent
Sangha.*" "Sangha" originally referred to the assembly of monks and
nuns, but today, especially in the United States, it has come to mean a
group that includes the lay people, who gather to study and practice
Buddhism.

Professor Prebish has made an interesting observation that colleges are now serving as a kind of a Sangha for students interested in
learning about Buddhism. He ingeniously called it "silent," since the
students are obviously not going to Buddhist temples or meditation
centers but are still able to get some guidance about Buddhism.

This is reflected in the significant growth in the number of colleges and universities in the last 30 years that now offer courses on Buddhism, from "*Buddhism 101" to Ph.D. programs* in Buddhist Studies. As
of a few years ago, it was reported that in a two-year period eighty-
eight *doctorate-level dissertations* focusing on Buddhism were written
by individuals attending U.S. universities. This likely *surpasses* that
of the Buddhist countries of Asia.

Today, Professor Linda Penkower, who teaches Buddhism at the
University of Pittsburgh is here to tell us a bit more about Buddhist
Studies in the U.S.

KT: Well, Professor Penkower, it's a real pleasure to have you
with us.

Prof. Penkower: Thanks for having me.

KT: I'd like to begin by asking, "How did you get started in your
formal study of Buddhism?"

Prof. Penkower: I had just happened to take a course on Buddhism when I was an undergraduate, and I was hooked.

KT: So, once you got hooked, where did you do your studies, especially your graduate program?

Prof. Penkower: I finished up my undergraduate program in philosophy with a minor in Buddhism, and then I did my graduate work in Columbia University in New York. Columbia at that time was just moving—it was one of the first universities to move—the study of Buddhism out of area studies departments into religious studies departments. And we were very fortunate to have four Buddhologists with whom I studied.

KT: Four Buddhologists? Who are Buddhologists?

Prof. Penkower: I am a Buddologist. A Buddhologist is anyone who studies, in a scholarly fashion, Buddhist studies.

KT: Okay. So, what changes have you seen in the development of interest among students in American universities, more specifically at the University of Pittsburgh?

Prof. Penkower: I've been teaching for over fifteen years now and quite frankly the level of interest in Buddhism has been always very high. I think that most students coming out of their parents' home for the first time, are interested in and figuring out who they are and what they want to be independent of their parents' ideas. And Buddhism is always very attractive in helping kids figure out a little bit about how they want to present themselves to the world.

However, in recent times, I think that students come to Buddhism with a greater understanding and perhaps a greater exposure. There are many more books, for example, popular books as well as academic books that are available to them. They come through anime, they come through Kung-fu movies, comic books, "how to" manuals, business manuals, the visual arts, [etc.]. And more and more students are traveling. So they come to it with some knowledge often of Asia, for example, and not just as an isolated incidence of a topic in religion.

KT: And of course, recently Buddhism is perceived *as one of the American religions* and no longer as foreign as before. And with more and more people who are Buddhists, Richard Gere, for example, so I would say that young people look at Buddhism as an American religion. Would you say that?

Prof. Penkower: Absolutely. I think that we can see that, not just as an American religion, but people are interested in it as a *contemporary religion* and not something just historically in the background.

KT: That's an important point.

Prof. Penkower: But kids come [because] they are interested in meditation. They are interested in philosophy. They've looked at some of it. They know some Buddhists. They've seen some Buddhists. the Dalai Lama, for example, has been to America, et cetera.

KT: Especially, the Dalai Lama

Prof. Penkower: Especially the Dalai Lama.

KT: Now, how do you, as a professor of religion, the Buddhologist, feel about this kind of activities or involvement on a popular level?

Prof. Penkower: I think whatever draws students in to take a serious look at Buddhism is perfectly all right. There's certainly students who come to Buddhism with more serious ideas about enlightenment [and] wanting to know what enlightenment is, et cetera. But I think that we have to communicate, and if this is an entry for them into the world of Buddhism, I think it's terrific.

KT: What are some of the courses that you are teaching at the University of Pittsburgh?

Prof. Penkower: Well, I think to keep students' interest, and I think religion in general has more a serious side and a lighter side, and has a *theoretical side* and has a *practical side* and how one lives one's life. Theory is not divorced from how we behave. So, in my courses I teach general introduction to Buddhism, and I teach introduction to East-Asian Buddhism in particular. And I also teach a very popular Chan, Zen meditation course or meditative tradition course. And we, for example, go to a Zen monastery to spend a day or sometimes overnight at a local Zen monastery to do that.

KT: How interesting! I think perhaps we have already touched upon this, but what are some of the motivations for taking interest in Buddhism?

Prof. Penkower: I think students come from remarkably different angles when they come to classes like this. As I said before, a lot of students are very interested in looking for a religious tradition or a *philosophy of life*, if you will, a way to behave that would complement their own ideas and their own Western traditions, Judeo-Christian traditions that they may have come out of. Other students are interested as a part of the larger picture of the *cultural heritage of Asia*. Some of the students are interested in it as a *new religion in America*, for example. So, there are many different reasons for students to come and take a look at these courses.

KT: So, when they take these courses, what are some of the most often asked questions that they bring to you?

Prof. Penkower: I think students have a real interest in *enlightenment experience*. They really want to know what it feels like, what it looks like to be enlightened. And unfortunately, in that particular regard, I'm on the same side of the desk as they are. But I think that is one of the biggest driving forces for students. They are also interested in questions of good and evil, right and wrong, the *ethical questions* that are guided by Buddhist ideas in juxtaposition to what they've been taught up until now.

KT: I see. So, now, we talked about what attracts them. What are some of the problems they may have with Buddhism? What are the difficult questions that they encounter as they study Buddhism?

Prof. Penkower: Remarkably, I think the students are very *open to this idea of impermanence*, to the idea of not having a "soul." There's very little resistance I find to that. And there's very little [resistance.] I'm always surprised. They start, of course, by filtering Buddhist ideas through their own ethical and religious understandings and systems, but somewhere about midway through the course, usually you see a change and you can see them starting to think about Buddhism in its own terms rather than in their terms.

KT: I see. So, you mentioned that some of the students are there to look at Buddhism as a way of helping them personally. You know, 18-, 19- or 20-year-olds are often going through difficult times. Have you seen any evidence of Buddhism helping their search?

Prof. Penkower: I think as part of the human experience, Buddhism certainly is a contributor to how we live in this world. Unfortunately, of course, in the academy, it is not our position to be proselytizers. So, my job is to accurately explain Buddhism to them to get them involved in an understanding of what it means for Buddhists to be Buddhists but certainly not, in the classroom setting, to help them figure out [their personal problems].

KT: That's true. That's true. So, you must then refer students to the centers or temples.

Prof. Penkower: Students are constantly asking where they can go locally to meditate, and certainly I've had students who have gone on to spend some time in a monastery. I have students who've gone on to graduate school in the academies. So, you get both.

KT: I see. So, what are your thoughts about the future of Buddhism in the U.S.?

Prof. Penkower: I think Buddhism is quite healthy in the United States. I think students are starting to explore greater and greater topics in the area.

KT: I see. Good. So, you are optimistic.

Prof. Penkower: I certainly am.

KT: Well, Professor Penkower, thank you for joining us and for giving us an overview of what's going on in American universities. Thank you.

Prof. Penkower: It was my pleasure. Thank you for inviting me.

As heard in our discussion with Professor Penkower, we are witnessing a thriving level of interest in the study of Buddhism in American universities. I would, therefore, like to encourage those interested to take advantage of the existence of "silent sangha"! You will be able to learn something about one of the three world religions in an atmosphere of objectivity and openness. And when you do, it's my sincere wish that you will also be touched by the spirit of compassion as expressed in today's opening passage:

As the light of a small candle spreads from one to another in succession, so the light of Buddha's compassion passes from one mind to another endlessly.

In our next show, we will explore the fascinating topic of the interaction of psychology and psychotherapy and Buddhism. See you then.

PROGRAM 45
Buddhism and Psychology:
Tapping the Jewel Together

Like the drunken man of the story, people wander about suffering in this life of birth and death, unconscious of what is hidden away in their nature, pure and untarnished, the priceless treasure of Buddha-nature.

(The Teaching of Buddha, pp. 144-146)

Hello. We're glad you could join us for today's show.

Buddhism and Psychology

I like to talk about how Buddhism and psychology have a lot in common and how they can be used to complement each other to foster our inner well-being. This concept is evident by the hundreds of books in English that promote self-contentment by applying Buddhism and psychology together. I should mention that I am using "psychology" in the broad sense of the term to also include "psychotherapy."

Of course, Buddhism and psychology are not exactly the same in their methods and ultimate goals, as one is an ancient spiritual tradition from Asia and the other is a modern scientific approach developed in the West. However, in North America, it has long been recognized that the two overlap.

For example, about 100 years ago, *William James*, the father of scientific study of religious experience, was lecturing on psychology at Harvard University. He noticed *Anagārika Dharmapāla*, a well-known Buddhist monk (in reality, he was a lay Buddhist) from Sri Lanka, in the audience. It's been reported that Professor James then called out to Dharmapāla and said, "Take my chair. You are better equipped to lecture on psychology than I am. This is the psychology everybody will be studying 25 years from now."

Let me give a tangible example of how the two can work together to address human needs.

Loss of Confidence

No matter how successful we are in schoolwork or at our job, one time or another, we have all experienced a loss of confidence or a sense of being inferior to others. Everyone has felt this way. No one is exempt.

We experience this feeling when we are criticized, or when our efforts fall miserably, or even when hardly anyone notices or pays any attention. In the future, when you experience such let downs, try to remember a simple Buddhist parable that I'd like to share with you.

Parable of the Hidden Jewel

This well-known parable comes from the *Lotus Sutra*, one of the important scriptures from the Mahayana branch of Buddhism. I'm going to take the liberty of slightly modifying the original story for our purpose.

Once there was a man named Jiva who fell into a drunken sleep. His good friend Kumar tried to stay with him until he woke up, but after remaining as long as he could, he had to leave him when Jiva still did not wake up. Worried that Jiva would be in need to support himself, Kumar hid a jewel in his drunken friend's garment. When at last Jiva finally woke up and found his supportive friend gone, he was at a loss and began looking for Kumar, for he felt he truly could not live without his friend. He kept looking for him and wandered about, poor and hungry. He didn't know that Kumar had hidden a jewel in his garment. After a long time, the two friends met again, and Kumar told Jiva about the jewel and told him to look for it. Sure enough, the jewel was there—where it had always been all along.

How do you like this parable?

Aren't we all like Jiva when we experience a loss of confidence, self-doubt, self-pity, or a feeling of inferiority? At such times, rather than looking for the jewel within ourselves, we turn outward to find someone to support and validate us. Jiva finally found his friend but had wasted so much time. And even if he had found Kumar right away, that would have satisfied him only temporarily. In other words, having a reliable friend is important, but does not provide a real solution, for in the end we need to find the answer in ourselves and for ourselves.

The Jewel is the Teachings

The jewel represents the Dharma, the teachings, in its two aspects. One is in the form of *principles*, such as the *Four Marks of Existence*, for us to actualize in our lives through personal cultivation. The jewel as a principle points us in the right direction.

The second comes in the form of *spiritual assurance* expressed as *Buddha nature*. All sentient beings are equally endowed with Buddha nature. It does not matter whether you are rich or poor, man or woman, young or old, or even human or non-human. This Buddha nature assures us that we all possess the potentiality to become fully awakened. We are all future Buddhas. Being future Buddhas, we are all precious and worthy of respect.

The Buddhist teachings represented by the jewel can help people such as Jiva find themselves. They are directed toward the ultimate truth or, metaphorically, the vertical dimension.

Psychology in Support of Buddhism

However, according to psychologist *John Wellwood*, there are many people who are not able to benefit from these spiritual truths because they suffer from a fragile ego, which shows up as an extreme lack of confidence in oneself or self-hatred, insecurity, or self-doubt.

For example, Dr. Wellwood cites a case of a woman—let us call her Jackie—who had gone to a Buddhist teacher seeking advice about her anger toward her husband. The teacher advised Jackie to be a compassionate friend to her husband rather than to be angry with him. This advice to be compassionate initially made her feel relieved, for Jackie did not have to confront her anger, which was too painful and threatening to her fragile ego.

However, according to Dr. Wellwood, Jackie actually needed to *confront* her anger because she had suppressed it all her life. Her father was extremely abusive and punished her whenever she expressed her discontent, so Jackie soon learned to hold everything back and instead always tried to please others by being "a good girl."

From an absolute spiritual perspective of the *vertical dimension*, the advice for her to be compassionate was correct. However, on the relative everyday *horizontal level*, being compassionate without addressing the rage inside left her unhappy. She needed to first acknowledge her anger before she could express genuine compassion and love.

And it is at this relative truth that psychological inquiry operates. Dr. Wellwood says that as a therapist, he helped Jackie to be open to the experience of anger, letting it unfold without judgment and then gently exploring its meaning within her life experience. After she had attended to her psychological wounds from the past, she was then ready to benefit from the spiritual teachings. This is psychology at work in further serving to lead one toward spiritual development.

Integration

Some psychologists as well as Buddhists feel that these two concepts have little to do with each other. Fortunately, however, there are psychologists, who are open to integrating psychology and religion.

Many of them support a branch that has come to be known as *"transpersonal psychology."* As the word *"transpersonal"* implies, it not only attends to the "personal" but also to what transcends it by affirming and integrating religious aspects, including Buddhism.

In my view, psychology aims to assist individuals to develop the "personal" dimension. In other words, the aim of psychological work is the healthy ego or individuality for living effectively in the world, as was done in Jackie's case.

However, for many of us, it's not enough to be fulfilled only at this "personal" level. After all, the personal dimension is limited in terms of time and space. In terms of *time*, we are finite and eventually we all must die. Death and the afterlife have been a perennial issue throughout much of human history. In terms of *space*, we cannot live alone physically or mentally for long. We depend on others, human and non-human, for our very survival.

Within this human predicament, many of us experience a strong and powerful urge to go beyond this "personal" level to connect with what is sacred and real. This comes in the form of ultimate spiritual reality, human community and the world of nature, wherein we find greater fulfillment in resolving the limitations of the self.

And so, it is heartening to see this kind of greater integration of psychology with the spiritual and the sacred taking place, since in the end the two are not separate. In actuality, we live in both dimensions. We need to cultivate both if we are to be truly fulfilled.

In the 21st century, the ancient Buddhist tradition is blessed to be in a position to work closely with the modern discipline of psychology toward a more effective way of assisting humankind to realize their potential. Therefore, we must allow the two, Buddhism and psychology, to *work together to tap the jewel within*, while recalling today's opening passage!

> *Like the drunken man of the story, people wander about suffering in this life of birth and death, unconscious of what is hidden away in their nature, pure and untarnished, the priceless treasure of Buddha-nature.*

Next week, we will explore the topic of Buddhist social action with an interesting guest. Please be sure to join us. Also, please visit our website for a listing of the various Buddhist centers in your area.

PROGRAM 46
Social Action: Bodhisattva Spirit of Compassion for Others

Now I wish to realize enlightenment
For the sake of all beings in the world of the Dharma.
With an unwavering mind of great compassion
I am determined to throw off the body, which people cling to.
(Buddha-Dharma, p. 651)

Hi, how are you doing today? I hope you had a wonderful week, one filled with great learning experiences and discoveries.

Today, we'll explore the topic of *Buddhist social action*, rooted in the *Bodhisattva spirit of compassion* for others. "Bodhisattva" can mean many things in Buddhism. One main meaning refers to those human beings who seek to help others out of immense compassion for others. This compassion is the result of virtue that they have cultivated through learning and practice. So, the Bodhisattva spirit of compassion does not stem from a sense of obligation or a need to be ethically correct, but rather a *heartfelt, automatic selfless response* to those in need.

An ultimate example of this selfless action is seen in a well-known story of *The Hungry Tigress*. The tale, as retold by *Rafe Martin* in a book of the same title for contemporary audiences, goes as follows:

Once, long, long ago, the Buddha came to life as a noble prince named Mahasattva in a land where the country of Nepal exists today.

One day, when he was grown, he went walking in a wild forest with his two brothers. The land was dry and the leaves brittle from extreme drought. The sky seemed alight with flames.

Suddenly, they saw a tigress. The brothers turned to flee, but the tigress stumbled and fell. She was starving, and her cubs were starving, too. She eyed her cubs miserably and, in that dark glance, the prince sensed her long months of hunger and pain. He saw, too, that unless she found food soon, she might even be driven to devour her own cubs. He was moved to compassion by the extreme hardness of their lives.

"What, after all, is this life for?" he thought.

Stepping forward, he calmly removed his outer garments and lay down before her. He tore his skin with a stone and let the starving tigress smell the blood. Mahasattva's brothers fled.

Hungrily, the tigress devoured the prince's body and chewed the bones. She and her cubs lived on, and for many years, the forest was filled with a golden light.

Centuries later, a mighty king raised a pillar of carved stone on this spot, and the pilgrims still go there to make offerings even today.

Deeds of compassion live forever.

The story is, of course, an *extreme and dramatic* example of selfless compassion, and sacrificing oneself as the Prince did may even strike some people today as being bizarre. In telling this story, of course, no one is being encouraged to sacrifice himself or herself in the same way. Rather, its aim is to convey the importance of compassionate caring for others in need. That is the *Bodhisattva spirit*!

Today, we are happy to have *Jonathan Watts* back as our guest. Jon is an active member of the *International Network of Engaged Buddhists*, an organization that is dedicated to establishing a more compassionate society, and in my view, motivated by the Bodhisattva spirit. Jon has also written extensively on the topic of Buddhist participation in the world, commonly referred to as "engaged Buddhism."

KT: Well, welcome back to our show, Jon.

Jonathan Watts: Thank you. Good to be back.

KT: Today, our topic is Bodhisattva spirit. Is there anyone in your life who exemplifies that spirit?

Jonathan Watts: Well, there are actually quite a number of people, but for today's program I'd like to choose Joanna Macy.

KT: Oh, Joanna Macy. Yes, she is well known, and I've met her too. So, how did you come to meet her?

Jonathan Watts: Well, I met her about five years ago in Berkeley, California, through an event sponsored by Buddhist Peace Fellowship. Since then I've been kept in contact with her through my group and my work called "Think Sangha." But actually I first encountered her and her works through her books about 15 years ago, and that had a big effect on me in the beginning of my work in engaged Buddhism.

KT: I see. Now, how do you think Joanna Macy exemplifies that Bodhisattva spirit?

Jonathan Watts: Well, I really appreciate her work because she has this wonderful balance of two Buddhist virtues of wisdom and compassion. On the wisdom side she spent a number of years in the '60s and '70s in India studying Sanskrit and Buddhism, and she produced a book called *Mutual Causality in Buddhism and General Systems Theory*. In this book, she talks about causality, which is how the universe systematically works. And she compares the Buddhist view of this, the views of other religions and the views of science. And this book is really a stunning piece of scholarship, but actually I found it much more important for what it means for our daily lives.

KT: So, what does she say in that book?

Jonathan Watts: Well, she says, in short, that the universe is a web of life, in which ethical action is actually systematically embedded.

KT: Embedded? Okay, what does it mean, "embedded"?

Jonathan Watts: What it means is that usually we make organizational systems, and we don't think about the emotive and human emotive inputs into it. But actually when we act ethically, this is a positive input into any system that makes the system work more efficiently.

KT: And leaves an imprint?

Jonathan Watts: Yes, it leaves an imprint.

KT: I see. I'm sorry to have interrupted you. You're saying …?

Jonathan Watts: Well, so this is the basic gist of the book. I mean it's quite complex, but it's had a lot of impact on the people I know, specifically a friend in our group who is a consultant for the British government. And he is trying to use the ideas in this book to see how government policies can be better developed and implemented.

KT: I see. So, what else does she advocate to improve the world?

Jonathan Watts: Well, that was the wisdom side of her. And she's probably better known for her compassion work, which is … I think it's very important for our country. Since the latter days of the Cold War, she started developing what are called despair and empowerment workshops. And she developed at that time for all of us who were living with sort of the repressed fear and anxiety of a society like ours that was on the brink of nuclear holocaust. So, using a deeply Buddhist model, she teaches us not to run from our repressed fears or anesthetize these fears.

KT: I see, I see. So, besides not running from our fears, what does she propose?

Jonathan Watts: Well, what she proposes is based a lot on the book that I was telling you from before, which is not to see fear or despair as a problem or problematize it, but to see it as a resource. It's actually just trapped energy, and it's energy that if we go into and transform and harness, it actually gives forth a tremendous amount of positive energy, a compassionate energy, an energy to be active and engaged in the world. So, basically she's developed a model for Bodhisattva training. And I think today in our country with so much fear and despair and anxiety being churned up in our lives, this is a very important work.

KT: I see. So, how about yourself, personally? What motivates you to be involved in engaged Buddhism?

Jonathan Watts: Well, I think I first got interested when I was in university and I came across the writings of Gandhi. And I remember clearly him talking about the path of Karma Yoga, which is spirituality and finding one's spiritual salvation through working in the world and aiding others and helping others. And he said this path was a higher path than just doing religious rituals or studying Holy Scriptures. And that really struck a chord with me at a young age.

KT: And how is that youthful inspiration playing out in your life today?

Jonathan Watts: After college, I got serious about becoming a Buddhist, and I started doing meditation practice. Through these experiences I had glimpses of this lack of break between self and others, that we're actually deeply interconnected and one. And when you have that realization, then you know that you really want to work for others in your life. And as the Buddha said to help others is to help oneself, and to help oneself is to help others.

KT: So, finally, can you tell me a little bit more about your work in INEB, the International Network of Engaged Buddhists?

Jonathan Watts: Well, INEB is basically a non-sectarian, ecumenical network that includes even people who aren't Buddhists. And it's a network of people who are supporting each other in Bodhisattva work. Specifically, we do a lot of work in trying to train people at the local level, in conflict resolution, gender awareness, environmental action on using a specifically Buddhist understanding and approach to this kind of work.

KT: I see, very good. Well, thank you for coming in to share your experiences with us about a topic that's not talked about very much as it should. Thank you.

Jonathan Watts: Thank you.

Well, I hope that the discussion with Jon Watts has given you a better understanding of the Bodhisattva spirit in action, and has inspired you to do what you can do to carry it out in your lives.

Again, you are not being asked to sacrifice your body like the prince in the Hungry Tigress parable, but to be mindful of the Bodhisattva spirit of sharing out of a deep understanding of the oneness and interconnectedness of all life. I would like to close with today's passage, uttered by that Bodhisattva prince:

> *Now I wish to realize enlightenment*
> *For the sake of all beings in the world of the Dharma.*
> *With an unwavering mind of great compassion*
> *I am determined to throw off the body, which people cling to.*

Next week, we'll address the topic of Buddhism and science. We look forward to seeing you then.

PROGRAM 47
Buddhism and Science

Buddhism teaches wisdom and compassion, but another important teaching is upāya, which means expediency or choosing the right means to accomplish an end.

(Mutually Sustaining Life, p. 140)

Hello. We're glad you've joined us.

Conflicts Between Science and Religion

As all of us know, the relationship between religion and science has not always been a harmonious one, particularly for Christianity in Europe where modern science began. For example, the Catholic Church condemned Galileo for his views, and it was not until 1995 that the church pardoned him for what were once considered "incorrect" ways.

And in North America in the late 19th century, the theory of evolution proposed by Charles Darwin clashed with the traditional Christian view of creation. A similar kind of conflict continues even to this day in the area of school curriculum. In many of the public school districts throughout America, some Christian groups are vigorously opposing the teaching of the theory of evolution in favor of the creationist or the so-called "intelligent design" position.

Buddhist Perspective

When dissension surfaced in the late 19th century, some Americans were no longer satisfied with the traditional Christian understanding of the origin of the universe and its development. Some sought answers in other religions, such as Buddhism.

One such person was Paul Carus. He found himself unable to reconcile science and theology of the time. He desperately sought what he called a "religion of science" that could accommodate science and its worldview. He found the answer in Buddhism.

Regarding his views on science, he once stated, "Buddhism is a religion which recognizes no other revelation except for the truth that can be proved by science." And he spoke of the Buddha as "the first prophet of the Religion of Science."

We can feel the enthusiasm that Carus felt for having found the right religion, but we also realize that he had reduced Buddhism to what he wanted to see. For example, he focused on the "karmic law of cause and effect" as a law of nature, but ignored the less scientific elements of traditional Buddhism, such as meditation practices and the esoteric and "miraculous" elements. We continue to see the same kind of approach and conclusion by more recent thinkers, such as Fritjof Capra in his landmark book *The Tao of Physics*.

While not very many Buddhists would go so far as Carus or Capra to equate Buddhism with science, they are in line with the basic view held today by most Buddhists that Buddhism does not conflict with science.

The Dalai Lama's Dialogue with Scientists

One such person is the Dalai Lama, who has been at the forefront of dialogue between Buddhists and scientists. One statement he made really caught my attention. The Dalai Lama announced that in the domain of the natural realm, Buddhists should adjust any traditional understanding if it is refuted by science.

So, for example, he would have no problem abandoning the classical Buddhist worldview that sees the towering Mt. Sumeru at the center of the world, surrounded by seven to eight concentric circles of mountains and oceans, and four main continents. In the same vein, the Dalai Lama would be fully open to the latest theories regarding the origins of the universe attributed to the mechanism of subatomic particles.

Some may find the Dalai Lama's position to be too compromising, but his view is in keeping with the basic Buddhist position that scientific findings do not weaken or negate Buddhist truth and its message. This is because Buddhism is a religion of awakening, concerned foremost with "how we experience life" rather than "how things happen," which is the realm of science. Put another way, Buddhism seeks spiritual awakening, while science seeks verifiable knowledge about the natural realm.

Despite the differences, Buddhism has always attracted me for its openness to encompass both the spiritual and the natural. And I am happy to learn that Albert Einstein had made similar observations about Buddhism when he stated:

> Buddhism has the characteristics of what would be expected in a cosmic religion for the future: it transcends a personal God, avoids dogmas and theology; it covers both the natural and spiritual, and it is based on a religious sense aspiring from the experience of all things, natural and spiritual, as a meaningful unity.

Why Do Bad Things Happen to Good People?

So what does all this talk about Buddhism and science have to do with the problems of life? Well, I'd like to take the example of a fatal illness.

Some years ago when I was serving as a minister of a temple in California, a member in her 50s died of cancer. She was an extremely devout and hardworking member of the temple. Plus, she was a wonderful person, liked by everyone who knew her.

Many people asked, "Why her?" Behind the dismay was the nagging question that people everywhere have asked from time immemorial, "Why do bad things happen to good people?"

Perhaps in other religions, the answer might be, "It's God's will." However, in Buddhism, we wouldn't say, "It's Buddha's will," since Buddha is not a creator, designer or judge.

Cause and Effect Relationship

In my view, there are two categories of a cause and effect relationship that can possibly provide an adequate response to the question of "how could this happen to her?"

One is objective conditions (niyāma) and the second is personal karma. In my view, her cancer was not due to her personal karma.

Her illness and death must be explained within the category of objective conditions or laws that determine such things as environment, weather, and heredity.

In her case, objective conditions point to a myriad of circumstances that contributed to the illness. These could include a genetic disposition to the disease, her past exposure to some carcinogenic chemicals, her eating habits, and her stress level. But there are numerous other possible contributions that can rarely be accurately isolated.

This is the natural realm, as distinct from the spiritual realm. As the natural realm, it's the domain where science can provide us with the best possible understanding of how she became afflicted with the disease.

Personal Karma

If the causes of the cancer lie in the natural realm, then what role does personal karma play? Well, personal karma functions in the realm of the spiritual or the vertical plane, while science functions in the natural realm or the horizontal plane. We live each moment where the two planes intersect. Karma determines "how we experience life," while science attempts to determine "how things happen."

Karma is a Sanskrit word that has now become part of the everyday English language, but unfortunately it's often misunderstood as "fate." Karma is often used to justify misfortune, as in "Well, that was his karma." In such usage, suffering is retribution or punishment for some negative deeds previously committed, either in this life or in prior lives. This idea is absolutely wrong and must be rectified!

The correct Buddhist meaning of karma is "action" in what a person thinks, says, and does, mostly in the context of spiritual and moral cultivation. By diligently following the correct teachings, karma can lead to positive results as manifested in a life of wisdom, compassion and joy. Here, however, we must be careful in noting that the "positive result" we speak about is from the spiritual perspective on the vertical plane. On the other hand, when measured from the mundane perspective on the horizontal plane, her short life would not be judged "positive."

Spiritual Over the Natural

However, I believe that we cannot judge whether one's life was positive or negative, or a success or failure, from the mere perspective of the natural and the horizontal. In the final analysis, only she, and no one else, can make that final determination. Would it have been more positive had she lived another 20 years, but without the kind of spiritual understanding and peace she had come to realize? She lived life fully with wisdom and compassion, and she faced death with understanding and courage; she was at peace with herself.

Inclusion of Science

As one proof of this, she decided to donate her body to a research hospital. She was determined to make a contribution to medical science to find a cure for her kind of cancer. Even in death, she thought about the welfare of others!

Here, we have an excellent example of an open and inclusive Buddhist attitude toward science, since she knew that science does not undermine her Buddhist faith. On this point, her understanding reflects Albert Einstein's observation that Buddhism encompasses the "natural and spiritual, as a meaningful unity."

Thanks for joining us, and please tune in again next week when we learn about Project Dana, a Buddhist social service program in Hawai'i.

PROGRAM 48
Social Welfare: Project Dana of Hawai'i

Thousands of people may live in a community, but it is not of real fellowship until they know each other and have sympathy for one another.

(*The Teaching of Buddha, p. 448*)

Hello. Welcome to our program.

Project Dana

Today's show is about a project in the area of Buddhist *social welfare* that has captured the interest and attention of many people, as well as exemplifies the *Bodhisattva spirit of compassion* for others that we explored a couple of shows back. It's called *Project Dana* and is being carried out in Hawai'i.

Founded in 1989 at Mō'ili'ili Hongwanji, a temple affiliated with *Jodo Shinshu Buddhism* located in Honolulu, Project Dana has since expanded statewide as an interfaith volunteer coalition that now also includes other Buddhist denominations, Christians and those of the Jewish faith. Many awards since its inception attest to the project's effectiveness, including the first *Rosalynn Carter Caregiving Award* bestowed in 1993.

The goal of Project Dana is to provide support services for the frail elderly, disabled persons, and their caregivers. Volunteers from 30 different congregations across the State of Hawai'i have unified under the guiding principle of *dana—selfless giving of time and energy* —in order to put their faith into action. Project Dana volunteers are trained to offer spiritual, emotional and social support. Volunteers also offer a range of services including friendly home visits, telephone reassurance, help with grocery shopping, light housekeeping, and transportation to stores, church services, and medical appointments.

To give us more insight into Project Dana, we're fortunate to have *Rev. Clyde Whitworth* as our guest today. Rev. Whitworth, who is a *Jodoshu priest,* had been both a volunteer and an Assistant Project

Coordinator at the Project Dana headquarters for a number of years.

KT: Well, Clyde, thanks for coming to this program to share your experience and knowledge about this wonderful program.

Rev. Whitworth: My pleasure.

KT: So, can you tell me a little bit about your experience, volunteering for this Project?

Rev. Whitworth: So, I first began to volunteer for Project Dana back in the '90s. And at that time I was assisting a young man with severe developmental disabilities and saw the Project's volunteer services to be something he might enjoy doing with me. So, my friend really liked grocery shopping, and since, as you had mentioned, grocery shopping is something that Project Dana offers as a service, we approached the co-founder and Chief Administrator, Rose Nakamura (*co-founder of Project Dana*), to inquire if it would be possible for us to volunteer.

Well, they trained me and then set us up with an assignment. Every week or two for two years, we assisted an elderly Native Hawaiian man, who was virtually homebound, with his grocery shopping needs. After some months we began to feel like family. And we always looked forward to shopping day, and had a lot of fun doing it.

KT: Sounds like a lot of fun.

Rev. Whitworth: Yes. It was great.

KT: Typically Hawaiian attitude!

Rev. Whitworth: Yes, absolutely, Aloha type attitude. Yes.

KT: Good, good. You know, I've always liked the word, "Dana." In fact, I was going to name my daughter Dana, but it didn't quite work out. So, I'm sure that the audience would be interested in knowing what Dana means. I said earlier that it meant "selfless giving of time and energy." So, I wonder if you could elaborate on that word.

Rev. Whitworth: Certainly, the term Dana can be found in both Theravadin and Mahayana schools of Buddhism, and has several definitions. The Mahayana teachings of Shakyamuni Buddha recorded in Sanskrit mention Dana as being one of the *Ten Paramitas or Perfections*, the first six of which are practiced by both lay and monastic communities alike.

Dana in this context means the attempt to perfect selfless giving. When the late *Ruth Tabrah* of the *Honpa Hongwanji Betsuin* suggested that the term be used as the name for the Project, the concept was integrated in the formation of the Mission Statement, and the name quickly adopted.

KT: So, how do the project's Buddhist volunteers actualize Dana in their efforts to help the elderly, the disabled, and their caregivers in this program?

Rev. Whitworth: The goal of attempting to perfect selfless giving is one that the Project Dana volunteers all hold in common. Getting to the point where we don't even expect the recipient to say "thank you" for our efforts … .

KT: But you know it's awfully hard sometimes, isn't it?

Rev. Whitworth: It's true. It's very difficult, but it's key to our particular type of volunteerism. So, putting our faith into action is something that naturally comes to our volunteers, because through the Buddhist teachings we recognize our interdependence with others and apply it through our volunteerism.

So, our compassion for others is quickly transformed into a sense of interconnectedness, which enables us to recognize the common ground we share in regard to the effects of aging. So, in this sense, Dana is not based upon pity for others, but upon a feeling of wanting to assist others because we see ourselves as being a part of the whole of humanity.

KT: Now you are a priest of the Jodoshu tradition. And, so how does the concept of Dana relate to your personal understanding of the Pure Land [Buddhist] tradition, especially of the Jodoshu tradition?

Rev. Whitworth: In Pure Land Buddhism we have the concept that we are all *bonbu*. Bonbu means that we are all sort of deluded and remain largely unaware of our true nature for the most part. As a bonbu being, perfecting the most difficult practices of Buddhism upon our own powers is kind of recognized to be something that we have very little hope of doing in this lifetime. So we turn to the power of *Amitabha Buddha* to lead us to enlightenment. However, in the Jodoshu tradition, Honen Shōnin … .

KT: Excuse me. Honen is the founder of Jodoshu who lived around the year 1200? So, he is the founder of your tradition?

Rev. Whitworth: Yes. So, Honen emphasized that once we have firmly established the practice of reciting Amitabha Buddha's holy name within our daily lives, then the other practices adhered to by other traditions of Mahayana Buddhism can be implemented as long as they are supportive of our recitation practice.

KT: I know in Pure Land Buddhism the reciting the holy name, as you said, is very important. It's the central teaching. And sometimes many Pure Land Buddhists of the past or traditional Pure Land Buddhists do *only* that. But now you are kind of bringing out another aspect of Honen's teaching of supplementary practice that's involved in the world and participating in the world.

Rev. Whitworth: Absolutely. And in this regard, the Project Dana and socially engaged activities that the Project Dana is involved in can be considered a form of supplemental practice. But it should be clear that this type of practices don't, in any way, compromise the integrity of our complete reliance upon Amitabha Buddha to lead us to enlightenment.

KT: I understand that the Project Dana has gone beyond the Buddhist community and is well known in the general public. And I'm wondering how members of other traditions take Dana and apply it to their lives or how they understand Dana as they participate in the volunteer work?

Rev. Whitworth: That's a good question. I've met with many of the Christian Project Dana site-coordinators and their ministers over the past couple of years.

KT: Oh, good. So, you have Christians. About how many would you say [in terms of] the numbers [of Christian groups]?

Rev. Whitworth: We have roughly eight groups at this point.

KT: Eight groups, I see. Mainly in Honolulu?

Rev. Whitworth: In the Honolulu area.

KT: I see. But it's still great.

Rev. Whitworth: So, when we discuss this issue [of inter-religious cooperation,] it kind of confirmed my belief that the concept of Dana is not unique to our religion. There are several quotes from the Bible that convey the same concept, such as, "Do unto others as you would have them do unto you."

KT: Yes, I've heard of that.

Rev. Whitworth: The "Golden Rule," right? So, it's incredibly similar to the concept of Dana, and in that it points out the recognizing the effect of our actions have on the lives of others. At the same time, we kind of contemplate exactly what it must be like for those on the receiving end of our actions.

KT: I see, I see. So, let me ask you what were some of the rewarding experiences that you have being a part of this project?

Rev. Whitworth: There's been so many but … .

KT: I'm sure.

Rev. Whitworth: But on several occasions I had wonderful opportunity to assist people who are terminally ill. And one delightful lady in particular was stricken with malignant cancer, cancer throughout most of her body. And I learned so much from her during our month together. I learned a lot about her, and I learned a lot about myself. But I know the goal is the ideal to give my time and energy without expecting any reward, but that does not mean that rewards don't just naturally come to you. Most certainly do. In volunteer experience such as this, reward is quite unexpected and often kind of life-changing experiences.

KT: Well, good. I'm glad that you had a wonderful experience, particularly in your spiritual quest. So, well, thank you very much for being with us to share this experience with us on this very important project called, Project Dana in Hawai'i.

Rev. Whitworth: My pleasure.

KT: Thank you.

Project Dana has certainly brought joy and assurances to many in need of support in Hawai'i, regardless of their religious, ethnic or economic background. And in keeping with the spirit of selfless-giving of Dana, the volunteers not only grow personally and spiritually, but also contribute to the building of a real community, as described in today's opening passage:

Thousands of people may live in a community, but it is not of real fellowship until they know each other and have sympathy for one another.

This concludes today's show. Thanks for joining us. Next week, we'll examine the odyssey of a person in search of awakening.

CHAPTER TEN:
Searching and Sharing with Others

PROGRAM 49
Seeking Awakening: A Spiritual Journey

"If a person keeps her eyes open, she will see the teachings every-where, and so her opportunities for awakening are endless."
(The Teaching of Buddha, p. 346)

Hello. I hope we find you well.

Today, I wish to explore the topic of the importance of *seeking* in the Buddhist search for awakening. To reinforce its importance, Buddhists have always placed enormous value on one's *"aspiration for awakening"* (bodhicitta). It refers to a firm resolve to realize awakening. This mental commitment then serves as the fuel that drives one to learn and practice.

Sudhana's Spiritual Journey

The importance of seeking is illustrated in a story from the *Flower Garland Sutra* about a spiritual journey of a young man named *Sudhana*. The journey begins with Sudhana going to *Bodhisattva of Wisdom, Manjushri* for guidance. However, rather than imparting the teaching to Sudhana, Manjushri sends him off on a journey to meet people and experience life.

During his odyssey, Sudhana meets up with 53 or so individuals from all walks of life. Some are religious figures, such as saint, goddess, monk, nun, Brahmin, and ascetic. Others are those with high worldly status, such as a king and wealthy merchant. Others include those with little social status or power, such as a prostitute, children, and slaves.

What inspires me about his spiritual journey is that Sudhana learns from the most *unlikely of teachers*, such as a young boy and a girl, and even from a slave and a prostitute. He seeks answers from a wide range of people and situations, no matter how socially lowly or experientially ordinary. Every encounter is a source of learning.

This story also reinforces the importance of *learning first hand*.

Bodhisattva Manjusri could have given Sudhana the answers, but knew that he had to find out for himself. So, Sudhana was sent off to learn directly from his own experiences.

Sudhana's search exemplifies the importance of the *process* of the search itself, just as much as the goal. Sometimes, we get so wrapped up in the goal that we forget to relish the process. During this process, we find Sudhana already exhibiting a great deal of curiosity and energy, which are the same qualities to be found in a person who has reached the goal of awakening.

Guest

To get a better glimpse into what it means and feels to seek, we have invited *Mr. Jeff Kriger* as our guest. Jeff is a member of *Sokagakkai International—USA*, one of the largest Buddhist denominations in North America. He serves as a senior advisor in the SGI-USA Study Department and has been working recently on the English translation of the next volume of the *Writings of Nichiren Daishonin*. Nichiren is the 13th century Japanese founder of the tradition

KT: Jeff, welcome to our program, and thank you for being here.

Jeff Kriger: Thank you very much for inviting me

KT: Sure. Now, how long have you been a member, and can you tell us something about your organization?

Jeff Kriger: Well, I've been practicing Buddhism for about 30 years now, which is a great part of my life. And the organization, SGI-USA, is a part of SGI, which is Sokagakkai International. It's an association of independent lay organizations of *Nichiren Buddhism* around the world. Nichiren's teachings were based on the *Lotus Sutra*, the essence of which is that the *Buddha-nature* or the enlightened nature of human beings is universal and accessible to every person; and also that people through awakening that nature [they] can have a profound influence or impact on their environment, on their community and society.

KT: Today's topic is focused on the topic of "seeking." So, I was wondering what circumstances led you to seek the Buddhist path?

Jeff Kriger: I didn't start out specifically seeking the Buddhist path, but I was looking for a solution to great *dissatisfaction or suffer-*

ing. In my teen years, I couldn't seem to get out of it. I loved nature, but I was sort of discouraged by urban society. And as a child of the sixties, I was influenced by a lot of those things.

KT: Me, too. I remember that, too.

Jeff Kriger: But I remember listening to the radio on one occasion and hearing *Alan Watts*, who as you know was a pioneer of introducing Buddhism to [the West].

KT: Yes, he influenced a lot of people.

Jeff Kriger: He was talking about something kind of obscure. He was talking about how the earth is like a living organism and can be compared to a tree. And just like a tree has blossoms that bear fruit, the earth bears people. In other words, it bears "blossoms of humanity." And it kind of struck me because …

KT: It struck a chord in you.

Jeff Kriger: That's right. From that point on, I started—when someone would ask me about my religion—I would tell them I was a Buddhist even though I knew nothing about Buddhism. But at one point I happen to run into some friends who were practicing this particular form of Buddhism, and they invited me to a meeting. The first thing is that when I approached the meeting place, there was a powerful sound of chanting. And to my sort of depressed condition, it sounded very refreshing.

KT: How did the chanting sound?

Jeff Kriger: The basic practice is chanting the words "*Nam-myoho-renge-kyo*" and also reciting the portion of the *Lotus Sutra*.

KT: What does that mean?

Jeff Kriger: "Nam-myoho-renge-kyo" is … Nichiren defines it as the essence of the *Lotus Sutra*. It actually derives from the title of the Sutra. "Nam-myoho-renge-kyo" is actually the title of the Sutra pronounced in Japanese. And that's the basic practice. I didn't know at the time; I just heard it. And, as you mentioned, it struck a chord. Then after the meeting, I encountered some of the members, and they seemed upbeat and warm, and kind of opposite of where my life was at the time. So it took me a while to try it (chanting), but after encountering several individuals who were practicing it, I decided to give it a chance since I had already considered myself a Buddhist!

KT: So Jeff, what were some of the problems or concerns that you had as you embarked on your search. And also did you run into some problems or obstacles in your searching?

Jeff Kriger: Well, one of the hesitations that I had was I had kind of rejected religion. [It was] mainly because I felt that the people I knew, the more religious they became, the more *judgmental* [they became.] That was my perception. And so in looking back at myself then, maybe they were right in [having] judged me, but it wasn't comfortable. So, the idea that Buddhism was a religion was a point of hesitation for me. But with the SGI members, there were so many different kinds of people that it seemed impractical for them to be judgmental. And I didn't feel that I was judged. I felt encouraged to improve myself, and gradually I became more comfortable with the idea.

And as far as the obstacles, I would say the biggest obstacle was within myself; I was basically very lazy.

KT: [So it was] a personal issue?

Jeff Kriger: Yes, [it was] internal. Buddhism kind of defines obstacles as originating from inside anyway, but the basic practice of chanting and reciting the sutra is called *gongyo* in Japanese, which means in Japanese, *"assiduous or dedicated practice."* But I wasn't very disciplined, and it was hard for me to get up early in the morning and do it. But by just trying, I felt I became stronger through that effort and became more consistent. And also I became more consistent in other aspects of my life as well.

KT: Great. So, how did your seeking translate into changes in your personal life?

Jeff Kriger: Well, I think [as for] seeking, at least I've learned in my study of Buddhism—in Mahayana Buddhism—that seeking means not only seeking our own path but also means seeking to *empower or help others*. And I think through my Buddhist practice and within SGI-USA, even though I was kind of a loner, early on I was given responsibility to take care of other people. And I think I had to come out of myself, and, to me, the opportunity to consider the *sufferings of other people* to chant or to pray for them to win over their suffering had been one of the most fulfilling aspects that I've gained through Buddhism. And that's changed me personally as well, I feel.

KT: So, you changed because other people changed.

Jeff Kriger: Yeah, and other people in turn helped me, and I'm able to appreciate the *interconnectedness* of the Buddhist family.

KT: Well, it looks like we are out of time. We really appreciate you sharing your personal story about your search in your tradition.

Jeff Kriger: Thank you very much, again, for the opportunity.

The quality and level of seeking, will naturally differ according to respective individuals. We need not compare with others but be true to ourselves and seek within our means. What is called for is our sincerity and openness in seeking as suggested in today's sacred passage:

> *If a person keeps her eyes open, she will see the teachings everywhere, and so her opportunities for awakening are endless.*

In our next show, we will be looking at the so-called Buddhist sympathizers or Nightstand Buddhists, who don't claim to be Buddhists but are Buddhistic in many ways. So, do join us again.

PROGRAM 50
Sympathizers or "Night-stand" Buddhists:
Not Buddhist, Yet Buddhistic

One who sees merely my body does not truly see me. Only one who understands my teaching truly sees me.

(The Teaching of Buddha, pp. 24-26)

For today's show, we'd like to find out more about people, who do not claim to be Buddhists but show strong interest in Buddhism. They make up a category of people whom some experts refer to as *sympathizers*.

Most experts estimate there are around 3 million Buddhists in the U.S. However, this number would be much higher if the Buddhist "sympathizers" were to be included.

In describing these sympathizers, one expert on American Buddhism, *Prof. Thomas Tweed* states:

> "Sympathizers are those who have some sympathy for Buddhism but do not embrace it exclusively or fully. When asked, they would *not* identify themselves as Buddhists. They would say they are Methodists, or Jewish, or unaffiliated. If we could talk to them long enough—or, better yet, visit their homes and observe their daily routine—we would notice signs of an interest in Buddhism. They might practice *zazen* (sitting Zen meditation), subscribe to a Buddhist periodical, or read books about the tradition. They might attend lectures at the local university. They might visit a Buddhist center's web page or participate in an on-line Buddhist discussion group. They might consciously decorate their homes with Buddhist artifacts."

American Buddhism, edited by D. Williams and S. Queen. Curzon, 1999, p. 74.

Prof. Tweed also refers to the sympathizers with another, a flashier, term *"Night-stand Buddhists."* The "Night-stand Buddhists" derive their name from their practice of placing a Buddhist meditation book on the nightstand and reading it before they go to sleep. Then, they get up next morning to practice to the best of their ability the meditation they had read about the night before.

These sympathizers or Night-stand Buddhists, who practice and read in the privacy of their homes, do not show up in any statistics on Buddhist population. However, they are thought to have been an important part of the story of Buddhism in North America from its beginning and continue to be so today.

Today we're lucky to have as our guests two people, who, in my view, qualify as sympathizers. They are *Nienke Klaver* and *Ed Staples*, who are husband and wife and are both school teachers, specializing in music.

KT: Well, Nienke, thank you for coming on our show.

Nienke Klaver: Thank you. Nice to be here.

KT: And Ed, thank you for being here.

Ed Staples: Thanks, Ken. My pleasure.

KT: My first question to you is, "How long ago did you begin to take interest in Buddhism?"

Nienke Klaver: We've always been interested in world religions including Buddhism. But about seven years ago, we started to travel extensively in Asia. We went to many Buddhist countries, visited a lot of places, Buddhist places and got more interested. We wanted to know more about the religion.

KT: So, it was through your travels then.

Nienke Klaver: Yes.

KT: I know that you have some artifacts, Buddhist artifacts, in your home. Can you tell us something about them?

Ed Staples: Probably the most prominent display would be the statues that we have, the Buddhist statues. We have four of them in our home. One of them is a very large stone statue from Korea; a wooden one that we purchased when we were in Cambodia. And probably the one I like the best is a very small one, a few inches high, that we purchased in Thailand. And it's what is known as *Ayutthaya* style, Thai style. And it has a very serene and very peaceful feeling about it.

We also have several musical instruments we've collected, a lot of them from Tibet. One of them is a trumpet that's used ceremonially by the Tibetan Buddhist monks. And [we have] cymbals [and] instruments played like an oboe with a double reed. And when we were in Tibet most recently, we saw these instruments performed as part of the ceremonies.

KT: I see. You said that you visited some Buddhist places, and I'm wondering which are some of the places that really stand out in your mind?

Nienke Klaver: Mmm …, that's a difficult question. I would have to say our last experience this last summer [when] we traveled to Tibet. And we were invited by two monks to come with them to their monastery. And as it happened, the youngest monk was the 6th reincarnation of the *Bo Gangkar Rinpoche*.

KT: Oh, Rinpoche! A reincarnated lama.

Ed Staples: Reincarnated lama. That's right. And so we traveled to their monastery. And this monastery (*Minyak Gangkar Monastery*) is in a very remote area. There is no electricity. There's no telephone, of course. But somehow people had heard about this, and everyone was out and welcoming the Rinpoche-to-be. It was a very incredible experience. What impressed us most was *devoutness* of the people.

Nienke Klaver: [For] the installation of the Rinpoche, people waited in a very hot sun for two or three hours. And after the Rinpoche was installed, everybody went through and received a blessing from him. And we went through at the very end as well and received his blessings; it was a very memorable experience, once in a lifetime experience.

KT: Did you know these two Rinpoches or these monks?

Nienke Klaver: No, we just met them [while] walking in a marketplace.

KT: Even better.

Nienke Klaver: Yes. And they had just come back from three years in India and come back to the monastery.

KT: Do you meditate or do you participate in Buddhist services at all?

Nienke Klaver: I don't meditate as such, but I do yoga. And through yoga sometimes I get into a meditative state.

KT: I see, I see. How about you, Ed?

Ed Staples: No, I don't meditate. We've attended several Buddhist services over the years, none recently I guess. The most recent one would be the ceremony that we attended in Tibet, which was this past summer.

KT: And did you feel anything at the service?

Ed Staples: Oh, yes, very much. It's hard not to, when you're surrounded by hundreds of devout people. And all of them [were] there because their spiritual leader was there. You get caught up with that. You get the same feeling, perhaps at the different level than they might, but definitely.

KT: Okay, what attracted you to Buddhism?

Nienke Klaver: For me it's the *non-aggressive life*. It is the *acceptance* of everyone and everything. *Non-violence*. As far as the acceptance goes, I will never forget [the time] I walked in Lhasa, [and] we passed an old lady. We looked at each other, and she started to laugh and grabbed my hand. And we couldn't talk. We could not talk each other's language, but we walked like that through the streets, and she was just holding my hand and looking at me and laughing. And I felt very accepted.

KT: How about you, Ed?

Ed Staples: Like Nienke mentioned earlier, I've always had an interest in world religions, and I believe that everybody is going through some sort of *personal search* or some sort of spiritual search. And in my search, I was open to all sorts of beliefs. Right now Buddhism seems to be the one that interests me the most. I like the non-aggressive part of it. I also like the *compassionate* side of it. And I like the way teachings help me to be a good person or a better person.

KT: Well, since you've been very attracted to Buddhism, have you considered being Buddhists?

Nienke Klaver: With that, if you mean, have I considered being a part of ritual and becoming a part of a sect, "No." I would say, "No." But if you mean, to try to *live a good life* in a Buddhist way, I would say, "Yes."

Ed Staples: I guess my answer would be, "Yes." I have thought a little bit about what it would be like to be Buddhist. I'm not sure what that would take. And if it means trying to follow the teachings of Buddha and trying to be a more compassionate understanding tolerant person, and if that's what it means to be a Buddhist, then I guess, in some ways, I am a Buddhist.

KT: Well, thank you for joining us, and I believe we've gotten a very good idea, a glimpse into a real live Buddhist sympathizer! Thank you for coming in.

Nienke and Ed: Thank you.

If *you* happen to be a Night-stand Buddhist, please know that most Buddhists would not feel compelled to "convert" you. In this vein, the *Dalai Lama* has repeatedly encouraged the thousands of people who come to hear his talks in North America to be the best possible Jew, Catholic, or Methodist they can be! What we need in today's world is not for religions to be competing for members, but for as many people as possible to live up to the ideals of their current affiliated traditions.

Now having said so, the "declared" Buddhists, like me, would certainly welcome anyone interested in becoming Buddhist with wide open arms.

However, in the final analysis, I would prefer to see one strong Night-stand Buddhist than ten "Couch Potato" Buddhists, since it's more important to understand the teachings than to merely identify with the outward forms of one's religion, as expressed in today's sacred passage by the Buddha!

> One who sees merely my body does not truly see me. Only one who understands my teaching truly sees me.

In our next show, we will look at the topic of sharing the Buddhist teachings with others. We look forward to seeing you then.

PROGRAM 51

Sharing the Teachings with Others:
Yehan Numata's Spirit and Contribution

When a Buddha Land is founded upon the pure mind of a single person, that single pure mind draws other kindred minds to itself in the fellowship of like-minded people. Faith in Buddha spreads from individual to family, from family to village, from village to towns, to cities, to countries, and finally to the whole world.

(The Teaching of Buddha, p. 466)

Hello. We're pleased that you could join us as we continue to explore the fascinating facets of Buddhism.

The Buddhist Tradition of Sharing

Our topic today is *"sharing the teachings with others."* This forms a natural set with the act of *"seeking awakening,"* a topic we discussed a couple of shows back. Seeking and sharing go hand in hand.

In Buddhism, when a person attains some level of awakening, that person *automatically* begins to share the teachings with others. The Buddha exemplified this, for after awakening he dedicated the rest of his life to share his understanding with others. He chose a life of a wandering monk to travel the kingdoms of the lower Ganges River, in order to take the message to as many people as possible.

During the long Buddhist history, there have been innumerable Buddhists who dedicated their lives to sharing the teaching with others. They include King Ashoka of the 3rd century B.C.E. who spread Buddhism throughout the Indian subcontinent and beyond, and ordinary people who made donations to temples.

In Buddhism, there is a doctrine of *benefit for oneself* (svārtha) and *benefit for others* (parārtha). Once a person has benefited oneself by realizing some level of awakening, that person then makes a spontaneous effort to benefit others.

Rev. Dr. Yehan Numata

One person who exemplifies the spirit of sharing and benefiting others is Yehan Numata. He founded the *Society for the Promotion of Buddhism*, the sponsor of this program series. I believe that his enormous contribution is worthy of dedicating today's show to him.

Born in Hiroshima, Japan in 1897, he lived a long and productive life that spanned almost a century, when he died in 1994 at the age of 97. He was born a third son of a Jodo Shinshu Buddhist priest.

Upon graduating from a middle school, Yehan felt a strong urge to further his education, but knew that his family could not afford a higher education for him. He, then, accepted an offer to go to Hawai'i as an assistant missionary priest. After a few years in Hawai'i working as a priest, he moved to Los Angeles, where he worked his way through high school.

Once earning his diploma from Hollywood High School, he enrolled at the University of California at Berkeley. He majored in economics, and then went on to earn his Masters in economic statistics.

During his college life, he met a number of Buddhist priests in California who impressed Yehan Numata by their personal virtues for transmitting the teachings. He found himself lacking in such qualities and decided, then, that he would not become a full-time priest but, instead, support the spread of Buddhism through other means.

Pacific World Journal

Soon after completing his undergraduate work, Yehan Numata embarked on his first major effort directed toward propagation of Buddhism in 1925, when he began *Pacific World*, a journal in English targeting the learned American audience interested in Buddhism. The first issue of *Pacific World* included articles by an impressive group of contributors. They included David S. Jordon, President of Stanford University, several faculty members of the University of California faculty, and Buddhist historian [Prof.] *Kenneth K. Saunders*. Prof. Saunders' essay was entitled, *"Buddhism and Christianity and the Historical Shakyamuni."*

However, after four years Yehan Numata ran out of funds and

was forced to abandon his project. This bitter experience convinced him even more of the importance of financial resources for sharing the teachings with others. Yehan Numata, then, decided to return to Japan to establish a business with the intent to direct portions of its earnings toward disseminating the Buddhist teachings. Back in Japan, he worked for a few years with the Japanese government before leaving the stable and prestigious job in order to focus on his start-up business, *Mitutoyo Corporation*, a company for manufacturing *precision measuring instruments.*

Society for the Promotion of Buddhism

The company grew and flourished, and by the mid-1960s there were branch factories in other countries, including Germany, Brazil and the U.S. With the prosperous business supporting his long held dream, Mr. Numata was able to establish in 1965 *Bukkyo Dendo Kyokai*, the Society for the Promotion of Buddhism, a non-sectarian, non-profit organization for the promotion of Buddhism internationally.

He understood the need to employ *methods other than books and words* to share the Buddhist message. He commissioned an artist to depict through paintings the major events in the life of the Buddha. He also funded a production of a movie about a prominent Buddhist figure. He promoted modern music, which was quite rare for Buddhists. For example, he donated a huge pipe organ to a prominent Buddhist temple in Tokyo. He also realized the importance of practicing the teachings, not just reading about them, which led him to establish annual retreats for interested people to participate in the practices of various denominations.

Distribution of *The Teaching of Buddha*

I have found his *non-sectarian, ecumenical spirit* most impressive. Though he was born into a Jodo Shinshu temple family, he sought to promote Buddhism *as a whole*. This attitude is reflected in the primary project of the Society for the Promotion of Buddhism: the distribution free of charge of *The Teaching of Buddha* in hotel rooms. Since 1975 this book has been translated into 41 different languages and is found in 1,100,000 rooms in 55 countries.

The Society has also promoted Buddhism in the academic area. For example, it has established scholarships for young Buddhist scholars as well as establishing *academic chairs of Buddhist Studies* at 14 institutions in Europe and North America, which include Oxford University, the University of California at Berkeley, the Institute of Buddhist Studies at the Graduate Theological Union in Berkeley, Harvard University, and the University of Calgary.

Another project which began in 1982 seeks to translate into English 139 main scriptures from the *Chinese Buddhist Canon*, which when completed will contain close to 150 volumes. This is a project that is unprecedented, requiring about 150 international scholars.

For all of these accomplishments, he was awarded Honorary Doctorate degrees from the University of Hawai'i and Ryukoku University in Kyoto.

The Inner Source

We have looked at his accomplishments, which by any standard are impressive to say the least. He began with nothing, paid his own way through high school, college and graduate school in a foreign country, and founded a profitable international company, while keeping his promise of sharing the teachings with the world. Many who knew him wondered, "Where does he get his drive?"

Well, I got a hint for the answer to that question during my one encounter with him. He once visited Berkeley at the Institute of Buddhist Studies, where I was teaching. He invited some of the faculty out for dinner at a traditional Japanese restaurant, where we sat on *tatami* mats. The lively and enjoyable dinner lasted close to two hours, but after half an hour or so, all of us had our legs thrown out and were leaning against the walls.

The one exception was Mr. Numata who was 91 years old at the time! He sat in a dignified manner the whole time in the traditional Japanese style on his knees with his legs folded under him and his back straight. I could not be more impressed by his stamina and discipline, undoubtedly derived from his inner calm and strength.

Beginner's Mind

And this mind of calm and strength is none other than the *"beginner's mind"* (shoshin), which he often spoke of as his guiding light in his life. Yehan Numata, indeed, faced life with the beginner's mind.

With the beginner's mind, he *avoided preconceived attitudes* and, instead, lay open to consider all possibilities. He had firm convictions about his goals but was flexible in his methods.

Despite his seniority and all his accomplishments, the beginner's mind also made him see himself on an equal footing with others. His *humble demeanor* was evident at that dinner, when he spoke to my much younger colleagues and I with respect and concern.

The beginner's mind further manifested itself in the form of his *compassion for others and his optimism* for the world. He expressed this, when the once defunct *Pacific World* was revived in 1982 after more than 50 years:

> *Throughout my life, I have sincerely believed that Buddhism is a religion of peace and compassion, a teaching that will bring spiritual tranquility to the individual, and contribute to the promotion of harmony and peace in society. ... For the opportunity to be able to contribute to the propagation of Buddhism and the betterment of humankind, I am eternally grateful. (Yehan Numata, 1897-1994)*

Today, through the distribution of the books and a host of other projects, Rev. Dr. Yehan Numata's wish to share the teachings with others lives on.

In our final show next week, we plan to explore with a distinguished guest the topic of the distinctive contribution that Buddhism can make to this troubled world. Please join us again.

PROGRAM 52
Buddhist Contribution in the Troubled World

If one speaks or acts with a pure mind, happiness follows him like the shadow that never leaves him.

(*Buddha-Dharma, p. 428*)

Hello. We're especially glad that you've joined us for our final show.

We would like to conclude by pointing out some of the distinctive teachings of Buddhism that can help to address the problems and challenges that lie before us, as reflected in the title of our program series, "Mutually Sustaining Life: A Call to a Troubled World."

For this purpose, I have invited a guest whose studies make him eminently qualified to provide us with a valuable perspective. Our guest is *Dr. Sengaku Mayeda, Professor Emeritus of Tokyo University* as well as of *Musashino University* in Japan. His area of expertise is in Indian Philosophy and Buddhist thought. Dr. Mayeda has traveled widely and has lectured and taught in several countries.

It's a great honor to have this distinguished scholar share his thoughts, focusing on the distinctive qualities of Buddhism. Plus it's an extra pleasure for me, since Dr. Mayeda was one of my professors in graduate school a few years ago … okay … some 30 years ago. Hard to imagine it was that long ago!

KT: Well, Dr. Mayeda, welcome to our show, and thank you for being with us today.

Dr. Mayeda: It's my pleasure.

KT: In my introduction I mentioned that you've taught in several countries, and I was wondering, "where did you teach the longest?"

Dr. Mayeda: I was in India for some time, but I taught the longest at University of Pennsylvania. It was for 3 years in the mid-1960s.

KT: I see. In those days in the U.S., there were far fewer courses on Asian religions than today.

Dr. Mayeda: Yes, that's true. It's hard to believe how the interest in Asian religions has grown in America, especially in Buddhism.

KT: Since Buddhism emerged in India, it shares some teachings with Hinduism, such as the idea of *karma, reincarnation,* [and] *enlightenment.* However, what distinguishes Buddhism from Hinduism? Can you give one example?

Dr. Mayeda: If I need to choose just one, I would have to say *non-attachment to the self or what you consider your own,* **anatman** in Sanskrit.

KT: Can you give us an example of what you mean by non-attachment to the self?

Dr. Mayeda: It means *not to be attached even to the Buddhist teaching itself.*

KT: But shouldn't Buddhists consider their teachings to be very important?

Dr. Mayeda: Yes, of course, it's important, but once you've attained some level of awakening, you should no longer be attached to it.

KT: So, can you explain that a little more?

Dr. Mayeda: There is a famous Buddhist *metaphor of the raft.* The teaching is like a raft to get you from this shore to the other shore. You rely on the raft to get to the other shore, but once you land on the other shore, you must let go of it. It would be foolish of you if you carried the raft on your head as you walked to your destination, just because you liked it so much. That would be an attachment to the self or what you consider your own.

KT: I see, I see. I really think that the image of the raft is pretty clever and effective. Actually it would be pretty awkward and quite a heavy burden, wouldn't it? So, how can this apply to our daily life?

Dr. Mayeda: It means *not* to be so attached to Buddhism to think that Buddhism is the only true religion for everyone. For *me* Buddhism is the best, but I cannot speak so for everyone.

KT: And that's an important and critical point for people in the world to get along. Anything else?

Dr. Mayeda: Also, when you are not attached to yourself or what you consider your own, then you would be able to *see beyond yourself.* You would be able to put yourself in the shoes of another person. This is *compassion,* the real heart of Buddhism.

KT: Compassion! I see. So, speaking of Buddhism, why did

Buddhism become a world religion, while Hinduism remained largely a religion for the Indians?

Dr. Mayeda: *Buddhism is "Hinduism for export."*

KT: Ah, Hinduism for export! I've never heard that term before. That's an interesting way of putting it. And what made it exportable, then?

Dr. Mayeda: I believe it was largely because Buddhists opposed the caste system. This meant that the *teaching was available to everyone.*

KT: That reminds me of the famous words of the Buddha, to the effect that the worth of a person is determined *not by one's birth but by one's deeds.* So, what message does Buddhism provide to the "call to a troubled world" that is the subtitle of our program?

Dr. Mayeda: I believe that the two teachings we talked about can be an important asset.

KT: You mean *non-attachment to self* as seen even in regards to its Buddhist teachings and also the *non-discrimination* in the abandonment of the caste system? Are those the two that you are referring to?

Dr. Mayeda: Yes, especially the first is distinct, if not unique, to Buddhism. And please do not forget about *compassion for others* that arises from the two.

KT: Yes, I think that's an important point: compassion. And compassion is very important but also the point you brought up earlier about not being attached to even one's own teaching. And I really think that is a very radical position. Though very radical, it can be a moderating influence on the relationship between different religions.

Well, Dr. Mayeda, thank you so very much for being with us to share your thoughts, especially on the distinctive qualities and teachings of Buddhism and how it can contribute to [solving] the problems of the world.

Dr. Mayeda: It was a pleasure to be here, especially with my former student, Ken!

KT: Oh well, thank you! I appreciate that very much. Really great to have you here. Thank you.

I would like to offer some concluding thoughts within the framework of the title of our program series, "Mutually Sustaining Life: A Call to a Troubled World."

A Call to a Troubled World

Many things are troubling in our world, such as the constant fear of terrorism. I believe that no amount of stringent security will prevent terrorist acts, unless we address the underlying greed, hatred, ignorance that stem from the social and economic inequities among people and nations.

And religions can play a greater role in this. However, as we discussed in an earlier show, the attitude of *superiority and exclusion* is rampant among many people in all religions and denominations, including Buddhism. This has prevented religions from interacting meaningfully to make any significant difference.

I believe, however, that the Buddhist teaching of non-attachment, cited by Dr. Mayeda, can serve as a moderating influence in a world where religions and nations are at odds based on unyielding positions of good and evil. These rigid attitudes are based on attachment to self or what you consider your own. Therefore, the Buddhist teaching of non-attachment can foster an outlook in which one's own religion is affirmed as most precious for that person, *yet not regarded as the **only** true way* or *the right way for everyone.*

Mutually Sustaining Life

I feel that we have adequately conveyed the Buddhist teaching of interdependence to show that our lives, our communities, and our world are "mutually sustaining." No one person or one community or one country can survive on its own.

This realization of our connectedness should foster greater understanding of the intrinsic value of others and encourage us to work together even when the differences seem insurmountable. This outlook is none other than the expression of compassion that Dr. Mayeda spoke of.

And this "mutually sustaining" nature of our existence refers also to humanity's *relationship with the environment*. I believe that the Buddhist understanding serves as an important reminder of the urgent need to radically change the way we relate to the environment. We can no longer afford to let our planet Earth deteriorate any further.

Words of Farewell

As we conclude, all of us sincerely hope that you, the viewers, were able to gain something meaningful to be applied to your lives. This series has been an extremely challenging task, and at times I was not sure if I could be ready for some shows. Yet *remarkably* when difficulties arose, I felt the guidance of a "spiritual force" that did not come from *me* but rather from a source beyond me!

I'd like you to keep in mind that while life is, indeed, a bumpy road, with our sincere effort we all awaken to the shining jewel within us, as well as those jewels that surround and embrace us. And when you do, "Yes, life is, indeed, great!" Your happiness is in your hands, as proclaimed by the Buddha in today's sacred passage:

> *If one speaks or acts with a pure mind, happiness follows him like*
> *the shadow that never leaves him."*

Best wishes to you all!

Questions Often Asked

About the Teachings and Practices

- How do you meditate? *See* Index on "meditation"

- What kinds of meditation are there? *See* Index on "meditation"

- What kind of life did the Buddha lead? *See* Index on "Shakyamuni Buddha"

- How do you depict the Buddhas and saints? *See* Index on images and statues"

- What are the most basic teachings of Buddhism? *See* Index on "Four Noble Truths" and "Four Marks of Existence"

- What the Four Noble Truths? *See* Index on "Four Noble Truths"

- What is the Eightfold Path? *See* Index on "Eightfold Path"

- Why do we suffer? *See* pp. 50, 75-76.

- Can you explain the meaning of "emptiness"? *See* Index on "emptiness"

- Tell me more about "non-self" and "no soul." *See* Index on "non-self"

- Doesn't karma mean fate? *See* Index on "karma"

- What happens when a person is enlightened? *See* Index on "awakening" and "awakened persons"

- Why do bad things happen to good people? *See* p. 252

- Wouldn't a life of an enlightened person be dull? *See* p. 171

- What do the chants say? *See* Index on "chanting"

- What are some examples of Buddhist art, including songs and music? *See* Index on "art or images" and "songs or music"

About the Institution or its Role in Society

- How many Buddhists are there in America? *See* p. 5.

- What kinds of Buddhism are there? *See* pp. 5-6.

- Why is Buddhism growing? *See* p. 8.

- When did Buddhism begin? *See* pp. 13-15.

- What kind of life does monks and nuns lead?
  See Index on "monks" and "nuns"

- What do all the schools have in common? *See* p. 92.

- Aren't Buddhists supposed to be indifferent to the world?
  See pp. 34, 51, 88, 127. *See* also Index on "engaged Buddhism"

- What are the roles and status of women?
  See Index on "women" and "nuns"

- How compatible is Buddhism with science?
  See Index on "science and Buddhism"

- How different is Buddhism from Psychology?
  See Index on "Psychology and Buddhism"

- What is Buddhist humor like? *See* Index on "humor"

Index

Bulk Rate Information

A discount of 20% OFF the regular price is available for orders of 10 or more books.

Order through:

Buddhist Churches of America Bookstore
2140 Durant Avenue
Berkeley, CA 94704
510-809-1435

Email contact: sales@bcabookstore.com
http://bcabookstore.mybigcommerce.com/index.php

About the Author

Kenneth Kenshin Tanaka is Professor and Dean of Buddhist Education at Musashino University in Tokyo. Earlier in his life, he became a monk in Thailand and also served as a minister in a California temple. He studied at Stanford University (B.A., Cultural Anthropology), Institute of Buddhist Studies, Berkeley (M.A. Buddhist Studies), Tokyo University (M.A., Indian Philosophy), and University of California at Berkeley (Ph.D., Buddhist Studies). He currently serves as president of two academic associations, the International Association of Shin Buddhist Studies and

Kenneth Kenshin Tanaka
Courtesy of: Bits Magazine, Toronto

the Japanese Association for the Study of Buddhism and Psychology. His publications include, *The Dawn of Chinese Pure Land Buddhist Doctrine* (State University of New York Press, 1990), *Ocean: An Introduction to Jodo Shinshu Buddhism in America* (Wisdom Ocean Publications, 1997), and *American Buddhism* (written in Japanese) (Musashino University Press, 2010). Dr. Tanaka has lectured in numerous countries, and his books have been translated into Chinese, Japanese and Portuguese.